Canaan Bound

Canaan Bound

The African-American

Great Migration Novel

Lawrence R. Rodgers

University of Illinois Press

Urbana and Chicago

© 1997 by the Board of Trustees of the University of Illinois
Manufactured in the United States of America
1 2 3 4 5 C P 5 4 3 2 1

This book is printed on acid-free paper.

Library of Congress Cataloging-in-Publication Data
Rodgers, Lawrence R. (Lawrence Richard), 1960–
    Canaan bound : the African-American great migration
novel / Lawrence R. Rodgers.
      p.   cm.
Includes bibliographical references and index.
ISBN 0-252-02304-8 (alk. paper). —
ISBN 0-252-06605-7 (pbk. : alk. paper)
1. American fiction—Afro-American authors—History
and criticism. 2. Afro-Americans in literature. 3. Rural-
urban migration in literature. 4. Migration, Internal, in
literature. 5. City and town life in literature. 6. Literature
and society—United States—History—20th century.
7. Southern States in literature. 8. Narration (Rhetoric)
I. Title.
PS374.N4R57   1997
813.009'896073—dc20   96-25270
                                                  CIP

For Rob (1957–90)

Perhaps to lose a sense of *where* you are implies
the danger of losing a sense of *who* you are.

Ralph Ellison

Contents

Preface

As a form, what I call the Great Migration novel began as a response to the limitations of American racial geography. My general goal in *Canaan Bound* is to map the many ways in which African-American novelists have written about and participated in the largest common experience uniting the African-American population after slavery, the mass movement that saw millions of black southerners resettle in the Northeast and Midwest during the first half of this century. The challenge of completing a successful migration is invoked in the book's title. The phrase *Canaan bound* intentionally foregrounds the promise embodied in the migrants' destination and also recognizes that the effort to fulfill this promise has remained very much in process.

When I first began seriously exploring the connection between novels and the Great Migration in the mid-1980s, I was struck by what seemed to be the discrepancy between the movement's significance and the limited attention it had generally been paid both inside and outside academic circles. Depending on whom one asked, even the name itself was under some dispute. The term *Great Migration* was often reserved for describing the waves of eastern and western European immigrants arriving in the United States in the nineteenth century. When used in conjunction with the domestic migration of black southerners, the term tended to be understood as referring to the several-year period in which approximately five hundred thousand people moved to midwestern and northern cities in response to World War I's industrial labor demands. By such measures, the Great Migration happened well in the past, involved a relatively small and anonymous group of people, and was now over.

Overcoming the severe limitations of this view involved the labors of several generations of sociologists and historians, ably studying the Great

Migration in far more expansive terms, who were able to register the staggering degree to which the movement shaped, and continues to shape, many of the basic structures of American urban life. But like much that is addressed by a specialized community of scholars, the Great Migration, for many years, remained primarily an academic sideshow displaying only limited signs of penetrating the realm of national popular discourse and culture.

In the past few years the picture has changed significantly. In 1989 the University of Chicago Press published James Grossman's excellent *Land of Hope: Chicago, Black Southerners, and the Great Migration*. During the early 1990s academic conferences at Carnegie Mellon and Washington universities drew national audiences to discuss the history and culture of migration, and the Modern Language Association hosted a session on literature and the Great Migration. Even more interesting than the burgeoning scholarly attention was the startling range of cultural venues that looked to the experience of migration as a source of inspiration and an object of scrutiny. The phenomenon has been addressed in intellectual and imaginative ways that have finally begun to come to terms with its ongoing historical importance.

If there was an initiating moment of general public awareness, it no doubt came in 1988 with the opening of an exhibit, "From Field to Factory," at the Smithsonian Museum of American History. By putting several hundred thousand Washington tourists in touch with some of the basic facts of the Great Migration and allowing them to observe the visual differences between a sharecropper's shack on a Mississippi farm and Chicago's South Side tenements, this walk-through diorama publicly sanctioned the migration experience on a vast national scale. In 1991, during February's Black History Month, Knopf, a respected popular press, released Nicholas Lemann's *The Promised Land: The Great Black Migration and How It Changed America*. After capturing an enthusiastic review on the front page of the *New York Times Book Review*, the book moved onto several bestseller lists. As important as demonstrating that the general public was indeed interested in learning more about the Great Migration, Lemann's captivating and stylish work built on the labors of his scholarly predecessors to make a persuasive case for the most consequential part of the Great Migration occurring following World War II. It was not, Lemann narratively documented, a moment in history that quietly ended decades ago. It has played, since the war, an ever-enlarging and more influential role in shaping the contours of both the country's cities and southern rural towns.

By organizing the study around the lives of individuals in three locations—Clarksdale, Mississippi (the home of blues king Muddy Waters), Chicago (the destination of choice for Mississippi migrants), and Washington (the faraway seat of government, where well-intentioned bureaucrats argued endlessly over how to win the war on poverty)—Lemann risked reducing his characters to mere emblems of their larger world but still managed to evoke the Great Migration's sense of character, plot, and narrative tension well enough to make the book read like a riveting novel. In fact, the result was so successful that *Promised Land* inspired a 1995 multiday miniseries on cable television's Discovery Channel, which itself led to a compact disc release of music of the same title. Part of the show's appeal came from the interviews with Lemann's subjects, allowing readers to match faces and voices to the book's rich characterizations. Unfortunately, the migration CD, in contrast to the much-talked-about prior release of Delta bluesman Robert Johnson's two-volume collection, was not a serious exploration of the migrant roots of black music, but rather a curiously cobbled together soundtrack designed to tap into residual market interest in the miniseries.

If the events surrounding the Smithsonian exhibit and Lemann's work showcased the intellectual appeal of the exodus, the public was also ready to be immersed in the culture of migrants as a form of entertainment. In 1989 Gloria Naylor's novel of migrant women living in a northern project, *The Women of Brewster Place* (1984), was turned into a soap opera-esque miniseries starring an ensemble cast that included Oprah Winfrey, Cicely Tyson, and Robin Givens. The fact that viewers were asked to envision such widely recognized actresses and celebrities playing a cadre of outcasts who were meant to represent a sector of black America invisible to dominant culture had little effect in dampening television and video audiences' general enthusiasm for the show. Probing considerably more deeply into the impact of migration, August Wilson won the 1990 Pulitzer Prize for Drama with *The Piano Lesson*. Set in Pittsburgh in 1936, the play measures the striking degree to which postmigration northern opportunity has been challenged by the ongoing erosion of southern memory. Equally profound was writer-director Julie Dash's *Daughters of the Dust* (1992). Set in 1902 in one of the Sea Islands off Georgia and North Carolina, the film beautifully captured the events surrounding a ceremony preceding a family's journey north.

The roots of one of the most powerful cultural displays of the Great Migration extend well before the 1980s. In 1940 the eminent African-American painter Jacob Lawrence applied for and received the first of three consecutive annual Rosenwald Foundation Fellowships. The fellowship, which allowed him to set up a studio on 125th Street in Harlem (and share a building with Romare Bearden, Claude McKay, and William Attaway), was awarded so that he could create a series of paintings on the Great Migration. Following a period of sustained research, Lawrence spent about a year executing a sequence of sixty small (twelve-by-eighteen-inch) gesso panels that, in harsh primary colors, brilliantly evoked the epic scale of the movement amid the personal experience of its individual participants. He wrote his own captions for the group of panels, which he entitled "And the Migrants Kept Coming." Displaying the artist's characteristic lack of sentimentality, the series documents the entire range of migrant activity— from a portrait of featureless, anonymous migrants at a southern train station, followed by several panels recording their arrival in the North, to a rendering of the domestic activity of reading mail from relatives down home juxtaposed with scenes of hauntingly stark northern housing (Bearden and Henderson, *A History of African-American Artists;* M. Brown, *Jacob Lawrence;* Wheat, *Jacob Lawrence* 59–63).

In a children's book made from the paintings, Lawrence explained his thinking as he worked:

> To me, migration means movement. While I was painting, I thought about trains and people walking to the stations. I thought about field hands leaving their farms to become factory workers, and about the families that sometimes got left behind. The choices made were hard ones, so I wanted to show what made the people get on those northbound trains. I also wanted to show just what it cost to ride them. Uprooting yourself from one way of life to make your way in another involves conflict and struggle. But out of the struggle comes a kind of power, and even beauty. (*The Great Migration* n.p.)

The children's book (itself a stylishly executed display of Lawrence's work) was published in 1992 in conjunction with a traveling exhibit of the paintings. The landmark exhibit brought together for the first time in decades all of the panels, which had been for many years divided between the Museum of Modern Art and the Phillips Collection. (The exhibit also produced what is no doubt one of the more idiosyncratic commercial homages to the Great Migration; refrigerator magnets emblazoned with the best-known panel of the series were on sale along with exhibit posters.) Both Lawrence's influence and the growing interest in migration extended into the world of dance, when in 1995 the Washington, D.C.–based Liz Lerman Dance Exchange premiered a "performatour" about the Great Migration at Washington's Kennedy Center and later at the Chicago Historical Society. Explicitly highlighting Lawrence's migration series as its inspiration, the show moved beyond the static artistic canvas and even the traditional fourth wall as dancers moved from room to room and audiences were encouraged to follow them from stages into galleries, corridors, and even toilets covered in "mobile art."

Inasmuch as a cultural movement can somehow be deemed fashionable, the Great Migration, sanctioned in Washington and documented in film, music, painting, and dance, has become so. When looked at in the proper perspective, however, such attention hardly constitutes a fad. What I try to record in this book is the century-long effort by a surprisingly diverse range of black writers to come to terms with this epic relocation of a culture. To the extent that issues surrounding movement and identity have, over the entire history of published black literature, occupied the center of African-American consciousness, the Great Migration, at least from the perspective of those who participated in it and wrote about it, has always been fashionable.

●

It is one of the more gratifying parts of the publishing process to be able to acknowledge the community of scholars, friends, and family who have helped me complete this project. I am led to believe, in paraphrasing Hillary Clinton invoking an old African proverb, that it takes an entire village to write a book. At least a first one.

Among my institutional supporters, I am grateful to that needlessly embattled institution, the National Endowment for the Humanities, for a travel grant, a summer fellowship, and funding to attend two summer research seminars. Program Officer Clayton Lewis has been especially helpful. It is no exaggeration to say that without the NEH's support this book would not exist. I also benefited from a University of Wisconsin dissertation fellowship and several grants-in-aid from Kansas State University.

Grateful acknowledgment goes to several libraries: The University of California, Berkeley, Boston University's Mugar Special Collections, Kansas State University's Farrell Library (especially their fine interlibrary loan department), Kansas University's Spencer Special Collections, the Newberry Library, the Schomburg Library, and Yale University's Beinecke and Sterling libraries.

Portions of two chapters are revised versions of previously published essays: Chapter 1 appeared as "Paul Laurence Dunbar's *The Sport of the Gods:* The Doubly Conscious World of Plantation Fiction, Migration and

Ascent," in *American Literary Realism* 24 (Spring 1992): 42–57, and chapter 4 appeared as "Dorothy West and the Ideal of Southern Folk Community" in *African American Review* 26 (Spring 1992): 161–72.

Early stages of this work were patiently guided by several people while I was still trying to gain the insight and knowledge to do this important subject the justice it deserved. John Lyons's understated, generous mentoring of my early career continues to serve me as a model on how professors ought to conduct themselves with students; Tom Schaub's penetrating critical acumen rescued me from dead-ends on several occasions; Stanley Schultz acquainted me with the discipline of urban history and taught classes in which I first realized I wanted to write a book on the Great Migration; and Bill Andrews, first as a Wisconsin professor and later as a fellow Kansan, provided and continues to provide support and friendship. Special thanks are due Craig Werner, who has read and commented on my work on many occasions throughout its evolution. He continues to set, as the large community of his devoted former students know so well, an ideal standard for what it means to be a scholar and teacher.

For five good years in Madison, Wisconsin, and for providing a wonderfully engaging intellectual and social community, I thank Jonathan Little, Ernest Suarez, Bob Grotjohn, Len Sancilio, Megan Loef, and many others. More recently, a number of colleagues, at home and around the country, discussed my work, argued with me about it, read small portions of the manuscript, and generally challenged my thinking to go forward. These friends include Angela Hubler, Linda Brigham, Tim Dayton, Elizabeth Dodd, Greg Eiselein, Carol Franko, Rob Grindell, Dean Hall, Cheryl Lester, Jim Machor, Anne Phillips, Joe Tabbi, and John Edgar Tidwell.

Several others deserve individual acknowledgement. R. W. B. Lewis, in the midst of providing a wonderful forum in which to write at his 1994 NEH seminar at Yale University, cast his sharp critical eye over my final chapter. He also kindly shared some personal reflections about his late friend Ralph Ellison. Bill Maxwell may not recall the gesture, but he generously gave me a copy of the excellent paper I heard him present, which helped gel my thinking on Richard Wright and William Attaway into its final stages. I first had the privilege of meeting Eric Sundquist as a participant in his 1990 NEH seminar on "The Concept of Race in American Literature," an eight-week residency at UC, Berkeley that so fully challenged my thinking and engaged my interests that it remains as a watershed in my intellectual development. In addition to setting the brilliant critical standard in his own writing that I and all of his readers have come to appreciate, Eric has taken the time, amid a staggering array of obligations, to read and comment on my work, give me the benefit of his counsel, and, in general, support my career in such a way that merely thanking him only taps the surface of my deeply felt gratitude.

If such an acknowledgment is appropriate for a man I sadly never met but whom I view as a hero, I want to thank Ralph Ellison. As a fellow native Oklahoman, he has, from my earliest reading of him, allowed me to take tremendous pride in the fact that such a man could have grown up just down the road apiece.

Many students in my African-American literature courses shared such engaging personal experiences with migration that their energy and interest kept me going amid my own sometimes flagging enthusiasm.

Several anonymous readers from the fields of American studies and history, as well as literature, offered careful readings of the manuscript that were jarringly on the mark and, therefore, both daunting to address and extremely helpful. Although I have, in the process of many revisions, tried to incorporate the collective wisdom of everyone I have named, I have likely failed to heed their sage advice in a number of places. Of the infelicities and mistakes (if not of fact, than of judgment) that remain, I alone am accountable.

My editor, Karen Hewitt, shepherded the book through the entire publication process. Mary Giles provided expert copyediting. I thank both of them.

Family is perhaps the hardest to thank because the obligations are deeper but less direct. Much love to Susan Jackson Rodgers, my wife, best friend, partner for life, favorite writer, and mother of Samuel and Margaret. This book has been enough of an intrusive third party in our marriage that her endless patience for listening, discussing, and editing—even when she had heard and read it all before—must be acknowledged. I also thank Joe, Jacci, Mary, Clark, Cyrena, Maggie, Paul, Mike, Mary, and my parents, Lee and Mary Joyce Rodgers, who gave me such an interesting world in which to grow up, I have never wanted to leave the university. By custom, first books are often dedicated to one's parents, and although such an expression of gratitude is appropriate here, they, better than anyone, will understand the different choice in that direction that I have made.

Canaan Bound

Introduction:
The Great Migration Novel Form

Folks, I come up North
Cause they told me de North was fine.
I come up North
Cause they told me de North was fine.
Been up here six months—
I'm about to lose my mind.

This mornin' for breakfast
I chawed de mornin' air.
This mornin' for breakfast
Chawed de mornin' air.
But this evenin' for supper,
I got evenin' air to spare.

Langston Hughes

America, and perhaps the rest of the world, can be divided into two classes: those who have reached the city, and those who have not yet arrived.

Robert Park

Buckley looked down at Bigger and said,
"Just a scared colored boy from Mississippi."

Richard Wright

Midway into Ralph Ellison's remarkable *Invisible Man* (1952), the narrator arrives in New York, fresh from college in the heart of Dixie.[1] Boarding the subway to Harlem, he is crammed into a car and finds himself crushed so closely against a white woman that he "might have brushed her lips with mine." He feels the "rubbery softness of her flesh" against the "length" of his body and feels himself pressed "hard against her" (158). Trapped in this lurid pose, the narrator is terrified that she will scream. But his alarm at having unwittingly violated the most sacred of all southern racial prohibitions gives way to the recognition that no one, including the woman, pays him the slightest attention. With this first lesson in urban invisibility, he concludes his ride in silence and, in a comically grotesque image of parturition, is "shot out" onto the subway platform and into the modern city.

Like generations of pastoral innocents, the narrator is eager to embrace city life, eager to "slough off" (164) the vestiges of his southern speech, eager to test his train companion Crenshaw's earlier pronouncement that "New York. . . . That's not a place, it's a dream" (152). Plainly echoing King Solomon Gillis's awe-struck entrance into Harlem in Rudolph Fisher's "The City of Refuge," the invisible man is both shocked and heartened by the existence of black police and retail clerks. But, like all his fellow southerners who left their homes to migrate north, he is an outsider, a marginal figure trying to comprehend his new surroundings within the limited modes of perception available through his southern experience.

He settles into a local rooming house to commence life in Harlem. Alone in his room, he picks up the universal signifier of the twentieth-century traveler, a Gideon Bible. Starting fresh so far from home, dazzled by the urban environment but finding "nothing familiar in [his] surroundings" (162), he logically opens to Genesis but cannot bring himself to read. His inability to confront the story of Adam's fall is more apt than he comprehends. Having yet to realize that he has been betrayed by the school's president and expelled from his own collegiate Eden, he thinks himself in the North for only a short time. He believes that economic opportunity, not freedom nor flight from oppression, has drawn him north. But he will soon learn a painful truth: In his earlier journey with the northern industrialist Mr. Norton into the murky racial backwater of the Deep South, he, in effect, conspired to aid the white man in sampling the fruit of a taboo tree, and for this the narrator will pay dearly.

His migration thus emblematizes his fall from grace. He enters the city not as the journeyer in search of Canaan, but as a nameless Adam, an outcast, a fugitive displaced from his roots. The narrator vacillates between euphoria and fear, between the prospect of a new beginning and the challenge of retaining his past. Ellison's conception of his young traveler's equivocal entrance into Harlem is well in keeping with the vision of migration drawn by a large number of African-American literary predecessors, many of whom will be examined in this volume. The narrator must confront the discrepancies between the actual and imagined consequences of his behavior in the South and between his perception and the reality of his condition in the North. His situation is a fitting point of departure for an extended survey of how novelists have imagined the Great Migration, a task that returns time and again to examining the burden of replacing one home with another.

As one of the most widely shared experiences of black America, migration, whether through force or volition, has remained a central subject of black literature and folklore. The dominant tropes of African-American experience encompass the African removal, escape from bondage, the journey to a promised land, and the challenge of recovering southern memory amid its constant erosion. To the extent that such freedom-seeking journeys have been portrayed in a range of slave songs, blues lyrics, folk poetry, and especially in the eighteenth- and nineteenth-century escape and travel narratives of slaves and former slaves (a group responsible for as much as half of all African-American written texts [Davis and Gates, Jr., eds., *Slave's Narrative* xv]), it might be asserted that almost all African-American literature is migration literature. Thus the boundaries limiting the novels that are to come under discussion are, to a degree, more temporal and historic than thematic and cultural. When Paul Laurence Dunbar introduced the first migration novel in 1902 with *The Sport of the Gods*, he wrote in a literary and cultural climate already steeped in multiple versions of migration as varied as the Middle Passage from Africa to the Americas, the Atlantic and Mississippi Valley interstate slave trades, the Underground Railroad, the settlement of Kansas Exodusters, the move north of many members of the "talented tenth," the large-scale, rural-to-urban migration, and the smaller Oklahoma land run. In addition to echoing earlier migration literature, Dunbar also introduced an original, pathbreaking work that prefigured much later twentieth-century African-American fiction. His novel was the first story published in the United States to focus on black urban life and the first to chart the impact of a south-to-north movement. As a form, the Great Migration novel commences at this juncture of tradition and innovation.

My definition of a migration novel is one in which a real—or, less frequently, a symbolic—journey from south to north, occurring either in the novel or figuring prominently in the narrative's recent past, strongly informs the protagonist's psychological constitution and his or her responses to the external environment. These novels explore the spatial, relational, and psychological differences between the present and former worlds inhabited by characters whose identities are shaped by their participation in a real or symbolic migration. Suspended between two fundamentally different ways of life, migrants are interjacent figures, who, like their slave forbears, see their journeys as pilgrimages. The act of migrating may, like the flight north of the fugitive slave, temporarily free the migrant from oppressive elements of his or her former home. For all migrants, however, leaving the South marks a point of critical separation from family, friends, and geographic identity that is difficult to reclaim.

The basic drive of migration is the search for a livable home. Because who one is relies on possessing a sense of one's place in the world—as the epigraph from *Invisible Man* commencing this book tells us—the process of migration is indelibly tied into the broader quest for identity. The Great Migration novel plumbs the depths of this relationship between geography and identity: How have writers since the turn of the century understood the idea of migration as it has affected the African-American self? As the migrating population has gone from the rural south to the urban north, how has this group reimagined its conception of identity in literature? How has a population that has been racially marginalized and economically disadvantaged also confronted geographic displacement from the foundational roots of its southern culture? How have migrants forged and retained human relations? And how have conceptions of identity changed as American racial and demographic circumstances have shifted over time? My task will be to examine migration novels in relation to such questions by exploring how they are defined in relation to each other and to the African-American literary corpus as a whole and how they are situated within the historical, cultural, and literary circumstances and the psychological and material environments that have shaped their production.

I have kept in mind three goals as I have approached the literature. The first is to use literary archaeology to identify the novels that focus on the Great Migration, justifying their inclusion within the form and then individually examining how each negotiates the subject of migration. Because the fictional form is principally determined by features of plot that grow out of the details of an ongoing mass cultural exodus rather than exclusively by specific formal characteristics, the novels demand to be read with a firm awareness of the conditions and relations that helped to shape and change them. The second goal, then, is to read the migration novel tradition within the historical situation of black America, particularly the endemic black-white racial conflict that has always affected that situation in profound, mostly negative ways. My third goal is to position the migration novel in relation to other African-American literary works, such as slave narratives and urban fiction. Establishing these connections continues the important critical project of mapping the contours of the African-American literary tradition. This tradition—as any number of seminal narrative studies have demonstrated—is characterized by unique literary forms and an ongoing chronology of authors and works, which is notably sizable given the oppositional climate in which these authors have always labored.[2] These forms are hybrids. Their distinctive heritage and vitality derives from a combination of African roots, black American folklore, and European-American literary genres. My intention is to establish the form of the Great Migration novel as well as to view it as a significant presence within the general canon of twentieth-century American fiction.

As I have written about Great Migration novels, I have continually recalled genre theorist Alastair Fowler's contention that the truest utility of clustering groups of literary works together has to do "with identifying and communicating rather than with defining and classifying" (*Kinds of Literature* 38). I am not interested in mapping out a rigid genre and thus entering a turbulent theoretical debate about categorizing novels. My purpose in asserting the importance of migration within the African-American literary tradition is generally less theoretical than formal and historical. My aim is not so much to provide an exhaustive analysis of every domestic national migration novel as to establish a general chronology of this literature that comprehensively catalogs the form and selectively examines its milestone novels in detail. Including both canonical and noncanonical works, the two novels in each literary chapter that receive extended treatment either illuminate a new direction in the development of the form or provide exemplars of some important feature of the overall pattern.

Novelists have written about the Great Migration with varying degrees of directness. There are novels such as Waters Turpin's *O'Canaan!* (1939), Carl Offord's *The White Face* (1943), and Dorothy West's *The Living Is Easy* (1948) that follow an easily recognizable migratory trajectory. They begin in the rural south, plot a migration journey, and follow their characters through a painful readjustment to northern urban life. Generally, my willingness to define a work as a migration novel is not limited to whether it snugly fits within this unidirectional structure. I have also included novels where the Great Migration plays a less conventional but no less important role. Although, for example, the protagonists of James Weldon Johnson's *The Autobiography of an Ex-Coloured Man* (1912) and Nella Larsen's *Quicksand* (1928) both migrate from south to north, they also travel to Europe as expatriates, remigrate back to the South, and move in and out of a range of social and class settings. Both novels still remain significant inclusions in the form, even though the particular version of migration that each portrays is without precedent. What remains significant is that both Johnson's narrator and Helga Crane in *Quicksand* are forced to confront the essential differences between the American south and north and then come to terms (with widely varying results) with how those differences undermine their respective assimilations into black urban culture.

In Richard Wright's *Native Son* (1940), the Thomas family's migration precedes the frame of action. Yet inasmuch as the novel seeks to account for Bigger's horrifying crimes in the context of his material limitations, his premigration sensibility, through which his responses to his slum environment are constantly filtered, emerges as a critical defining feature of his behavior. Jean Toomer's *Cane* (1923), likely the form's most controversial inclusion, exhibits neither a conventional migration sequence nor follows a traditional novelistic pattern. Nonetheless, within its south-to-north-to-south mode of organization it offers one of the century's profound commentaries on how African-American identity is affected by the ongoing need to accommodate the geography of one's surroundings. Coming to understand what it means to be a southerner in the North and a northerner in the South is central to unpacking the many layers of Toomer's text.

To put the matter differently, in weighing whether to include a novel I have looked as much to the depiction of character as to plot. Great Migration novels offer characters whose consciousness and actions are guided by having lived in the South before trying to adjust to the North. Less conventional novels such as *The Autobiography of an Ex-Coloured Man, Quicksand,* and *Cane* exemplify instances in which the authors' careers and cultural vantage points create a form of intellectual and imaginative migration that finds its way into each narrative. Putting such novels alongside more predictable inclusions foregrounds how the idea of migration is, critically, as much a state of mind as a state of movement. Everyone will surely not agree with all of my inclusions and omissions, but the provocative nature of the pattern invites refinements and new patterns to be established from the definitions I offer.

What follows from this is a survey of the primary details of the mass exodus and the basic historiographic and sociological issues that migration scholars have confronted as they have studied the shift from south to north. The historical circumstances of the experience are framed within a series of individual letters from potential migrants who add personalized, individual voices to what has often remained an invisible, generally face-less, and sweeping cultural experience. Following the introduction, chapter 1 establishes the beginning conventions of the form with Dunbar's *The Sport of the Gods* and Johnson's *The Autobiography of an Ex-Coloured Man.*

Dunbar's portrayal of the Hamilton family's move from its southern plantation to New York offers a structural and geographic prototype; Johnson's narrator serves as a character prototype. By mapping the initial boundaries of a new literary geography in the black urban north, Dunbar offers the first novelistic escape from the black literary south. Rather than identifying the North as an alternative to the southern literary setting, however, which was circumscribed by the turn of the century by demeaning stereotypes of racial minstrelsy, Dunbar concludes that neither the North nor the South offers the black population a realistic setting in which to progress. His damning conclusions about the limitations of American racial geography set the tone for the next half-century of migration fiction.

Johnson reaches a similar conclusion in *The Autobiography of an Ex-Coloured Man,* one of the century's most powerful delineations of a character whose desire to construct a southern folk consciousness consistently rules his quest for identity, no matter where he resides. *Autobiography* joins the large corpus of nineteenth- and twentieth-century novels focusing on characters who pass from one race into another. Passing is the most extreme form of ascent, which together with immersion constitutes the kinetic liberatory patterns of narrative formulated by Robert Stepto that will help to describe the migration novel form. The act of passing inevitably complicates the passer's ambiguous relationships to both races and is further complicated when the passer migrates and thus doubly alienates him- or herself by place as well as by race. If one's identity is neither wholly white nor black as culture constructs these binary conceptions of race, and one is geographically bound to neither the South nor the North, from where can American identity emanate? Far from resolving this far-reaching question, Johnson demonstrates that the social and psychological conditions framing his novel suggest that no answer is to be found until the internal and external geographies of intra- and inter-racial America change substantially.

Hazel Carby has written that "the dominant way of reading the cultural production of what is called the Harlem Renaissance is that black intellectuals assertively established a folk heritage as the source of, and inspiration for, authentic African-American art forms" (Carby, "Politics of Fiction" 30). Although she is somewhat critical of how this obscures other kinds of representation within the period, my reading of migration literature affirms the pervasive presence of a folk heritage. It also notes the curiously limited attention that writers of the 1920s gave to the experience of folk migration, given the critical role it played in setting the stage for the explosion of cultural energy that constitutes the Harlem Renaissance. Chapter 2 addresses this apparent anomaly in an extended discussion of how the era's principal writers were and were not connected to their migrant origins. The period's two most important novels, Toomer's *Cane* and Larsen's *Quicksand,* receive detailed treatment because they exemplify essential ways in which themes of geography and identity and patterns surrounding the migration novel form find their way into migration novels that are neither conventionally nor directly about the Great Migration.

Chapter 3 turns to a different kind of migration fiction that predominated during the depression and into the 1940s. Following up on Dunbar's and Johnson's conclusions about the limitations of American racial geography, Wright's *Native Son* and William Attaway's underappreciated *Blood on the Forge* (1941) offer the most potent expressions of the "fugitive migrant" impulse thematized around the same flight toward freedom as the fugitive slave narrative, their literary forebear. They even go so far as to incorporate the slave narratives' most frequently repeated incidents, particularly whipping scenes and perilous escapes to the North. The primary goal of the fugitive's migration is to achieve physical and spiritual freedom as a heroic response to violent white oppression. Driven by the quest for an inhabitable, nonmarginal place in which to reside and prosper, the fugitive migrant initially imagines a north free of racial and economic encumbrances. His utopian vision of a New Canaan disappears, however, amid a set of urban, industrial conditions that, although different from the racial pressures of the South, continually forestall his efforts toward assimilation. Written when economic opportunities in northern cities were at the century's all-time low, and betraying little hope for northern ascent as a mechanism to achieve racial and cultural advancement, fugitive migrant novels are the most pessimistic of the form.

Focusing on West's *The Living Is Easy* and Ellison's *Invisible Man,* chapter 4 addresses the ways in which migrant novelists continue the effort to recuperate southern experience into the postmigration setting. West and Ellison join Waters Turpin, Aldon Bland, and James Baldwin to offer a conditionally more positive view of the North than their fugitive migrant predecessors. Framing their characterization of migrant assimilation within African-American conceptions of community, these novelists look to the migrant cultures' shared history and kinship ties to combat the harsh urban environment. At the core of this communal notion of migration is the recognition that retaining racial and family bonds and ancestral connections to southern black culture is the most viable means of adjusting to the North. Although this insight is hardly new to these writers, coming to terms with its implications takes on, especially in *Invisible Man,* an urgency less evident in earlier works.

In identifying *Invisible Man* as the culmination of the form, I am recognizing several points, not the least of which is the sweeping role the novel has played as one of the most important, widely discussed, and often-taught works of postwar American fiction. More specifically, Ellison has provided the richest examination to date of the effect that going from one location to another has on the creation of African-American identity and community. Within the context of its hotly debated reception, *Invisible Man* set the terms of debate about black literature for decades—precisely when the national conversation surrounding African-American life was being reframed in the most sweeping fashion since Emancipation. The murder of Emmett Till in 1949 and *Brown v. Board of Education* in 1954 helped set in motion the general constitutional and social changes wrought by the civil rights movement, and the African-American population's gradual move from predominantly rural and southern to urban was beginning to turn around. By the late 1960s more blacks were moving southward than northward (mirroring the general nationwide shift toward the Sunbelt), which further exacerbated the continuing effects of migration in many northern ghettos even after the Great Migration had, at least in a demographic sense, officially ended.

Invisible Man is an appropriate terminus for my discussion. Even though the Great Migration has ended, however, writers have continued to fictionalize migration experiences and recast the ways in which they look on them. The epilogue positions a number of recent novels within several general trends that measure the ongoing relocation of African Americans from one home to another.

The Push and Pull of Migration

> It is not skin color which makes a Negro American but cultural heritage as shaped by the American experience, the social and political predicament; a sharing of the "concord of sensibilities" which the group expressed through historical circumstance and through which it has come to constitute a subdivision of larger American culture.
>
> Ralph Ellison

From the moment that John Rolf noted in his journal on August 20, 1619, that a Dutch man-of-war had arrived with "20 Negars" on board to be sold in Jamestown, Virginia, the history of African-American life is a history of migration. The runaway slave, the Kansas Exoduster, the Jamaican immigrant, the Birmingham minister and member of the talented tenth, the Mississippi Delta southerner bound for Chicago during World War I, the Harlem family moving south in the 1970s to return to its roots, each of these travelers joined other slaves, fugitives, wanderers, explorers, settlers, and wide-eyed newcomers to northern cities in a common experience that united them across time, class, gender, geography, and nationality.

The black population's migration experiences differ fundamentally from those of European Americans, many of whom descended from ancestors who elected to come to America and who, among the earliest immigrants, were themselves responsible for displacing the native inhabitants. For African Americans, migration has not been a process of discovery and domination—of encountering new cultures, conquering them, and establishing new orders. Instead, it has been about figuring out how to import old ways and adapt them into the existing orders of their new homes.[3]

Beginning during the sixteenth century and continuing until 1870, the transatlantic importation of slaves forced as many as nine and one-half million Africans to migrate from their homelands to various places in the New World; five hundred thousand of them were directed to what is now the United States (Franklin and Moss, Jr., *From Slavery to Freedom* 39). Once living and raising families there, more than eight hundred thousand African-American slaves were sold and involuntarily relocated as a part of the Atlantic Coast and Mississippi Valley interstate slave trades. During Reconstruction, the voluntary migration of recently freed slaves filled southern cities beyond their ability to provide jobs and resources. New Orleans alone admitted approximately ten thousand individuals from Louisiana plantations (Woodson, *A Century of Negro Migration* 119). In the first planned, voluntary black migration, Benjamin "Pap" Singleton led the Kansas Exodus of 1879, increasing the black population of the state from 627 at the beginning of the Civil War to more than forty-three thousand by the 1880 census. In 1889 more than seven thousand land hungry black frontier farmers participated in the Oklahoma land rush, and over the next twenty years approximately a hundred thousand more followed (Grossman, *Land of Hope* 24; Painter, *Exodusters*).

These post-Emancipation migrations were the early flow of what would by World War I become a surging stream of men and women leaving rural areas in the South and heading to the cities of the North in search of

jobs and social equality. This mass internal migration, the largest in
ican history, is the most important African-American event after s
It has had as much effect in shaping the aspirations, attitudes, and life-styles
of urban black America as anything following slavery. Far more than simply a geographic relocation, the Great Migration transformed a rural farm
folk to an industrial city folk. It reshaped a culture from one that measured
time by the sun and seasons, counting its successes and failures in inches
of rain and bales of cotton, into a northern labor force sounding off the
beat of its day to the slow and steady tick of the factory time clock. In his
insightful Introduction to Horace Cayton and St. Clair Drake's *Black
Metropolis* (1945), Richard Wright explains that throughout history as
people left their rural homes "their kinship with the soil altered, men became atoms crowding great industrial cities, bewildered as to their duties
and meaning. . . . Holy days became holidays. . . . As the authority of the
family waned, the meaning of reality, emotion, experience, action and God
assumed the guise of teasing questions" (xxii).

What aspects of the Great Migration raised these monumental questions? Although the historiographic and social implications are still subject to debate, the major facts are well known. Ninety percent of the black
population lived in the South in 1900, and 80 percent of these residents
lived in rural areas. Fewer than one in four blacks lived in American cities. At the height of the wartime migration between 1916 and 1919, half
a million black southerners resettled in the North, and more than a million followed during the next decade. Between 1910 and 1930 nearly one
out of every ten black southerners migrated to the North and Midwest.
New York's black population grew from around thirty thousand to more
than one hundred thousand residents, and Chicago's increased from sixty
thousand to more than 150,000.

Despite the size and impact of the migration, it remains a surprisingly
invisible part of American history. Although the limited attention given to
black subjects in general accounts for part of the omission, the movement's
unique nature also accounts for the absence. As Melvin Drimmer notes,
the Great Migration was for the most part leaderless and without forceful personalities; it "went by relatively quietly. It had no philosophy, no
messianic beliefs, no revolutionary ardor" (*Issues in Black History* 171).
Not monolithic, it flowed northward through thousands of separate migrant streams. These streams so realigned the African-American demographic composition that by the 1960s half of the black population in the
United States lived outside the South. Nine out of every ten African Americans in the North and West lived in urban areas. From 1916 through the

1960s more than six million black southerners left their homes and migrated to various urban locations outside of the South.[4] Although that number is relatively small when compared to the nineteenth-century waves of European immigration, measured in terms of its impact on contemporary urban life the Great Migration has had an equally profound effect.

African-American responses to migration were predictably varied. Despite their substantial ideological differences, the two most famous former slaves in the country, Frederick Douglass and Booker T. Washington, argued more than a half century apart that black America was better off remaining in the South. By 1841 Douglass had distanced himself from the "scorching anti-southern attitudes expressed by Northern abolitionists," contending, in the words of his biographer William McFeely, that "if only his South could be granted the 'quietness' of emancipation, it would be preferable to the North." "The northern people," Douglass told one audience, "think that if slavery were abolished, we would all come north. They may be more afraid of the free colored people and the runaways going South. We would all seek our home and our friends, but, more than all, to escape from northern prejudice, would we go to the south" (*Frederick Douglass* 94–95). Echoing a similar sentiment, Washington wrote in 1915 that he had "never seen any part of the world where it seemed to me the masses of the Negro people would be better off than right here in these southern states."[5]

Washington's opinions were affirmed not only by many southern black businessmen, who viewed agriculture not industry as the basis for black progress, but also by black intellectuals. Howard University's Kelly Miller declared that "the Negro's industrial opportunities lie in the black belts," and Sutton Griggs, the black Memphis novelist, who, in a view of migration bordering on apocalyptic paranoia, argued that high urban death rates foretold the forthcoming extinction of American blacks.[6]

On the other side of the issue, Massachusetts-born W. E. B. Du Bois, in his pioneering study *The Philadelphia Negro* (1899), emphasized migration as an important element of population growth and community definition. Although not convinced that migration was the entire answer to the southern racial dilemma, Du Bois still found the prospect of black advancement more promising in the North than in the southern black belt. Alain Locke was champion of the postmigration, urban sophisticate known as the "New Negro" and one of the intellectual midwives of the Harlem Renaissance. He recognized the importance of this extraordinary movement and wholeheartedly joined in the contemporary debate among black leaders over the wisdom of the mass exodus. Locke set the tone for advocates of migration by describing it as "a new vision of opportunity, of social and economic freedom, of a spirit to seize, even in the face of an extortionate and heavy toll, the improvement of conditions" (*The New Negro* 16). James Weldon Johnson concluded that the exodus was "tantamount to a general strike" and joined a host of black southern leaders who realized that the threat of migration offered a forceful lever to political and social change (Johnson quoted in Grossman, *Land of Hope* 60).

No doubt the most vocal proponent of migration was Robert Abbott, the *Chicago Defender* editor who used the paper to publicize the North's economic and social opportunities. Abbott's overwhelming faith in northern migration was an antithetical response to Washington's famous advice to black southerners to cast down their buckets where they were. By 1916, the year after Washington's death, Abbott's position prevailed. As African-American sections of southern towns began to empty by the thousands onto northbound trains, it became clear that Washington's counsel went unheeded. No amount of persuasion could convince an ever-expanding number to remain in the South.

The debate over migration went well beyond arguments over whether it should or should not take place. Even before the war ended and the migration stream slowed, it had become the subject of much academic interest. William Cohen notes that "the Great Migration occurred just as the movement for the study of black history was taking root and the two became intertwined with one another" (Harrison, *Black Exodus* 77). Two of the earliest important books were Carter Woodson's *A Century of Negro Migration* (1900), which focused on migration before World War I, and Emmett Scott's *The Negro Migration during the War* (1920), an extensive study developed under a Carnegie Corporation grant. Included in the latter book were studies Scott commissioned by Monroe N. Work, Charles S. Johnson, and T. Thomas Fortune. These early migration scholars, joined by other contemporary observers such as Du Bois and Henderson Donald, a student at Yale University, were united by their awareness that they were witnessing an event of profound importance.[7] As individuals interested in examining the roots of the exodus, they came to a number of different conclusions about its causes. As a group, however, they arrived at some unified general conclusions that, although defined by earlier methods of historical scholarship, still remain valid.

The large-scale conditions that sparked this mass hegira were, of course, as varied as the individual aspirations and identities of each migrant; nonetheless, they can be summarized by what early students of the movement described as southern "push" and northern "pull" factors.[8] The combination of deteriorating life in the South, what James Weldon Johnson called "the tremendous shore of southern barbarism" (Grossman, *Land of Hope* 16), together with the sudden wartime need for northern laborers, stimulated the largest surge of migration. There are dozens of accounts of the Great Migration, ranging from the brief descriptions it receives in most conventional American histories to the extensive, focussed, region-specific accounts favored by recent social scientists and historians. As contemporary scholars have learned from, built upon, and moved beyond the assertions of the early studies of Scott, Woodson, and Charles Johnson, the recognition of migration's importance continues to grow. Any present-day bibliography on the subject runs to dozens of pages. James Grossman's impressive *Land of Hope: Chicago, Black Southerners, and the Great Migration* (1989), which brought migration historiography up to date and should remain the standard treatment for some time to come, summarizes a balanced means by which to comprehend the array of arguments that seek to account for the motives behind the exodus:

> Regardless of how much priority is placed on which factor, lists of "push" and "pull" forces suggest mainly the range of injustices and privations driving blacks from the South. No list can implicitly weave together its various components to compose an image of the fabric of social and economic relationships which drove black southerners to look elsewhere for a better life. Nor can lists communicate the fears, disgusts, hopes, and goals that combined to propel blacks from the South and draw them northward.
>
> An explanation of motivation, of the decision to move North, lies in the continuity of southern black life, as much as in the changes caused by the wartime economy. (18)

Blacks from both rural and urban environments in the South were pushed away from a way of life characterized by an isolated, primarily feudal, underdeveloped, rural agricultural economy. The South as a whole had fewer schools, fewer basic services, and higher unemployment than the rest of the country. It also had an underindustrialized, sagging labor market critically dependent on cotton, which by the early 1900s had been severely ravaged by a calamitous influx of boll weevils and widespread flooding throughout the Mississippi Delta. As additional burdens, the black population had to endure Jim Crow, the legacy of the Supreme Court's 1896 "separate but equal" *Plessy v. Ferguson* decision, and various forms of disfranchisement enforced by harassment and prohibitively high poll taxes. In addition to those supposedly legal means of stripping black southerners of their civil rights, the white majority also relied on the invisible empire of the Ku Klux Klan to keep order and, when deemed necessary, impose the draconian authority of lynching. For southern blacks, the bitter fruit of reconstruction ripened only into peonage, discrimination, and neo-slavery, leaving little doubt that the decades before and after the turn of the century remain the nadir of African-American history.

Despite such racial woes, African Americans of the South were often loathe to exercise their right to leave their homes, partly because of the various schemes developed by white southerners to harass potential migrants into staying. Many towns hurriedly passed ordinances limiting black mobility. Because most sharecroppers were technically entrapped by a cycle of perpetual debt, local sheriffs pulled them off trains and even jailed them to try to keep them at home. When labor agents appeared throughout the South offering blacks free passage on special northbound freight cars, many of the agents were driven from town at gun point and occasionally even tarred and feathered. Because generations of southern blacks had found ways to circumvent an array of obstacles, however, white resistance alone did little to stem the northward tide.

Many rural residents had never ventured further from home than they could walk in a day and, despite whatever they learned about Chicago or New York through barber and beauty shop talk, letters from relatives, and general local gossip, they lacked any real conception of northern city life. The journey almost always meant leaving a supportive network of family, friends, community, and church. Faced with the prospect of such losses, the difficult part of their decision had little to do with white oppression.

Nonetheless, thousands found the courage to venture into the unknown. When European immigration dropped sharply from 1.2 million in 1914 to a hundred thousand in 1918, the American war industry's desperate need for laborers forced northern factories to lift their bans on black employees. The same year, Henry Ford reinforced the trend by announcing that his Detroit auto plant would hire blacks and pay the unheard of minimum wage of $5 a day. Although Ford's motives for employing blacks were allegedly connected to a life-long pattern of anti-Semitism, individual workers had no knowledge of his prejudices and were happy to benefit from their good fortune. Blind Blake was one of several migrant bluesmen who put his satisfaction with Ford into song:

> I'm goin' to Detroit, get myself a good job, [*twice*]
> Tried to stay around here with the starvation mob.

> I'm goin' to get a job, up there in Mr. Ford's place, [*twice*]
> Stop these eatless days from starin' me in the face.
> (Oliver, *Blues Fell This Morning* 30)

As more and more southerners were, like Blind Blake, pulled toward factory jobs, the arteries of kinship, which since slavery, had buttressed life in the rural south, expanded rapidly into various points in the North. These community connections channeled migrants toward specific destinations, jobs, residential districts, and even specific boardinghouses and homes (Trotter, *The Great Migration* 72).

The message was clear: The large number of opportunities and higher wages offered in the North made migration a real alternative for every black southerner to consider. There are any number of individual explanations that account for the "exterior facets of migration—the causes, destinations, numbers of migrants, and living conditions in origin and destinations areas" as well as numerous new studies focusing on the experience itself that examine the "structures of group life and the values, attitudes, perceptions, and status that migrants brought to their movement" (Gottlieb, *Making Their Own Way* 69).

Among the myriad firsthand analysts of the Great Migration, no observer was more qualified to assess its importance than James Weldon Johnson, whose penetrating description of the migration's causes was presented in *Black Manhattan* (1930), his classic study of African-American life in New York from its earliest days:

> With the outbreak of the war there came a sudden change. One of the first effects of the war was to draw thousands of aliens out of this country back to their native lands to join the colours. Naturally, there was also an almost total cessation of immigration. Moreover, the United States was almost immediately called upon to furnish munitions and supplies of all kinds to the warring countries. The result of these converging causes was an unprecedented shortage of labour and a demand that was imperative. From whence could the necessary supply be drawn? There was only one source, and that was the reservoir of black labour in the South. And it was at once drawn on to fill the existing vacuum in the great industries of the North. Every available method was used to get these black hands, the most effective being the sending of labour agents into the South, who dealt directly with the Negroes, arranged for their transportation, and shipped them North, often in single consignments running high up into the hundreds. I witnessed the sending North from a Southern city in one day a crowd estimated at twenty-five hundred. They were shipped on a train run in three sections, packed in day coaches, with all their baggage and other impediments. The exodus was on, and migrants came North in thousands, tens of thousands, hundreds of thousands—from the docks of Norfolk, Savannah, Jacksonville, Tampa, Mobile, New Orleans, and Galveston; from the cotton-fields of Mississippi, and the coal-mines and steel-mills of Alabama and Tennessee; from workshops and wash-tubs and brick-yards and kitchens they came,

until the number, by conservative estimate, went well over the million and a half mark. For the Negroes of the South this was a happy blending of desire with opportunity. (151–52)

The appeal of Johnson's description is found in its emphasis on the vast magnitude of migration, yet it stops short of viewing the movement as a fluid historical process. Up through the 1960s and 1970s, historians tended to represent migration as a series of one-way movements to the North that helped explain the formation of urban ghettoes. Whether pushed or pulled to the city, migrants once there were trapped in the economic and environmental limitations of their surroundings. From within this "ghetto model," they were represented as passive victims of larger forces. The most recent generation of historians has counteracted the biases of this model, however, by considering the dynamic connection between northern residents and their southern roots. Migrants, they have concluded, rarely stayed in the North without returning south, sometimes for weeks or months at a time.[9] Yet regardless of whether they traveled there physically, the South remained central to their collective urban consciousness.

A summary of where migration historiography stands can be measured in Joe William Trotter's *The Great Migration in Historical Perspective* (1991), a collection of essays that, even within its wide field of analysis, shares two important theses. First, migrants have always relied on access to premigration cultural resources that have at least blunted if not overturned the force of economic and social discrimination in the North. Second, migrants have, from their earliest arrival in the North, exerted substantially more personal control over their lives than may have been previously granted. Although scholars were, perhaps, slower than they should have been in coming to understand these points, African-American writers, who over the past century have incorporated migration into their stories, as example after example bears out, knew them to be true all along.

Migration's Individual Voicings

Beyond the debates, the explanations, and the statistics, who were the individuals who made up this epic movement? One of the difficulties in describing the Great Migration is balancing the large with the small, the general with the particular. Social science's tendency to reduce individuals to numbers and mute singular modulations in favor of the voice of a greater, collective personality is balanced against the hazard—more recurrent in literary scholarship—of too freely positing the words of one person as universally representative of a collective consciousness. How to avoid such generalizations, particularly within the sociological framework that writers such as Richard Wright have favored, has been a recurring dilemma for black writers; how to read black literature in light of this problem has been the burden of critics. Offered only selective and frequently skewed representations of black humanity, the white reading public has, over the years, mistakenly looked to the characters of black fiction as racial spokespersons and representative types of black humanity and thus reduced them to curious others and essentialized them within racial boundaries. Zora Neale Hurston was so frustrated by the constant pressure to use the yardstick of race as an aesthetic measure of her art that she told a black critic that she was interested in "writing a novel and not a treatise on sociology" (Hemenway, *Zora Neale Hurston* 42).

To comprehend the Great Migration on Hurston's terms is to localize the sociological generalizations and numbers of the movement. The push and pull impulses were well understood by individual migrants, who articulated personal versions of them in several distinct formats. The most available and wide-ranging of these individual folk responses are reflected in blues lyrics. Although the following chapters emphasize published literary responses to migration, the blues were one of the most significant cultural by-products of the Great Migration; its music (and lyrics) provided artistic outlets and new kinds of expressive agency, particularly for women and the disadvantaged.[10] In his classic *Blues Fell This Morning*, Paul Oliver, a British blues historian, points out that "a folk music reflects the environment of the people who create it, and when their background is a constant varying one it is scarcely surprising that the images that are mirrored in the blues have much to do with the movement of the black workers" (43–44).

The spread and development of the blues was dependent on the itinerant habits of its practitioners. Thus it is to be expected that many of the primary themes of migration recur with some frequency in the lyrics of pre–World War II blues songs. In her "Freight Train Blues," Trixie Smith reproduced the migrant's sense of placelessness and loneliness. Bill Casey's "WPA Blues" documented the struggle to find good work, as did Gene Campbell in his "Levee Camp Man Blues" (1930): "These contractors they are getting so slack, / They'll pay you half of your money and hold the other half back." The burden of constant travel was a widely repeated subject. In "Hard Road Blues," Blind Blake lamented that "walkin' down the hard road done wore the soles off my shoes, / . . . My soles are ragged, I got those hard road blues" (Barlow, *Looking Up at Down* 197). Petey Wheatstraw likewise sang in "Road Tramp Blues" that "my feet is too sore to walk" and "my tongue is too stiff to talk."

One of the more widespread feelings was the vital sense of liberation from the South. Although Alabama-born Charles "Cow Cow" Davenport overlooks his failure to be liberated from Chicago's famously cold winters in the last line of the appropriately titled "Jim Crow Blues," he still conveys spirited enthusiasm for putting distance between himself and Dixie:

> I'm tired of being Jim Crowed, gonna leave this Jim Crow town,
> Doggone my black soul, I'm sweet Chicago bound,
> Yes I'm leavin' here, from this ole Jim Crow town.
>
> I'm goin' up north where they say money grows on trees,
> I don't give a doggone, if ma black soul leaves,
> I'm goin' where I don't need no B.V.D.s.
> (Barlow, *Looking Up at Down* 297)

Conversely, Roosevelt Sykes was among the many migrant singers who, once in the North, longed for home: "Well I'm going back down South . . . Old Dixieland is jumping—I've got those Southern blues."[11] Although such examples constitute only a starting point for recording the dramatic dimension of migration-influenced blues (which helped pave the way for the later explosive popularity of black music during World War II), they hint at a cultural legacy that is less easy to register than published literature but remains every bit as important. Contemporary popular music, unfolding as it did out of the postwar migration, is one of the movement's most dominant and visible products.

A more self-contained set of migrant expressions and an interesting companion piece to blues lyrics is found in the best-known historical document of folk responses to leaving the South: a collection of letters received by the *Chicago Defender,* the nation's most widely read black newspaper, and later published in the *Journal of Negro History.* Carter Woodson, son of former slaves and a Harvard Ph.D., began editing the journal for the newly formed Association for the Study of Negro Life and History in January 1916. As the leading figure of a group interested in promoting the study of black history, Woodson envisioned a journal that would apply the same rigorous research standards to scholarship on black subjects in America and Africa that were commonplace in other historical, sociological, and anthropological areas. His goal was to combat the pseudo-scientific, propagandistic, and avowedly racist treatments of the African-American population throughout Reconstruction and the turn-of-the-century racial nadir.

In addition to standard academic articles, Woodson included a documents section that reprinted primary material, often with no editing or explanation. As he intended, the feature provides a critical source of primary information, including one of the richest, most revealing, and widely cited group of documents of the migration. For the fall and spring documents sections in 1919, Emmett Scott, long-time private secretary to the recently deceased Booker T. Washington, collected some 140 pages of letters written by black southerners. The letters came from Charles Johnson, who worked for Scott and was the research director for the Chicago Urban League. Johnson had poured through some four thousand letters "written by Negroes from all parts of the South to northern persons and agencies expressing a desire to move" (Johnson, "Negro Migration" 323). Most of the letters were originally mailed to the *Defender,* which had held them, unpublished, in its files before giving them to the journal. Scott wrote a brief headnote for each letter, organized them thematically under descriptive headlines, and presented them exactly as they had been written, grammar and misspellings intact.[12]

The letters arrived at the newspaper from everywhere, from the coasts of Georgia and Florida to small towns in Oklahoma. Most were dated and signed, but their exact origins are difficult to pin down. Although many were composed and signed by the same person, some had been no doubt written and sold by professional letter-writers, others had been transcribed by more literate friends and neighbors, and still others had been copied from form letters. Regardless of their origins, the letters told an overwhelmingly similar story: The southern black population desperately wanted out of the South, and northern and midwestern cities were the destinations of choice. They conceived of migration in complex terms long before they boarded northbound trains or set foot in Grand Central Station. Like their blues-singing relatives and like characters of migration fiction, the writer of each letter had an individual story to tell.

One of the reasons for Scott having a large choice of letters was Robert Abbott's personal crusade to liberate the black south. Measuring all issues in terms of racial self-interest, the *Defender*'s editor, a migrant from Georgia, as late as 1916 still urged black southerners to remain at home. He converted almost overnight, however, as the demand for black laborers in the North increased dramatically, and he became the country's most relentless promoter of migration.

Abbott's strategy to lure migrants north was simple and effective. Every issue of the *Defender* stressed the wretched state of affairs in the South and contrasted what Abbott portrayed as a southern economic and social wasteland with the land of infinite opportunity that lay at the other end of the Illinois Central Railroad. Not above yellow journalism, he often documented southern lynchings and other acts of white terrorism with tabloid-sized headlines and luridly descriptive prose. Such stories were complemented by employment notices for factory work and manual labor, which specifically targeted black southerners. Eager inquiries poured in. When a southern family accepted what must have seemed to be a personal invitation from Abbott to come north, the *Defender* was there with equally candid advice about how they were to behave in their new home. A typical editorial page exemplifies the paper's mission: The left half scabrously denounces a southern lynch mob and the right half reminds recently arrived migrants of the necessity of bathing.

Abbott sold readers a vision of Chicago and the North as nothing short of a promised land. Channeling distribution through itinerant singers, well-known black orators, and especially the thousands of Pullman porters based out of Chicago whose routes took them throughout the South, Abbott ensured a wide southern readership. Between 1916 and 1918, the height of the Great Migration, the *Defender* became so popular that its distribution increased tenfold, and it reached a paid circulation of more than 230,000 (Ottley, *The Lonely Warrior* 130–40; Tuttle, *Race Riot* 90).

By turning the letters over to Scott and the *Journal of Negro History,* Abbott functioned as an antebellum abolitionist acting as amanuensis for fugitive slaves. He transformed fragmented, exploited, unheard voices into a collective argument for reform by drawing on the power of their presence on the page. As with slave narratives, present readers must negotiate an unfamiliar rhetorical mode favoring propaganda and persuasion over the factual and more lyrical recounting of a true life story.

The letters are a powerful, unique conjunction of autobiography and original social history. They include personal histories, character references, train-fare requests, employment applications, and accounts of beatings, lynchings, and other southern white hostility. Rather than marking unconventional lives, each offers an unconventional mode of telling about an ordinary life. Like more traditional autobiographical forms, they must be read through the filter of their writers' biases. As William Andrews has observed, autobiography as a general form "stems more often than not from a need to explain and justify the self" (*To Tell a Free Story* 1). If the writers can clarify their circumstances in the South to the sympathetic ear of the *Defender,* they qualify as potential migrants. Denied access to conventional autobiographical forms, they explain and justify themselves in letters. The letter form is as notable as the context of the writers' individual situations. It is reminiscent of an earlier text of the written black self, the fugitive slave narrative, and shares the same agenda—the impelling drive toward literacy and freedom.

As detailed, fragmented, highly personal stories of black folk life in the South, the letters are epistolary creations of the self. They provide details and insight into the desires, fears, and motivations of a population whose written biographical legacy was sparse because of low levels of literacy, isolation from publishing enterprises, and estrangement from white power structures. Like other autobiographies, the letters are linked by a common intent, interlinked themes and strategies, and a common chronology; moreover, they have been arranged, validated by an authenticating document, printed as a unified work, and presented to a public readership.

The letters' introductions are conventional. The writer introduces himself or herself to the paper and then inquires about the "labor situation," "information concerning positions," the "need of employees," whether "you will send me a transportation," and other like requests. But beyond their concerns for work, they voice strong emotions about how they are being treated, demonstrating their intense anxiety about day-to-day interaction with the white population.

It was hardly surprising that many letter-writers inquired about job opportunities from a publication that contained more employment notices targeted at black readers than any other source in the country. That the writers confided details of their oppression (information that would put them at risk if white neighbors were to intercept the letters) indicates just how important and trustworthy the *Defender* was. A frightened and repressed population was willing to take such a chance for the prospect of a better life. A Troy, Alabama, writer, for example, addressed the unknown recipient of the letter as a sympathetic ally and confidante: "I am enclosing a clipping of a lynching again which speaks for itself. I do wish there could be sufficient presure brought about to have federal investigation of such work" (Scott, "Additional Letters" 440). Requests for anonymity were assumed to be honored: "This is not as a testimony—don't publish" (Scott, "Letters" 334); "i follow publick work untill now would not like for my name to be publish in the paper" (Scott, "Letters" 335); "because things is afful hear in the south let me here from you soon as poseble what ever you do dont publish my name in your paper" (335); and "I will do most anything to get our family out of *Bam*. Please let this be confidential" (Scott, "Letters" 312).

A stronger truth is found in the letters' subtext, which concerns white prejudice and social conditions in the South. A Macon, Georgia, resident, for example, asked for "transportation" because "we are down here where we have to be shot down here like rabbits for every little orfence" (Scott, "Additional Letters" 438). A Bham, Alabama, writer pleaded, "O please help me to get out of this low down county i am counted no more thin a dog help me please help me," and opened his letter with a powerfully suggestive metaphor: "i am in the darkness of the south and i am trying my best to get out" (Scott, "Additional Letters" 440). A college-educated teacher from Lexington, Mississippi, wrote that "I am so sick I am so tired of such conditions that I sometime think that life for me is not worth while and most eminently believe with Patrick Henry 'Give me liberty or give me death'" (Scott, "Letters" 304), a severely ironic reference if one recalls that Henry owned slaves. A Sanford, Florida, resident similarly demanded his rights as an American: "I still have a desire to seek for myself a section of this country where I can poserably better my condishion in as much as beaing asshured some protection as a good citizen under the Stars and Stripes" (Scott, "Additional Letters" 439).

The writers often expressed a desire for employment as a way of achieving social equality and betterment. A seventeen-year-old girl from Selma, Alabama, was simple and direct: "Sirs I am writeing to see if You all will please get me a job. And Sir I can wash dishes, wash iron nursing work in groceries and dry good stores. Just any of these I can do." Even direct requests for employment revealed much about conditions in the South. A letter written from Newbern, Alabama, read in part: "I wish to say that we are forced to go when one things of a grown man wages is only fifty to seventy five cents per day for all grades of work. He is compelled to go where there is better wages and sociable conditions, believe me" (Scott, "Additional Letters" 419–20). The writer, a minister, was "forced" to move because he made too little money, but he also addressed poor southern "sociable conditions": "The white man is saying that you must not go but they are not doing anything by way of assisting the black man to stay" (Scott, "Additional Letters" 420). Another letter concentrated on details: "I am a Negro, age 37, and am an all round foundry man. I am a cone maker by trade having had about 10 years experience at the business, and hold good references from several shops, in which I have been employed" (Scott, "Additional Letters" 425). Regardless of his qualifications, he could not overcome the fact that "it is hard for a black man to hold a job here, as prejudice is very strong. I have never been discharged on account of dissatisfaction with my work, but I have been 'let out' on account of my color." A job in the North would allow this writer to leave, but his social status clearly spells out why he was "anxious to get busy and be on my way" (Scott, "Additional Letters" 425).

The migrants were a disgruntled, underpaid, and ready work force, but the economic environment from which they wanted to flee was borne out of southern prejudice and exploitation as much as failed crops and unfair interest rates. Other letters point to the wide range of respectable and responsible jobs the writers held, their managerial skills, particularly their overwhelming desire for education for themselves and their children; demonstrate the intensity of the population's desire to migrate; fix the cause of this desire for social improvement, bringing sharp relief to theories based principally on economic betterment; and forcefully spell out the widespread feelings of repression and fear that governed daily life in the South.

Although the gate of entry looked inviting, for only a few migrants did the North prove to be the black promised land as Abbott sold it and the writers optimistically pictured it. Racism was less overt in the North than in the South, but its economic and social exclusion was just as strong and intensified by the hostility of established northern blacks. The new migrants represented stiff labor competition, and, as a largely undereducated agrarian work force that brought often-crude habits and folkways to the city, they reminded the black middle class of stereotypes that had been painful to overcome. Yet the *Defender*'s letters suggest that the new urbanites, despite their obvious lack of sophistication, were not so different from their more entrenched neighbors. Before migrating, they had held a multitude of responsible jobs, and they offered a wide range of labor skills to northern employers. Some were well educated, and almost without exception they exhibited sufficient rhetorical skills to make a case for why they deserved more than the South offered. The letters indicate that the migrants were not ignorant country bumpkins, as their northern urban neighbors came to characterize them.

The concept of migration took shape and gained importance throughout the South even before the migrants departed. Black southerners did not simply react to white oppression. They seized the opportunity to overcome oppression through a conscious act, meaningfully planned and executed. Asserting both autonomy and ambition, the migrant's decision to leave the South, as Grossman notes, "could be taken as a challenge, an aggressive statement of dissatisfaction" (*Land of Hope* 38). As Leroi Jones [Amiri Baraka] would write, "It was a decision Negroes made to leave the South, not an historical imperative" (*Blues People* 96).

Baraka suggests that southern blacks were, in a larger sense than is usually granted, the agents of their own fortune. But there is another implication: The overtly sociological interpretation of the Great Migration has conditioned a view that favors sweeping conclusions over individual experience. Viewed on what Grossman terms a "macro-historical scale" (*Land of Hope* 14), the migration seems a vast human tide rolling north-ward. As Edward Relph observes in the preface to *Place and Placelessness,* however, "Place and sense of place do not lend themselves to scientific analysis for they are inextricably bound up with all the hopes, frustrations, and confusions of life." The latest generation of migration scholars have recognized this and demonstrated that an equally empirical and often more interesting voice is that of individual migrants. From these singular voic-es, a much richer, more personal, and more accurate historical picture of migration emerges. Through such voices, migration has come to represent far more than simply a cultural change, a shift in the labor tide, and a mass physical movement. Articulated by individuals, this matrix of shared ex-perience is a series of symbolic possibilities; it is a trope and, finally, an art. The Great Migration has been thoroughly studied as history but not significantly enough as art. The novels of the Great Migration add to the effort to illuminate the many literary representations of this central Afri-can-American experience.

Fisher's "City of Refuge"

The signal features that characterize migration novels can be blocked out in a brief examination of Fisher's short story "The City of Refuge." As a model text, its movement and major tension summarize the principal con-flicts that grow out of the migrations of other protagonists/migrants in more fully developed novel-length migration fiction. First published in the *Atlan-tic Monthly* and reprinted in Alain Locke's anthology of Harlem writers, *The New Negro* (1925), Fisher's tableau of urban naiveté charts the tragi-comic path of a displaced southerner whose downfall comes from failing to com-prehend the differences between his old and new homes.[13] The story opens with the defining scene of the Great Migration: the arrival of a southerner who has come north to escape his past and improve his life. King Solomon Gillis stands "dazed and blinking." "Strange and terrible sounds" issue forth randomly from the nightmare that envelops him. Does he hear rifle shots? Distant thunder? Or is he to be consumed by the "shuffle of a thousand soles, clatter of a thousand heels, innumerable echoes"? The sound barrage is suddenly overwhelmed by "the screeching onslaught of the fiery hosts of hell." "Heat, oppression, suffocation" (57) grip him. Where is he? Snared inside this aural nightmare of technology? And how must he escape? Like thousands of migrants before and after him, young Gillis, fresh off the train from Waxhaw, North Carolina, stands inside New York City's Penn Station, transfixed by the cacophony of exotic sounds as he tries to navigate his way to Harlem. But like Jonah emerging from the belly of the whale (the image that Ellison later refigures in the same setting), he is spewed forth into "clean air, blue sky, bright sunlight," and the nightmare stage of his dreamstate is replaced by one of infinite possibility. Everywhere he looks, he sees "big, lanky Negroes, short, squat Negroes; black ones, brown ones, yellow ones; men standing idle on the curb, women, bundle-laden, trudging reluctantly homeward, children rattle-trapping about the sidewalks; here and there a white face drifting along, but Negroes predominantly, overwhelmingly everywhere" (57–58).

Gillis, like so many fugitive migrants, has hastily departed "with the aid of prayer and an automobile" from the fictional Waxhaw, where he narrowly avoided a lynching for shooting a white man. Although the North represents a new beginning for him, his initial euphoria is short-lived. Unschooled in urban ways, he mistakenly puts himself under the instruction of a North Carolina homeboy, Mouse Uggams, who wastes no time putting his gullible friend to work selling narcotics. Gillis, a rube assuming that motives and loyalties are the same in Harlem as they were in North Carolina, can only express gratitude at being included in Uggams's "medicine" business. Needing someone to sacrifice to the police to draw attention away from his own illegal activities, Uggams has lured Gillis into the action only to set him up for a fall. When the police come to arrest him, Gillis puts up a fierce fight until a "cullud" officer steps in. Stunned and filled with pride at the opportunity of being arrested by a black with such status, he happily submits and is led away.

From its initial scene, Fisher's narrative underwrites a series of critical oppositions of the kind that recur throughout migration novels. Even from the sparse textual clues, it is clear that Gillis has left behind an agrarian setting within a homogeneous community that is, like other segregated black settings in the South, circumscribed by racial marginality, a shared history rooted in slavery, and relationally connected through a common language and similar folk culture. The source of his downfall (and the basis of some of the story's more humorous moments) is his failure to recognize that the North is structured around a different, even antithetical, set of conditions. In Harlem, Gillis encounters an urban, industrial, and culturally heterogeneous setting in which human relations are more associational than familial. The world of the story is characterized by progressive social structures, a gamut of different language features, and a well-entrenched black population that occupies the center rather than the margins of the culture. Gillis, like Ellison's narrator, views his new home through the eyes of an outsider. The story's, and the migration novel form's, ongoing conflict arises from the clash between the old culture and the new.

I am intentionally summarizing Gillis's literary migration with respect to monolithic binarisms such as north/south, rural/urban, agrarian/industrial, individual/relational, and kinetic/stationary because these oppositions are, in many instances, how migration novelists impose order on what is otherwise a diffuse, multifaceted, and ever-changing experience. Black migrants traveled from the West to the East, from southern cities to northern farms, and from positions of spatial freedom to stationary enslavement. Migration literature infrequently records these experiences, but the series of general oppositions upon which Fisher relies in "The City of Refuge" offers a useful shorthand outlining the structure from which the conflicts of migration novels emanate.

Gillis's complex social position can be clarified by two concepts—liminality and the marginal man—from social science that inform the discussions of individual novels. Liminality, an anthropological concept that Victor Turner has made well known, is useful as a means for talking about divided and marginal characters in literature. Detached in various degrees from personal and public history, from geography, from origins, and from much else that is familiar, migrants such as Gillis reside in a state of suspension, occupying a position that Turner has described as liminal. Modern investigations of liminality that began with the Belgian ethnographer Arnold van Gennep's *Les rites de passage* (1909) have been built upon substantially by Turner. In its original African context, the liminal moment marks a middle, interstitial stage of a three-step ritual initiation process. This phase of *rites de passage* is the tenuous period after which "an individual or group either from an earlier fixed point in the social structure, from a set of cultural conditions (a 'state'), or from both" has reached a "cultural realm that has few or none of the attributes of the past or coming state" (Turner, *Drama, Fields* 94). At this point in the transition, the limen (Latin for threshold) is alienated—by change in law, custom, convention, ceremony, or geography—in some way from the culture of the past but not yet fully attuned to the culture of the present.

In his characterization of liminality van Gennep emphasizes, according to Firmat, the "fleeting, ephemeral moment destined for supersession" (*Literature and Liminality* xiii). Turner expands van Gennep's definition by describing the synchronic possibilities of the concept. His fuller definition of the term makes a distinction important to migration, because, as Firmat writes, "Turner, in effect, supplements van Gennep's temporal, processual view of liminality with a spatial one. While for van Gennep the limen is always a threshold, for Turner it can also be a place of habitation" (*Literature and Liminality* xiv). As a liminal site, migration becomes more than a move between places. It charges the act of migration with a sacred cultural force that signifies a change in one's relationship to space. Liminality is, finally, to be understood not only as a position in which the "ritual subject . . . becomes ambiguous, neither here nor there, betwixt and between all fixed points of classification" (Turner, *Drama, Fields* 232) but also as the equivalent process of a journey of such symbolic force as to bear the full weight of a biblically inspired search for a new Canaan.[14]

The second concept, the marginal man, was developed early in the twentieth century by the most prominent member of the University of Chicago's sociology department, Robert Park. Drawing on the work of his predecessor, William Isaac Thomas, Park used his theory of social disorganization to note how the Great Migration propelled a number of ill-equipped southerners into an urban environment that was impersonal and constantly changing, which in turn accelerated the breakdown of personal and community identity and social mores. Caught between the cultures of the rural south and the urban north, the marginal man (which now must be read to include "marginal woman") was victim of this process. Unable to belong to either culture but possessing useful insight into both, his personality was constantly challenged as he tried to adapt to ways and values not his own. When he failed to adjust, he compensated with various kinds of antisocial behavior that threw the entire community further off balance. In spite of this seemingly grim prognosis for individual urban migrants such as King Solomon Gillis, Park also asserted that as old and new cultures interacted a race-relations cycle would grind forward that would eventually lead distanced migrants to more assimilated, better lives.[15]

Although contemporary urban sociologists accept Park's work as a pioneering explanation of urban dysfunction, few would accept his theory without taking into account the substantial refinements it has passed through over the years. As it pertains to migration literature, Park's devaluation of folk culture is the most notable defect of the school. It is, however, useful to consider the marginal man in its original formulation because it was in the writing of Park and his fellow Chicago academics that Richard Wright located a satisfying explanation for his postmigration marginality, which in turn played an integral role in Wright's conception of Bigger Thomas (chapter 3).

The plot of the migration novel reflects both the ordered, ritualized nature of liminality and the alienation of the marginal man. Following the example of "The City of Refuge," this plot may be generally summarized as a series of conventionalized events. A protagonist, more often male than female, leaves the South, either alone or with family, in order to escape from something—a series of farming misfortunes, a fateful encounter with a white man, a painful break with the black community, or, in the case of the female migrant, some form of gender exploitation—which has forced the migrant to sever the relationship to his or her former home. Either before or during the novel, the migrant arrives in the North, exultant in a newfound sense of freedom and confident of impending success. The new city-dweller, however, soon goes through an urban initiation that painfully demonstrates how poorly he or she is prepared for northern city life. The combination of environmental antipathy and a value system ill-equipped for successful urban assimilation ensures that the literary migrant must address a range of obstacles that can hardly be overcome. The migrant responds in various ways correlating to different conventions within the migration novel's various subforms: by finally rejecting the North and remigrating south, by rejecting his or her racial identity and recrossing the color line, by lashing out at forces beyond the migrant's control and falling victim to them, by submitting to the superior power of the environment, or, more rarely, by making a successful and triumphant transition from south to north.

African-American literature has been dominated throughout the twentieth century by what Hazel Carby, who is critical of the tendency, has called "an ideology of the 'folk.'" This construction of black literary consciousness, rooted in southern folk culture, favors vernacular expression and draws its imaginative configurations of black experience from a "mythology of the rural south that conflates . . . slavery and sharecropping, into one mythical rural folk existence" ("Ideologies of Black Folk" 126–27).[16] This ideology is as evident in "The City of Refuge" as it is in migration novels. Even Fisher, a middle-class physician who was born in Washington, D.C., and remained a northern urbanite throughout his life, suggests the limited possibilities available to King Solomon Gillis through the absence of strong folk representations. Despite whatever weaknesses Gillis displays, Fisher's sympathies lie more with him than with his Harlem neighbors. Fisher's ironic and somewhat gentle mocking of Gillis is balanced by a satiric appraisal of Harlem as an almost valueless urban landscape populated by an assortment of con men, frauds, and charlatans loosely held in check by the physical proximity of the police.

Missing for Gillis is what Toni Morrison has identified as a usable "ancestor." She has observed that "whether [a black novel] took place in the city or in the country, the presence or absence of that figure determined the success or the happiness of the character. It was the absence of an ancestor that was frightening, that was threatening, and it caused huge destruction and disarray in the work itself" ("Rootedness" 343). There is, for Gillis, no northern alternative to Mouse Uggams who can befriend and guide him. Able to take refuge only in the corrupt and false ancestor, Uggams, Gillis has no authentic part of his former culture to aid him. And lacking access to a usable southern model or misreading how an available model can be reconstituted in the North, as the Great Migration novel form emphasizes repeatedly, Gillis is as doomed in Harlem as if he had remained down home to face his white accusers.

The story makes only passing reference to Gillis's escape north; similarly, migration fiction places little emphasis on the actual details of the journey. The Great Migration designates much more than simply a geographic movement; it signals the need for a change of internal consciousness and an entirely new apprehension of external reality. This freighted conception of migration's impact grows out of the historical realities of slavery. The fugitive journey from south to north meant nothing less than the heroic flight from bondage to freedom, even if the journey's details may have been suppressed in the written accounts of escape so future fugitives would have opportunity to use a similar strategy to travel the same escape path.

Frederick Douglass, after escaping from slavery in September of 1838 in what is no doubt the most famous example of African-American domestic migration, characterized his arrival in New York as the culminating occasion of his life: "The dreams of my childhood and the purposes of my manhood were now fulfilled. A free state around me, and a free earth under my feet! What a moment was this to me!" (*My Bondage* 205). Whether fleeing the bonds of slavery, like Douglass, or eluding a North Carolina lynch mob, like Gillis, the migrant is propelled by a vision of liberty and privilege denied in the South. Realizing this vision, however variously it may be defined, becomes the symbolic quest of the narrative. The ability to move from one place to another has historically been, in the words of Howard Thurman, a black minister, "the most psychologically dramatic of all manifestations of freedom" (quoted in Levine, *Black Culture* 262). Even the earliest literary reference to migration by a black woman, "On Being Brought from Africa to America," a poem of Phillis Wheatley's from 1768, ironically portrays her middle passage as a voyage leading not to bondage but to religious liberation: "Twas mercy brought me from my Pagan land / Taught my benighted soul to understand" (Shields, ed.,

Collected Works 18). Numerous songs written by blacks and also blues lines repeat this pervasive need for mobility: "I jest came here to stay a little while," "Gwine whar' I never been befo'," "Oh, goin' down dat lonesome road," "Gone away, never come back no more," "My home ain't yere, / It's further down de road," and, as Robert Johnson sang in the famous lines, "I got to keep moving" because of a "Hellhound on my trail."[17] From these songs, through slave autobiographies, and into the literature of the twentieth-century Great Migration, African-American writers have viewed migration as the principal means of realizing physical and spiritual freedom.

The urban initiate views his or her migration as a movement from low-caste status toward a wholeness manifested in a vision of the North as the biblically inspired promised land. Turpin's title *O'Canaan!* reflects this view, and when the novel's main character, Joe Benson, explains the reference to a puzzled fellow north-bound traveler, he speaks for thousands of migrants: "'That's what they's callin' Chicago, man!'. . . . 'You know—like the Hebrew chillun in the Bible. This here's old Pharaoh's land an' the North is Canaan. See?'" (8). Donald, in one of the earliest studies of migration, could by 1921 already detect the symbolic force and biblical proportions of the mass exodus: "There are also Negroes of all classes who profoundly believe that God has opened the way for them out of the restrictions and oppressions that beset them on every hand in the South; moving out is an expression of their faith" ("The Negro Migration" 420). In Offord's *The White Face,* the "paradise" that Chris Woods envisions in the North finds "black people with rights just like any white man. Black people riding the trains, walking the sidewalk next-to-next with white folks. Black people talking back to white folks, man to man" (17).

Inevitably, such idealism fades as the migrant assumes a second-class citizenship in the North that resembles more familiar race, caste, and class exclusion in the South. Just as Douglass soon realized that even in the North he "was still in an enemy's land" (*My Bondage* 206), achieving the lofty goal of freedom by moving north is far from assured, and, in fact, the conclusion of the majority of migration novels more closely reflects Gillis's final ruin than Douglass's ultimate fame and distinction. Migration authors differ markedly from one another in where they locate the cause of the literary migrant's defeat. White racism, intra-racial rivalry, character flaws, immoral and deterministic cityscapes, industrial malice, political divisions, and gender exploitation are some of the major reasons for the migrant's downfall.

Migration, Ascent, and Immersion

Great Migration novels play an important role in establishing the formal literary relationship that runs throughout black literature. The relationship is an intertextual one characterized by the manner in which black writers respond to the various calls issued by earlier black works through imitation, revision, and that specifically African-American linguistic strategy of parody characterized as signifying. The migration novel is in many ways the most evident twentieth-century form of what Stepto defines in *From Behind the Veil*, his seminal diachronic theory of African-American narrative, as the ascent narrative. The strong presence of migration in twentieth-century fiction bolsters Stepto's line of argument by demonstrating the predominance of ascent narratives and affirming that this narrative pattern is not only limited to the male canonical writers he addresses but is also evident in women's narratives and in the large number of lesser-known migration novels that are mentioned or discussed throughout this book.[18]

Stepto has performed the most extensive analysis of the ways in which what he calls the "pre-generic myths" evident in the "prefiguring texts" of black literature's literary canon have issued calls to which major African-American narratives up through Ellison's have responded (ix–xv). Emphasizing the link between a wide range of oral and written sources, his project charts an African-American narrative tradition whose roots lie in the physical and spiritual journeys retold by slaves. Conjoining the impulses of freedom and literacy, this literary legacy clusters around narratives about moves from a "symbolic south" to a "symbolic north" (ascent), the reverse move from north to south (immersion), and narratives situated, like the concluding setting of *Invisible Man*, in a static space outside of the boundaries of traditional history (hibernation). The enduring quest of migration fiction, like that of the escaped slave, is to realize a positive version of ascent, which can be achieved only if migrants become literate enough in northern urban ways to attain a limited version of freedom, which in turn compensates for the inevitable sense of communal displacement that results from leaving the South. Said another way, to develop their identity in the urban north migrants must maintain a consciousness of their history and culture, an act that frames their tie to the past in liberatory not oppressive terms.[19]

By framing the narrative around a south-north polarity, Stepto stresses the importance of slavery as the constituting experience of black life, which in turn deemphasizes (although in no way ignores) the ancestral resonances of West Africa featured, for example, in Robert Ferris Thompson's *Flash of the Spirit* (1981) or Paul Gilroy's *The Black Atlantic* (1993). The result, to use Manning Marable's distinction, favors an integrationist over a nationalist view of African-American art by positioning black writers as Americans of African origin rather than Africans who happen to live in America.

In another vein, critics such as Deborah McDowell and Michael Awkward have pointed to the kinetic underpinnings of the ascent-immersion structure as a predominantly masculine paradigm that tends to exclude domestic fiction by women (although Larsen's *Quicksand* and West's *The Living Is Easy* suggest how women's narratives can remain both domestic and kinetic). In one sense, the criticism of McDowell and Awkward rests on a healthy suspicion of any totalizing theory of black narrative. The maturing and ever-burgeoning critical responses to the literature—whose result is very much an in-process assessment of the notion of a black literary tradition—have, over the past several decades, paralleled an unprecedented reclamation of previously lost and out-of-print texts. This expanding textual corpus helps put to rest misdirected assertions about black literature's overarching unity or universality of the kind that lay behind such flawed earlier studies as Roger Rosenblatt's much criticized *Black Fiction.* Stepto's work is a compelling attempt to document a narrative strategy that in the process of being mapped out has spurred the formation of persuasive complementary and competing theories.[20]

Furthermore, migration novels testify to the fact that narratives of ascent and immersion are more widespread than even Stepto's book maintains, particularly when his operative vocabulary is employed for its fullest meaning. Neither ascent nor immersion is limited exclusively by the geographic designations suggested by the terms *symbolic north* and *symbolic south* because each may also correspond to spatial movements occurring entirely within one geographic area. Contemporary versions of the ascent narrative move out of the South entirely, for example, in Lorraine Hansberry's *A Raisin in the Sun* (1959). The Younger family attempts to ascend from the black ghetto (the city's symbolic south) to the white suburbs (its symbolic north). As the final scene graphically conveys, their move typifies the double-edged nature of ascent. They forsake the comforts of a shared communal identity within the black ghetto, and even within the confines of their dilapidated apartment building, for the possibilities offered by a home in Clybourne Park, a white suburb so hostile to their presence that the neighborhood association is willing to pay them not to move. No matter how beneficial an act of ascent may seem—leaving slum housing for a nice home—the Youngers, like all slave/migrant/questing figures, must give up something, taking a risk to participate in the ritual.

Such a set of options emphasizes the ever-present equivocality of Stepto's pattern. In her astute critique of the pattern, Missy Dehn Kubitschek has noted that "ascent and immersion begin and end in an enslaved community, not in one that is free and fully functional" (*Claiming the Heritage* 135). This begins to explain the need for distinguishing Ellison's *Invisible Man* as a third kind of narrative, one of hibernation, and also suggests the need to identify other narrative structures—especially those occurring after *Invisible Man*—that figure the African-American urban landscape in terms of liberation and community rather than isolation and alienation. What is needed is an expansive consideration of "communal ascent," a term framed in response to Kubitschek's and Craig Werner's initial phrasings of "group ascent." Communal ascent, which in migration novels draws its energy from embracing the apparent contradictions that frame its construction, is a narrative pattern that conceives of spatial freedom within a rooted environment, mobility in terms of a fixed destination, and the formation of an autonomous subject within the context of local and national communities.

In one sense, the narrative of communal ascent is a response to the capaciousness of black literature; it also recognizes the way in which the migration novel form complicates any fixed, self-contained conceptions of ascent and immersion. Although migration fiction may superficially follow a set of variations on the pattern of ascent as the means of pursuing the quest for a livable home, the themes binding the novels to each other are almost always critical of the symbolic-south to symbolic-north movement in one way or another. In narrating the story of Elizabeth Grimes, the character whose migration to Harlem in 1920 precedes the birth of the novel's protagonist, John Grimes, James Baldwin writes in *Go Tell It on the Mountain* (1953) that "there was not, after all, a great difference between the world of the North and that of the South which she had fled; there was only this difference: the North promised more. And this similarity: what it promised it did not give, and what it gave, at length and grudgingly with one hand, it took back with the other" (163).

The power of *Go Tell It on the Mountain* draws from this view of the North as a fluid signifier. As writers have traced the ways in which the economic and social opportunities in the urban spaces inhabited by migrants have changed and gradually opened, these locations have become more complex, more nuanced bearers of meaning. And yet even as migration novelists have come to view migration in increasingly diverse ways, they have less often celebrated the North's narrow set of possibilities than explored its limitations. From Dunbar to Ellison to Morrison, the post-migration physical setting is characteristically represented in unfavorable terms, which migrant protagonists express in attitudes ranging from awe and fear to alienation and outright hostility.

If there are deep frustrations underlying the migration novelists' assessment of ascent, particularly in early migration novels, these frustrations are paralleled, with the most obvious exception of Larsen's *Quicksand* and Wright's *Native Son,* by a comparable commitment to the possibilities that immersion offers. When a migration novelist envisions the necessary conditions for an inhabitable northern setting, this location depends upon the economic potential and spatial freedom implied by ascent, but it must also be inscribed within the social and kinship networks and the historical roots of immersion. The migrant's goal is to find a means of bringing the black belt into the North. The readings of individual novels that follow will recognize the numerous instances in which characters strive toward communal ascent by trying to decipher and order their postmigration, post-ascent homes within the context of immersion's values.

Part of the migrant's urban initiation lies in discovering which attitudes and practices from the place of southern origin should be imported and which should be discarded. For example, Ellison's narrator exhibits no understanding of his need to disconnect himself from his southern college after arriving in New York until he begins to make such distinctions. As long as he relies on the seven letters of introduction given to him by Bledsoe, the president of the narrator's college, he not only continues to be associated with the demeaning and limited views of racial advancement extolled by Bledsoe but he also remains hindered by the letter's damning allusions to his supposed betrayal of the college's philosophy of racial capitulation. The narrator must contend with the horror of discovering that Bledsoe, Ellison's false vehicle of immersion, has deceived him.

But he is able to leave the incident behind and move on to a higher level of self-determination through the simple act of hearing a tune and recalling its lyrics, which begin, "O well they picked poor Robin clean." A traditional funeral dirge, the tune, as Ellison describes it in *Shadow and Act,* is "a jazz community joke, musically an extended 'signifying riff' or melodic naming of a recurring human situation, and was played to satirize some *betrayal of faith* or loss of love observed from the bandstand" (231, my emphasis). By analogizing the message of this "lugubrious little tune" to his own experience, the narrator comes to terms with Bledsoe's betrayal through the interpretive frame of an authentic and more utilitarian product of immersion than the sealed letters. The lyrics (only one of Ellison's multitude of references highlighting the practical as well as the expressive capacity of African-American vernacular culture) brim with the kind of comic functional wisdom that allows him to move beyond his fleeting urge to return and kill Bledsoe and begin instead to make a fresh start in the North.

The experience of many real migrants challenges the mostly critical literary view of northern ascent. By reconfiguring existing spatial and social arrangements, the act of migrating has historically been the way in which African Americans have freed themselves from the limitations of southern rural life; it has been the most widely called-upon means of elevating their economic and social standing. Until the contemporary era, however, the migration novel form has not fully registered this sociological and demographic reality. Even migration novels from the first half of the century that conclude by having established inhabitable, progressive northern settings achieve their satisfying endings through events aligned with the values of immersion. In Walter White's *Flight* (1926), Mimi Daquin finds happiness in Harlem after she "passes" back over to the black world and, more importantly, reclaims the child she earlier abandoned in the South. The final chapter of George Wylie Henderson's *Jule* (1946) begins as the title character arrives by train in Hannon, Alabama, for his mother's funeral. As he sets about to return to New York, he invites his girlfriend to go with him, thus ensuring his future happiness through the consoling prospect that "we'll be together" (234).

Both writers opt for sentimental conclusions that affirm the necessity of reconstituting northern versions of their protagonists' premigration families. Because earlier portions of each novel represent the New York setting as largely uninhabitable, the successful merging of ascent and immersion implied by these endings is achieved more by the artificial manipulations of the writer than by textual continuity that follows logically from previous episodes. Although such endings may point to formal weaknesses, they affirm the Georgia-born White and the Alabama-born Henderson's nostalgia for the folk origins of their native south and their unwillingness to sever those origins from the new urban cultures about which they write.

In Ellison's urban entrance scene that began this introduction, the thematic structure associated with the young narrator's journey to Harlem, within the broader context of black life, calls forth historical and cultural antecedents that are as charged as any in African-American literature. With such potent material at hand, it is no surprise that Ellison provides an image summarizing the principal thesis of this book. After arriving in Harlem, the narrator rents a room in the Harlem Men's House. Against a background of unfamiliar urban noise—traffic, the subway, and muffled voic-es—he sits on his bed, and his thoughts return to his past "and the attempts my father had made to institute family prayer, the gathering around the stove at mealtime and kneeling with heads bowed over the seats of our chairs, his voice quavering and full of church-house rhetoric and verbal humility" (*Invisible Man* 162).

With its vernacular expressive power, the narrator's memory-laden de-piction of home is one of the novel's only sentimental moments. But as if to deny a maudlin sense of loneliness, he cuts himself short by observing, "This is New York. I had to get a job and earn money" (162). The narra-tor's thoughts make a stylistic jump from his prosaic recollections of the past to the monosyllabic, staccato assessment of his current circumstanc-es. The contrast between past and present is striking. As a naive urbanite, now entirely on his own and subject to the strict laws of the northern marketplace, he has traveled a long way from his memories of prelapsar-ian family unity. Although he will more than once fail to heed the func-tional wisdom to be derived from such domestic recollections, the meal-time evocations of family, kinship, shared history and culture, and sacred communion finally express a set of values that is as close as Ellison will come to offering an urban ideal. Great Migration novels repeatedly rec-ognize southern black culture as essential to the core of African-Ameri-can life in the North.

Migration liberates migrants from the constraints of the South only if it can lead, in the North, to an authentic reattachment to an urbanized version of African-American community life that recognizes and draws from its undeniable connection to folk culture. Thus, to use the image that *Invisible Man* provides, the principal imperative of the African-American migration novel can be viewed as a century-long attempt to reconvene the family mealtime gathering in the heart of the modern city.

This ambition suggests that as the black population has made the tran-sition from country to city, and as writers have recorded this population shift, they have remained as committed to locating their essential geograph-ic connections to black life in the historically dynamic past and present worlds of the South as in the new urban environment. Migration to the urban north is one of the principal driving forces behind twentieth-centu-ry African-American fiction. And, as Charles Scruggs has shown through-out *Sweet Home: Invisible City in the Afro-American Novel* (1993), one of the principal drives of black writing in general has been a coming to terms with the ever-expanding importance of the city in African-Ameri-can experience and the recognition that the often-appalling conditions of modern black urban life, as well as the relatively short duration from which to trace out an urban past, make the process of writing about the city a delicate and difficult task. Any number of African-American city novels— Wright's *Native Son,* Ann Petry's *The Street* (1946), Gloria Naylor's *The Women of Brewster Place* (1983), and Terry McMillan's *Mama* (1991)— affirm that urban pathology can be transformed to the level of powerful art. Within the most depressed of settings, as the suggestive image of a cleansing rain concluding Naylor's novel so well illustrates, a community of people can find numerous ways, if only momentarily, to transcend the heavy burden of their surroundings. Scruggs argues that in African-American fiction, even in the "city of brute fact," writers locate the idea of a protean visionary city, which although at times heavily qualified is always present in the tradition of black urban writing (4–6).

My examination of migration fiction finds the quest for an inhabitable geography, especially in the urban north, to be an elusive and at times impossible goal, particularly from the turn of the century through the depression. Migration literature testifies to the fact, however, that for migrants in the urban north, the South is more than "nostalgia expressed for some pastoral past" (Scruggs, *Sweet Home* 4). It represents a usable set of experiences, cultural artifacts, and values that exemplifies an ideal and a kind of salvation—even if only momentary—from the pressures of the North. Before the civil rights movement ushered in the seismic changes that have occurred in American racial life since the 1960s, an inhabitable urban geography was almost never realized. It was only conceivable to new migrants within the "usable past" of their imaginations.[21] As the racial landscape improved, particularly in migration novels following *Invisible Man,* that landscape shifted from the realm of the visionary and imagined to the existent and the real, but its genius loci still remained rooted in the South, still within the construct of Carby's "ideology of the 'folk.'"

While migration novels measure the difficulty of locating a site in the North that allows identity to develop and community to flourish, the endless stream of African-American freedom-seekers traveling north—and the numerous ongoing attempts to overcome the twin obstacles of race and place—testify to the strength of the desire to find a promised land. If the details of individual migration novels seem grim artistic reminders of the severe opposition that African Americans have faced in carving out livable homes, the body of migration fiction highlights the astonishing adaptability, amid circumstances more brutal than those met by any other group in the country's history, of a culture that traded the plow for the factory in only a few short decades.

1

The Early Migration Novel

Indeed, [dialect-speaking "darkies"] are perhaps better known
in American literature than any other single picture of our
national life. . . . they form an ideal and exclusive literary
concept of the American negro to such an extent that it is
almost impossible to get the reading public to recognize him in
any other setting. . . . This generally accepted literary ideal of
the American Negro constitutes what is really an obstacle in
the way of the thoughtful and progressive element of the race.

James Weldon Johnson

Much of the Afro-American literary tradition can be read as
successive attempts to create a new narrative space for
representing the recurring referent of Afro-American literature,
the so-called Black Experience.

Henry Louis Gates, Jr.

With the publication of *The Sport of the Gods* in 1902, Paul Laurence Dunbar initiated the form of the African-American Great Migration novel. Pushing beyond nineteenth-century southern stereotypes, he mapped a new literary terrain in the urban north that set the stage for twentieth-century African-American literature's emphasis on urban subject matter. The novel rests at a key juncture in the evolution of African-American fiction. Drawing on plantation literature and urban naturalism, Dunbar's tale is a turn-of-the-century novelistic litmus test measuring the limitations of these popular genres for black characterization. In a satiric narrative voice, far different from the dialect-speaking personae of his conventionalized plantation poetry, Dunbar subverts readers' expectations about black representation within the plantation tradition. He exposes the reigning notions of southern black-white equality as genteel romantic foolishness and reveals the South as an uninhabitable symbolic geography for the black population.[1]

In doing so, Dunbar justifies the need to initiate a literary migration northward. His deceptively simple, naturalistic melodrama of thievery, betrayed loyalties, dissipation, bigamy, and murder not only draws from the example of naturalism set by white contemporaries such as Theodore Dreiser and Stephen Crane, but the novel's fictional concerns were also to be taken up with striking regularity by later black voices such as Nella Larsen, Richard Wright, and Ralph Ellison.

As one of the best of the era's African-American protest novels and the first Great Migration novel, *The Sport of the Gods* initiates the fictional record of the difficult transition from south and north. It also launches the trope of the "fugitive migrant," which in recalling the literary antecedent of the fugitive slave narratives ties the forthcoming series of literary migrations to the manifold earlier geographic passages that had done so much to shape the collective experience of African-American life. The novel's range of implications, its force, its meaning, and its claim to a central place in the canon of African-American fiction can be measured, first, through the novel's veiled satire of the racist assumptions of plantation literature and, second, through the call it issued to chart the literary terrain of a northern city through migration from the South—a call answered time and again over the next ninety years.[2]

Dunbar's status as an important poet of his day is a critical commonplace, but he would seem an unlikely candidate to have introduced so pivotal a work of fiction, particularly about migration. Before *The Sport of the Gods,* he published three novels, each essentially romantic and each about white subjects—*The Uncalled: A Novel* (1898), *Love of Landry* (1900), and *The Fanatics* (1901)—but none of the three were commercial or critical successes. He turned to racial protest in *The Sport of the Gods* but still had to mine most of his fictional material indirectly. Although he was born in Ohio and did not travel south until well into adulthood, he was no doubt inspired by captivating boyhood memories of his mother's many stories of her slave childhood. She had come to Ohio and joined Dunbar's father, who had earlier escaped to Canada, after Emancipation.

The young Dunbar also loved to read dialect verse, and especially favored the poetry of James Whitcomb Riley, whom he soon surpassed when he began to compose verse of his own. Demonstrating unprecedented talent for creating southern "voices," he quickly rose, phoenix-like, from a

$4 a week elevator boy to the country's most popular poet, black or white. Together with Charles Chesnutt, his only African-American rival in popularity, Dunbar helped lay to rest any doubts about whether black writers could play legitimate and marketable roles in American literary life.

Success, however, came with a high cost. Dunbar's poetry celebrated what William Dean Howells, in his career-launching 1896 *Harper's Weekly* review of Dunbar's *Majors and Minors,* termed "the simple, sensuous, joyous nature of his race." But for Dunbar's white audience, who read his work through the veil of what George Fredrickson has appropriately termed "romantic racialism" (*Black Image* 101–2), this view of black life may have professed to celebrate black speech and customs but it also allowed non-blacks to affirm their perceptions of natural superiority.[3]

Whether Dunbar endorsed or undercut plantation-tradition stereotypes hardly seemed to matter because his readers, most of them white, were preconditioned to accept any linguistic and social designations of blackness as exotic at best and, more likely, as naturally inferior and bestial. For many, Dunbar helped maintain this racial hierarchy at the price of his birthright by appearing too willing to capitulate to popular, negative black stereotypes. As his body of dialect verse grew over the years, his significant accomplishments were tainted by the need to come to terms with his demeaning poetic portraitures and conventional plantation pieties. For example, "The Deserted Plantation" commemorates "de happy days gone by."

Dunbar, however, cannot simply be dismissed for his more overt plantation sympathies, especially when they are refracted through the publishing demands of his age. When he told James Weldon Johnson, "I've got to write dialect poetry, it's the only way I can get them to listen to me," he was expressing his ambivalence about dialect and his preference for writing poetry in standard English. Kenny Williams has pointedly described the limits of Dunbar's choices, given his situation: "He could become predominantly a protest writer and pay to have his work distributed among his own people in the manner of Sutton Griggs; he could stop writing because he did not get the kind of reception which he thought he deserved, as Chesnutt did; or he could veil his protests in such a way that they would prove to be acceptable."[4]

Dunbar's limited options were not his alone. All black artists were constrained by double consciousness. W. E. B. Du Bois first mentioned the famous phrase in "Strivings of the Negro People" (1897) and defined it in the *The Souls of Black Folk* (1903) as the "sense of always looking at one's self through the eyes of others, of measuring one's soul by the tape of a world that looks on in amused contempt and pity" (45). This capacity for double vision has been not only one of the dominant metaphors of African-American writing but also a paradigmatic representation of the divided African-American self. In his autobiography *Along This Way,* Johnson summed up the double bind for black artists:

> I could see that [Dunbar] writing in the conventionalized dialect, no matter how sincere he might be, was dominated by his audience; that his audience was a section of the white American reading public; that when he wrote he was expressing what often bore little relation, sometimes no relation at all, to actual Negro life; that he was really expressing only certain conceptions about Negro life that his audience was willing to accept and ready to enjoy; that, in fact, he wrote mainly for the delectation of an audience that was an outside group. (159)

The degree to which such "outside" groups dictated the direction of black cultural expression can be measured in the example of Dunbar's contemporary, the brilliant visual artist Henry O. Tanner, whom Johnson would praise as the "dean of American painters in Paris" (*Black Manhattan* 279). The early route of Tanner's painting, under the influence of his mentor Thomas Eakins, suggested that he would, like his white teacher, become an interpreter of everyday occurrences, perhaps achieving status as the first American painter to develop an entire career around black topics and subject matter. This promise is embodied in his well-known genre studies. Tanner's most famous work, *The Banjo Lesson* (1893), is an unsentimentalized, evocative rendering of an older man holding a child on his knee as he teaches the child to play the instrument. Equally suggestive, *The Young Sabot Maker* (1895) also depicts an elder tutoring his young protégé. By the time he exhibited these paintings, however, Tanner had refused, in contrast to Dunbar, to contain his art within a tacit premise of black servility. Finding the racial climate of the United States so limiting and patronage so difficult to obtain, he took the same avenue that Wright and James Baldwin would later travel. Tanner expatriated to France in 1891, where he began to make a career of tapping into his childhood religious memories. He eventually gained an international reputation as a painter of religious subjects, but he did so at the cost of abandoning black genre painting altogether. His success relied on his conscious decision to distance himself artistically and geographically from every angle of American racial politics. To Tanner, race had become, in Alain Locke's words, a "ghetto of isolation and neglect from which [black artists] must escape if they were to gain artistic freedom and recognition" (*Negro Art* 32).

That Tanner felt he had to leave American soil and reject racial subjects outright if he were to be considered a serious artist makes Dunbar's ongoing attempts to balance both sides of the racial equation all the more notable. Yet Dunbar still poses a thorny challenge for readers and critics. How can they grant him his obvious genius—appreciate his unrivaled popularity, recognize the high esteem he was accorded by other writers, and credit him for his pioneering and critical role in constructing the African-American literary tradition—and still come to terms with the fact that no small part of his career idealized and romanticized the same antebellum southern plantation world that had enslaved his parents?

The challenge is not simply to evaluate Dunbar's career as a writer, but to address the more complex question of how to measure him in light of the era's racial nadir, the turn-of-the-century environment of progress and resistance that paradoxically saw him become the country's first black literary celebrity for writing plantation poetry. Was Dunbar able to move beyond the limitations of double consciousness and find an acceptable voice, dialect or otherwise, without undermining his attempts to portray the power of black cultural representations? What did it take for him to steer African-American literature in a new direction? The answers to such questions are to be found in his use of migration in *The Sport of the Gods*.

The Racial Nadir

When *The Sport of the Gods* appeared, the major thrust of World War I migration was more than a decade away. Which is not to say that the post–Civil War migration had been inconsequential. The southern exodus increased from 156,000 in the 1870s and 1880s to 185,000 during the 1890s (Grossman, *Land of Hope* 32). But such record numbers did not significantly alter the general geographic distribution of the black population. The first census taken in 1790 had placed 91 percent of black Americans in the South; a century later the figure still hovered at around 90 percent. As the combined impact of migration's push and pull features became more pronounced, the proportion rapidly tilted northward. With U.S. industry grinding to life, the demand for labor in northern factories attracted an ever-enlarging stream of migrant workers who, amid southern racial conditions that had been deteriorating since Reconstruction, were joined by black leaders and professionals traveling north to preserve their safety.[5]

Racism was evident in seemingly every area of life. In all its manifestations, racial prejudice was designed to uphold the time-honored distinctions between the categories of "Anglo-Saxon" and "Negro" and maintain the latter's biological and cultural inferiority. By the late 1880s the South had initiated numerous attempts to replace slavery with Jim Crow.

As racial separation was institutionalized into law during the 1890s, the legal apparatus that ensured segregation—seemingly the most "natural" means for maintaining racial purity and enforcing racial difference—merely codified on paper what, despite surges of local resistance, had long been reality.[6] Contemporary intellectual issues entered the arena of race to justify the widening gap between black demands for full rights and citizenship and the realities of black lives. One broad movement, Social Darwinism, offered pseudo-scientific, laissez-faire justification for letting African Americans rest on the lowest end of the economic strata. As the argument went, the United States operated on a level economic and social playing field that encouraged the most fit to prosper. If blacks fell by the wayside, it was merely because of the immutable, if cruel, laws of the marketplace following their logical designs.

With a conspicuous lack of skepticism, the scientific community paid intellectual patronage to reigning theories of white supremacy by falling back on the same biological explanations of racial inferiority that had circulated since Thomas Jefferson's day. The voguish Higher Criticism attempted to prove white superiority through close reading of the Bible, ironically making the subject of black inferiority a peculiar instance of agreement for theorists of Darwinian evolution and biblical fundamentalism.

Southern race-baiters such as Thomas Dixon and Charles Carroll joined antebellum nostalgists—Thomas Nelson Page, for example—in using the literary marketplace to champion the necessity of retaining rigid racial distinctions. Dixon's highly popular novel *The Clansman* (1905), in 1915 to become the basis of D. W. Griffith's birth project for modern cinema, *Birth of a Nation,* rendered the consensual view of the African American as "half child, half animal, the sport of impulse, whim, and conceit" (Frederickson, *Black Image* 280). Carroll, a southern mulatto, was even more extreme in *The Negro as Beast* (1900). In this bizarre, quasi-religious tract, he waged a biblically inspired tirade against miscegenation and argued that blacks, more simian than human, were the original "tempter[s] of Eve." Although such extreme characterizations failed to be accepted by the majority of southerners, Fredrickson notes that even the more moderate and progressive white discussions of the "Negro question" rested on the assumption of black inferiority (*Black Image* 275–97).[7]

The general tenor of the age found its signal expression in 1896. Six years before the publication of *The Sport of the Gods,* two decades before the major thrust of the World War I migration, and one year after the death of Frederick Douglass, the most powerful nineteenth-century symbol of black America's ongoing attempts to secure the full privileges of

American citizenship, the Supreme Court case of *Plessy v. Ferguson,* registered the profound disequilibrium of black-white relations. By constitutionally sanctioning Jim Crow legislation, the decision remained for half a century the principal legal obstacle to civil rights in the United States. By inscribing the necessity of the segregated train car into the nation's law books, the decision also ensured that the principal conveyance for carrying generations of freedom-seeking migrants northward was also, ironically, the country's most potent symbol of their continued oppression.

The case had evolved from a challenge to an 1890 Louisiana statute requiring "equal but separate accommodations for the white and colored races" on its railroads. In 1892 Homer Adolph Plessy, seven-eighths white and one-eighth black, boarded the railroad to make the sixty-mile intrastate trip between New Orleans and Covington, Louisiana. According to a prearranged plan, he refused to ride in the Jim Crow car and was arrested as soon as he sat down. He was brought to trial before Judge John H. Ferguson of the Criminal Court of New Orleans, who found him guilty of violating the state law. Several of Louisiana's African-American leaders retained Albion W. Tourgée, the former North Carolina carpetbagger judge and current New York lawyer, as counsel to challenge the decision in the Supreme Court. The argument for instituting an action to restrain enforcement of the statute was based on the dual claims that it violated both the prohibition of involuntary servitude stated in the Thirteenth Amendment and the rights and privileges of national citizenship guaranteed by the Fourteenth Amendment.

The Supreme Court, by a seven-to-one vote, ruled Louisiana's statute constitutional. For the majority, Justice Henry B. Brown wrote that "the underlying fallacy" of Plessy's argument was its "assumption that the enforced separation of the two races stamps the colored race with a badge of inferiority." A law that "implies merely a legal distinction" between blacks and whites did not violate the Thirteenth Amendment. The Court decided that the Fourteenth Amendment "in the nature of things . . . could not have been intended to abolish distinctions based on color, or to enforce social, as distinguished from political equality, or a commingling of the two races upon terms unsatisfactory to either."[8] With no real legal authority upon which the Court could base such a conclusion, it rested the decision's validity on the nebulous tenets of scientific, sociological, and psychological racial theory.

Where *Plessy v. Ferguson* certified the legal continuation of segregation, the less influential but no less emphatic body of literature drawn under the heading of the plantation tradition ensured that the literary world was equally committed to legitimizing the artifice of racial hierarchies resting behind the Supreme Court decision. The legal and literary arenas were unified in the common belief that racial separation did not preclude the perception of equality because the dominant culture adequately provided for its less empowered black members through the illusion of benevolent paternalism—with the critical emphasis resting on a definition of "equality" that detoured through the mediating terms *perception* and *illusion.*

The plantation tradition's race-based conventions had gone through a long process of revision and fine-tuning since the publication of John Pendleton Kennedy's *Swallow Barn* (1832), generally considered the first important novel of the genre. The tradition included a diverse body of works and was influenced by different local-color traditions aimed toward both children and adults, used as evidence to support both sides of the slavery question, and varied as much in regional sensibility as in thematic emphasis.[9] Still, in its most stylized post–Reconstruction form it remained faithful to its original intent, converging around an idyllic vision of the prewar plantation economy of the South, where cotton was king and benevolent white caretakers watched over infantile, contented, and devoted slaves and servants who happily labored in the fields while gratefully bestowing their loyalty on their masters. Lamenting the demise of this heroic antebellum plantation world, writers such as Irwin Russell, Joel Chandler Harris, and Page were among the most successful plantation writers. Page's trend-setting collection of short fiction, *In Ole Virginia* (1887), has remained the most durable vessel of plantation images. Harris's well-known folk tales were collected in three volumes following the sensational popularity of his first book, *Uncle Remus: His Songs and His Sayings* (1880). His tales were less explicitly demeaning than Page's, but his kindly benevolent narrator, Uncle Remus (in his most popular persona), did little to challenge plantation orthodoxies.

Dunbar, like Chesnutt, recognized that the racism of his era was too entrenched to be assaulted directly. *The Sport of the Gods* represents his masked challenge of the array of forces exemplified in *Plessy v. Ferguson* and the plantation tradition. The novel dramatizes the tragic price paid by a black family who tries hard to live within a plantation framework ordered around *Plessy's* assertion that separate can, in fact, be equal. It is a narrative within a narrative. The frame story of the first four chapters focuses on the Hamiltons, a family of "typical, good living Negroes" who work for Maurice Oakley, a white southerner who has managed despite Reconstruction to maintain a prosperous antebellum-style plantation household. Berry Hamilton's thirty years of loyal service, since before

Emancipation, have brought the family financial comfort and made them the envy of their black neighbors. The Hamiltons appear to inhabit, like their plantation predecessors, a pastoral Eden indistinguishable from the settings Page and his fellow plantation writers detail. At every turn Berry shows his loyalty to the plantation system by imitating the middle-class white values of his employer. He furnishes a cottage that mimics the great house and follows Oakley's example in marriage by "taking a wife unto himself." By carefully heeding hierarchy of racial distinction, he is rewarded as the Oakley fortune rises.

In a quick turn of events, however, Dunbar subverts the harmony of Berry's world and undercuts the same plantation sensibility that had played so important a role in vaulting the author to national prominence. When a large sum of cash goes missing on the night of Oakley's farewell dinner for his brother traveling to Paris, Berry is immediately suspected, and, although he has a solid alibi, he is found guilty and sentenced to ten years at hard labor in prison for his supposed "peculations." Having deposited his life savings into the bank on the same day as the theft, he is convicted on false circumstantial evidence, which is, ironically, nothing more than the pecuniary fruits of his loyalty to his white "benefactors." In Dunbar's satire, the theft itself is a central plot development only insofar as it demonstrates such significant racial ironies.

For a poet accustomed to resting behind "the mask that grins and lies," Dunbar's point was both pessimistic and explicit: No matter how time-honored and deeply rooted a black-white relationship appears to be, white intra-racial loyalty in the South always dominates. In plantation fiction (as well as the real world of *Plessy*) harmony exists, and equality is maintained, only as long as nothing that the white world deems of value is seriously at risk. With Berry's conviction, Dunbar dramatizes a truth of racial distinction that was brought to national literary consciousness in the wake of *Plessy* through *Pudd'nhead Wilson* (1896), Mark Twain's flawed rendering of southern racial hypocrisies. There Tom Driscoll is sold down the river rather than imprisoned at the conclusion of Twain's parody of legal and social codes because pretending to be white is a worse crime than murder (Sundquist, "Plessy" 124). Although Berry, unlike Tom, has not passed as white, he has committed the equally serious offense of acting white while accepting the separate but equal barrier, modulating his behavior "based on an ideal of frugal, convivial Christian respectability that he assumes is the moving force of the southern white world" (Baker, *Blues, Ideology* 126). He is convicted finally because it can be proven that on the day of the theft he has occupied space in proximity to white money.

Dunbar's satire grows out of his keen insight into (and personal experience with) the veil, the brilliant metaphor that serves as Du Bois's descriptive linchpin of double consciousness. As a kind of a two-way mirror that allows the black population the "peculiar sensation" of "seeing through the revelation of the other [white] world" without being seen in return and without clearly seeing itself, the veil image describes the conceptual barrier between the two cultures (Du Bois, *Souls of Black Folk* 45). On the black side, the separation allows for a multitude of social and linguistic subversions. The most famous literary illustration of the veil as a subversive, empowering agent of second sight comes in Douglass's *Narrative of the Life of Frederick Douglass* (1845). The young slave, eager to learn to write, masks his ignorance in order to trick white boys into teaching him the letters of the alphabet, relying, of course, on the boys' inability to peer through the veil that separates them from Douglass and realize his true intentions.

One of the most damaging tactics of minstrelsy and plantation literature has been to present the black side of double consciousness as a deficient alternative to whiteness. Douglass brilliantly comments on this assumption by allowing the young boys to perceive that they are condescending to him, retaining their false perception of his mental deficiency while through his use of the veil he is able to elevate himself above them. For the Hamiltons, the veil's power is negated. Trained in the law of the plantation, they fail to embrace their blackness, favoring their white employer over their "less fortunate" black neighbors and thereby negating the veil's potential. It becomes transformed, if one extends Du Bois's metaphor, from a two-way mirror into a glass ceiling, with the Hamiltons liminally suspended between black and white.

For all the obvious differences between Dunbar, the northerner, and his southern protagonists, they share in their liminality a notable kinship. The Hamiltons' dilemma is surely one of the most personally charged that Dunbar would write about in his entire career, for it mirrors his personal situation. He wanted to align himself with the white cultural traditions of European poetic forms and language while drawing royalties from the white public's fascination with plantation sentimentality. After all, what subjects could be more important for Dunbar to explore than the potential dangers of black success achieved through white patronage, the possible betrayal by those seemingly admiring and benevolent white patrons, and the black population's smug response to that betrayal? Through Berry's false imprisonment Dunbar lashes out at the vertical social structure that denied the author and his protagonists an equal place in the dominant white world. The controlling white environment of the novel (functioning in part as the "gods" of the title) is guilty of the racist paternalism that leads to Berry's conviction. Dunbar moves well beyond simplistic fictional protest, however, to explore a more subtle point that may be traced in the reactions of the black community to the Hamiltons' fall.[10]

Even the early scenes of apparent plantation bliss are subtly undermined by Dunbar's portrayal of what goes on not between the neo-slaves and their master—the primary relationship of the plantation tradition—but within the black community itself. In aligning themselves with the Oakleys, the Hamiltons have earned the jealousy but grudging admiration of their fellow blacks. But their position of respect within the African-American community is predicated on their ties to the white community. When the latter is cut, the former disappears as well. Just as Dunbar's critics held him accountable for pandering to white tastes, Dunbar holds Berry and his family accountable for rejecting their blackness. Berry's conviction, from his black neighbors' point of view, comes because a black Icarus has flirted too closely with the white sun: "'Tell me, tell me,' said one, 'you needn't tell dat a bird kin fly so high dat he don' have to come down some time. An' w'en he do light, honey, my Lawd, how he flop!'" (*Sport of the Gods* 51).

When the Hamilton family is ostracized, their alienation from their black neighbors is dramatized in Joe's search for work after he is no longer welcome as a barber in whites-only "tonsorial parlours." Met by "the laughs and taunts of his tormenters," he suffers scorn reserved for a true traitor to his race. Even the narrator maintains a safe distance as he wryly notes, "It is strange how all the foolish little vaunting things that a man says in days of prosperity wax a giant crop around him in the days of his adversity" (*Sport of the Gods* 67). The novel's satire finds a voice among the Hamiltons' black neighbors in an "old crone, rolling her bleared and jealous eyes with glee" who notes, "'W'enevah you see niggahs gittin' so high dat dey own folks ain' good enough fu' 'em, look out'" (52). Worded in the folk dialect of the black south, the crone's voice is one that Dunbar viewed with a degree of ambivalence. Her message, no doubt representing the sentiment of some of Dunbar's contemporaries, is a pointed self-warning and a prescient forecast of his reception by critics (including his wife) when he was perceived to have distanced himself too much from the those about whom he wrote.[11] Had Dunbar better heeded the "old crone's" message throughout his career rather than often allowing his thirst for popularity to dictate his subject matter, his present critical status would no doubt be less contested.

Dunbar satirized the normative values of the novel's setting rather than reconstituting the characters who inhabited that setting. The Hamiltons are, like Uncle Remus, stock images in the storehouse of plantation figures. As fictional types they, along with Horatio Alger boys and urban working girls, were among the most popular characters of the day. The most important element of postbellum plantation romances was the black speaker (or mouthpiece), whose dialect voice dramatically authenticated the sentiment of nostalgia and, by implication, the correctness of the master-slave relationship. The speaker's departure from standard English into a substandard black dialect, however, was a mark of cultural and intellectual inferiority. When Dunbar effectively commanded the dialect voice in his poetry, its substandard diction and usage emphasized its distance from the "proper" English of his readers. With no small irony, the more Dunbar demonstrated his genius for language, the more effectively his poetry emphasized his subjects' inferiority.

Dunbar's only market competition among his black contemporaries was Chesnutt, whose own difficulty with negotiating the double bind of racial portraiture offers a useful parallel. Chesnutt's chief intent in the creation of his most famous character, Uncle Julius McAdoo, the shrewd, self-interested, dialect-speaking protagonist in *The Conjure Woman* (1899), was to advertise his "imaginative capabilities." Chesnutt firmly insisted that he was not simply imitating Harris (as the original cover depicting a balding old black man framed by two white rabbits would lead readers to believe) but was instead transcending the fading vogue of regional realism by offering familiar yet aesthetically purposeful, original stories.[12] However much Chesnutt championed social protest, he remained most interested in creating art. At the same time, in a short story such as "The Goophered Grapevine," Uncle Julius adapts his crafty story-telling powers to outwit his white employer and better his own lot in a shrewd reconfiguration of the exploited role of the typical black narrator. Chesnutt thereby subtly challenged his white readers' perceptions of black intelligence not through explicit protest but, in a case of showing rather than telling, by indirectly demonstrating the fact of black intelligence through the masked inventiveness of Uncle Julius.

In satirizing the plantation tradition from within its southern setting, however, Chesnutt may have been too subtle and crafty for his own good. The majority of reviewers overlooked or minimized his satire and chose to praise his talents as a promising new regionalist. Lumped in with Page and Harris, Chesnutt found it difficult to dislodge his association with the plantation tradition's lineage of black inferiority. It has taken recent critics, more distant from the damaging storehouse of racial impressions, to apprehend the subtle brilliance of Chesnutt's mask-wearing former slave.[13]

And yet William Andrews, Chesnutt's biographer, calls Uncle Julius "a functionary of some distinctive charm and interest, but essentially a static figure whose main activity outside of reciting tales is to reaffirm his endearingly mock-devious nature to an appreciative white audience" (*The Literary Career* 52).

This assessment suggests that despite the elaborate verbal masks that the old black man employs to subvert his listeners, he is stifled by the imposed linguistic limitations of speaking like a former slave. Even less conventionalized characterizations of blackness had difficulty transcending the stereotypes and prejudices of the southern setting they populated. The poor reception of *The Marrow of Tradition* (1901), Chesnutt's subtle novel of southern racial realities, compared to the overnight popularity of a Negro-phobic sensational novel such as Thomas Dixon's *The Leopard's Spots* (1902) points to how intolerant turn-of-the-century readers were to more complex renderings of the racial south. Chesnutt's failure to find a publisher after *The Colonel's Dream* (1905) is further evidence that black literature remained cursed by decades of demeaning representation that severely constricted the kind of characters that could be developed in the setting of the South.

For black writing to be freed from this prison, it needed more than the reconstituted version of the South that Chesnutt offered. He pushed black writing in a fruitful direction, but it also needed to begin charting an alternative geography. Where the fictional black south was defined by its tenaciously embedded negative representations of African-American characters—the tragic mulatto, the servile Uncle Tom, the bad nigger, the comic shuffling black, and the loyal ex-slave—the fictional black urban north offered a blank slate.[14] A host of antecedent white characters occupying northern cities were found in the hundreds of country-boy and country-girl novels and were more obviously on display in the fiction of white urban naturalists. In contrast, black writers had only peripherally begun to chart the cityscape by the century's end. Frank Webb's didactic novel of free blacks in Philadelphia, *The Garies and Their Friends* (1857), which was released in London; *Our Nig* (1859), Harriet Wilson's self-published, sentimental tale of northern racism; and *Contending Forces,* Pauline Hopkins's story of the color line, issued in 1900 by the Colored Cooperative Publishing Company, all unfolded in northern city settings. But as character dramas, none of the three addressed the urban north as a physical and cultural setting with anything approaching the level of interest shown by white realists. Black fiction, like the black population, needed to begin coming to terms with the city as the destined locus of twentieth-century black culture. This process commenced with *The Sport of the Gods*. Although Dunbar's anti-urban biases kept him from envisioning the urban north as a real solution to southern serfdom, the novel had the all-important effect of enlarging the terrain that African-American fiction explored.

Dunbar's African-American Cityscape

When they are displaced from the South, the Hamiltons become fugitives who travel to New York to escape the secret of their family shame. In the novel's treatment of migration as an act of geographic, cultural, and psychological displacement, Dunbar responded to an overriding thematic call of earlier black literature. He created a new version of the slave narrative's paradigmatic journey of plantation violence, escape, flight, family separation, and (failed) resettlement. Even within the historical changes and intervening years between the end of slavery and the appearance of *The Sport of the Gods*, Dunbar continued to echo one of the slave narrative's prominent themes: Although oppressed southerners may imagine the North as a land of infinite possibility, it is, in reality, merely a conditional improvement over southern slavery.

In Dunbar's north, ascent, as Robert Stepto defines it, is not possible. The Hamiltons fall prey to the environmentally determined cityscape and to their misdirected assumptions about how to read the complex urban codes—an inability to achieve what Stepto calls the "tribal literacy" required to function in that setting. In sending Berry to prison in the early part of the novel Dunbar cuts through the facade of loyalty buttressing the flawed foundation of the plantation house and liberates the rest of the family from the geographic bonds of plantation fiction. Their destination is a setting defined by urban naturalism that, with a few exceptions in the works of Crane and Howells, was previously occupied only by white characters. In a sweeping, chapter-opening passage, New York is a "cruel and cold and unfeeling" magnet that entices "provincials" such as the Hamiltons into its deadly charms.

Resonating with personifying adjectives such as "subtle," "insidious," and "unfeeling," Dunbar's characterization aligns his urban sensibility with those of Johnson, Dreiser, Frank Norris, and Upton Sinclair.[15] Dreiser's often-cited description that comes at the beginning of *Sister Carrie* typifies—and canonically embodies—the characteristic perspective on the power of urban geography that this generation of writers shared:

> The city has its cunning wiles, no less than the infinitely smaller and more human tempter. . . . There are large forces which allure with all the soulfulness of

expression possible in the most cultured human. The gleam of a thousand lights is often as effective as the persuasive light in a wooing and fascinating eye. . . . Half the undoing of the unsophisticated and natural mind is accomplished by forces wholly superhuman. . . . Without a counsellor at hand to whisper cautious interpretations, what falsehoods may not these things breathe into the unguarded ear! (1)

Dunbar finds this geography of urban naturalism to be no more promising as a literary terrain than the plantation south. It is less inscribed by racism—the Hamiltons' new Harlem-like home is entirely free of white interference—but its obstacles are no less daunting. After disentangling himself from the bind of racial double consciousness, Dunbar's attention shifts from race to a theme more in keeping with other naturalist writers: his characters' moral frailty when confronted by the charms of the city. If Dunbar's point is to demonstrate that Fannie, Joe, and Kitty Hamilton are victims of the grand causal forces at hand, the novel merely affirms a tired brand of realism. Its purpose remains confined to challenging the wisdom of migration by registering the horrors of the postindustrial cityscape. In *The Sport of the Gods,* however, geography and race are not the sole determinants of fate. The seeds of the Hamiltons' urban failure were sown long before their migration each time they distanced themselves from their southern black neighbors. Their ascent is frustrated as much by their failure to import a usable past as it is by the capricious determinism (the "sport") of their surroundings.

Having failed to immerse themselves in their own culture, Fannie, Joe, and Kitty have no model of behavior on which to order their experiences in their new home. They make various attempts at recreating their "pastoral" southern home life and replicating versions of their southern family, but each attempt leads only to further degeneration. Their first misstep is to invest energy in guarding their "fugitive" status by keeping Berry's fate hidden from their new neighbors. That his prison sentence is regarded as a point of honor when it becomes known aptly illustrates how badly the family has misread the values of their new home. Fannie tries to reproduce her happy southern home life early on by shielding her children from the city's temptations, and when that fails she bigamously marries a race-track man, Gibson, in a pathetic attempt to replace Berry. Having moved away from home, Joe takes up with the lowly denizens of the Banner Club, a "social cesspool" that feeds his thirst for alcohol, hunger for urban nightlife, and desire for a vicarious, much-improved "family." He meets a surrogate parent, Hattie Sterling, a rapidly aging chorus girl who tries to protect and educate him. As someone who has managed to negotiate the complexities of urban life without succumbing to the worst of its temptations, Hattie emerges as one of the few sympathetic characters in the novel. But no one is safe in Dunbar's city: Joe, in a jealous rage, murders her and is sent to prison. Kitty exchanges singing solos at her southern A.M.E. church for a career on the northern stage. In switching from "the simple old songs she knew to practice the detestable coon ditties which the stage demanded" (*Sport of the Gods* 130), Kitty leaves one racist code of behavior behind only to become engulfed in another. She is transformed from a stock southern plantation figure into the novel's northern minstrel reenactment of that same emblem.

Viewed within the evolution of the migration novel form, the Hamilton family's rapid deterioration marks a notable beginning point in the black southerner's ongoing struggle to make a new home in the northern city. Dunbar's prognosis for urban black assimilation is grim but no less so than the urban portraits drawn decades later by such literary grandsons as Chester Himes, John A. Williams, and Wright. It is significant that Dunbar, a northern-born plantation poet with tenuous personal connections to southern folk culture, wrote a novel about the high cost of repudiating southern black experience—and conversely the centrality of that experience as a necessity for formulating a northern identity—during a particularly hostile era of U.S. racial history. There were almost no literary models of black urban life, and the social, scientific, moral, and legal arenas charged with adjudicating the place of African Americans in American culture expressed no interest in poor black southerners. What Dunbar initiated, what recurs in *The Autobiography of an Ex-Coloured Man,* and what may be found again and again in later migration fiction right up to the recent migration fiction of Rosa Guy, Toni Morrison, and Marita Golden is a recognition that black southern culture provides the key that unlocks the possibilities of northern life.

Set against the decay of his family, Berry's release from prison is almost anticlimactic. The circumstances surrounding his exoneration provide Dunbar a forum to attack the hypocrisy of self-interested northern white liberalism. Berry's liberator is Skaggs, a northern newspaperman who represents himself as a crusading muckraker but is, in the end, no more than a greedy carpetbagger. Uncovering Berry's tragedy and securing his release from prison through a series of sensationalistic articles, Skaggs masterminds his scheme because "it would be a big thing for the paper" (*Sport of the Gods* 219). In a savagely ironic juxtaposition of description and dialogue, the narrator catalogs Berry's condition at the time of his freedom. His lips drooping pathetically, his hair grown gray, his "erstwhile quick wits . . . dulled and embruted," his memory of his family vanished from his mind amid his oxlike existence, he meets the white reporter, who remarks, "This is a very happy occasion" (243). Skaggs assumes that Berry's past can be atoned for merely by securing his release from prison (a deed motivated only by profit incentives and personal glory), offering him a pardon (rather than acknowledging his innocence, which the governor cannot bring himself to do), and allowing him and Fannie to move back into their former cottage without their children, where they must endure the now-insane Maurice Oakley.

Dunbar clears a space for future migration novels by undermining the reigning assumptions of how plantation geography dictates black characterization. In the brilliant image that concludes the novel, Berry and Fannie have returned south and joined the wife of their former master. Sitting together, hands clasped in a pitifully inadequate gesture of loyalty to the system that has failed them, the three pass their nights in a parodic imitation of their former existence. The punishment for their allegiance is to endure the continually shrieking voice of Maurice echoing across the yard. The price of maintaining loyalty to the plantation ideal has, for all of them, turned into madness. The novel thus ends as Berry and Fannie sit, waiting. Having neither made the transition from the southern neo-slave world that promised but failed to reward their devotion nor adapted to the urban north, they remain liminally situated in a setting soon to be forever altered by large-scale migration.

In the Hamiltons' reimmersion into the South, *The Sport of the Gods,* as forcefully as any event or document of the age, demonstrates that in turn-of-the-century racial America neither south nor north, city nor country, could accommodate African Americans unless they extended their aspirations beyond the limitations of nineteenth-century plantation ideals and looked to the guidance of their own culture.

The Passing Migrant: *The Autobiography of an Ex-Coloured Man*

James Weldon Johnson's only novel was begun shortly after the appearance of *The Sport of the Gods* in 1902 but not published until 1912. *Autobiography,* like *The Sport of the Gods,* focuses on the high cost of rejecting the black south in favor of adopting a northern white value system. Even more consciously than Dunbar, Johnson wanted to liberate black writers from the need to capitulate to negative representations of blackness. He joined Dunbar in recognizing that migration played a key role in furthering this difficult process. Through his act of literary migration, Dunbar had begun plotting a new narrative space uninscribed by popular stereotypes of minstrelsy in the new setting of the North. In his creation of character, however, he less successfully moved away from the kind of commonplace plantation portraits that his poetry had helped maintain. Johnson took the next important step. He annexed Dunbar's northern urban setting and, more important, introduced an entirely new character whose narrative posture allowed both author and teller-of-tale to address stereotypes directly.[16]

Into his curious fiction, Johnson added another variable to the migration novel's complicated equation of black identity: His narrator is racially as well as geographically suspended. Vacillating between the white world of his father and his black birthright, the protagonist assumes the role of American picaro, traveling from town to city, from south to north, from America to Europe, north to south, and back again; living on both sides of the color line; and cycling through multiple migrations in a circuitous, frustrated effort to claim a self-satisfying identity among two racial cultures that exist side by side in heated malevolence.

The combination of the narrator's racial liminality and his kinetic sense of self places him in a pivotal role in the development of the form. Following on the heels of his autobiographical antecedent, the nineteenth-century fugitive slave, the narrator is an important precursor to the fugitive migrants of the 1930s and 1940s. Part of Johnson's brilliance lay in understanding the relative benefits of being original as well as derivative.[17] He created a novel so different from anything American readers had seen from a black writer that it demanded to be taken entirely on its own terms. The novel's unnamed first-person narrator unapologetically recounts the events of his life that gradually alienate him from both sides of the color line. His detached voice is part philosophical treatise on the race question, part social history, part jarringly candid confession, and part autobiographical musing.

With almost no African-American fictional antecedent for its pseudo-autobiographical form or for Johnson's use of a first-person narrator, readers, not surprisingly, mistook the novel for the true life story of its author.[18] In spite of its originality, the odd amalgam of didactic ruminations, narrative digressions, tonal shifts, ellipses, and evasions that characterize the man's story is much indebted to Johnson's inventive reconfigurations of earlier African-American textual forms and tropes. The narrator's account commences with a transposed version of one of slavery's most tortuous scenes, the breakup of the family, follows with a series of failed quests, and concludes in the free soil of the North, where he has exchanged spiritual solace for the most extreme form of ascent, economic prosperity at the complete expense of avowing his black identity.

Born of a well-to-do southern gentleman and his mistress, a mulatto, the narrator assumes that he is white until a memorable incident in grade school informs him otherwise. As a young man, he eventually makes his roundabout way to New York, having been born "of the best blood of the South" (*Autobiography* 12) in a "little town of Georgia a few years after the close of the Civil War" (2). He and his mother migrate to Connecticut, where he spends his childhood going to school and studying music. After a thwarted plan to matriculate at Atlanta University, he does a stint as a laborer in a cigar factory in Jacksonville, Florida. When the factory shuts down, "a desire like a fever seized me to see the North again and I cast my lot with those bound for New York" (64).

He glides easily into a dissipated existence in the city's tenderloin district, distinguishing himself from the hordes of gambling fanatics among whom he lives by his talent for playing ragtime. After witnessing the cold-blooded murder of a white woman who has shown him particular favor, he flees New York by abruptly deciding to accompany an eccentric millionaire to Europe as a traveling companion and musical entertainer. Despite the narrator's attraction to the culture of Europe, he decides to return to the United States, acknowledge his black identity, and promote African-American culture via its contributions to American musical forms such as spirituals and rags. His grand intentions are short-lived, however. While traveling through Georgia, he witnesses a white mob burning a black man. The chilling spectacle has a profound and sobering impact on him, and he hurriedly returns to New York and the safety of the white world. Marrying a white woman, whose early death leaves him two children, he ends his wandering and settles in to live out the life of a racial coward, financially secure but spiritually empty.

This summary presents the events of the narrative and suggests its episodic nature but fails to indicate the more important element of the narrator's tale: his unresolved search for inward peace and happiness that his outward travels mask. What prompts the narrator to retell his story is his "savage and diabolical desire to gather up all the little tragedies of my life, and turn them into a practical joke on society" (1). He taunts readers by masking his identity, challenging them to wonder who among them carries the secret of being an "ex-coloured man." The narrative's force, however, as Robert Fleming has noted, lies less in the details that form this book-length "joke" on the white world than in documenting the dramatic irony "of a marginal man who narrates the story of his own life without fully realizing the significance of what he tells the reader" ("Irony as a Key" 83). His youthful ambition was "to be a great man, a great colored man, to reflect credit on the race and gain fame for myself" (*Autobiography* 82). Yet when he ends his protean wanderings, repudiates his black identity forever, and settles finally in the role of "an ordinarily successful white man who has made a little money" (154), the "joke" he plays on society doubles back on himself. By foregoing his opportunity as musician and musicologist to use his vast knowledge of black folk music forms, he fails to fashion a significant contribution to African-American art and in so doing negates the opportunity to use his greatest talent.

Again and again he leaves one home behind in search of another, trying but failing to come to terms with his racial identity until, finally, he concludes his narrative in an ambiguous state of self-professed racial limbo, willing to "neither disclaim the black race nor claim the white race" (139). He feels such isolation and failure that he must, like so many fugitive slave narrators, retell his story, "seeking relief" (2) through writing himself back into existence.

By documenting how the racially flexible narrator is transformed from a southern black boy to a northern white man, Johnson followed the lead of earlier stories from the popular genres of passing and miscegenation literature, including Twain's *Puddn'head Wilson.* Like Twain, Johnson mocked a culture that could think only in terms of binary racial categories. Where Twain forcefully demonstrated the contradictions, incongruities, and absurdities of contemporary race theory in a burlesque of national legal and social sensibilities, Johnson used the candid self-revelations of his narrator to examine the same arena in a more localized and personal way. Twain was only one of many writers, white and black, to whom Johnson could look as he sought to extend the conventions of the passing-for-white story. Measuring *Autobiography* against other contemporaneous African-American novels calls attention to Johnson's comparatively subtle comprehension of the psychological difficulties of operating in an either/or racial environment and to his unwillingness to view these difficulties within anything less than their fullest complexity.

Novels following on the heels of *Autobiography* included Oscar Micheaux's *The Conquest* (1913) and *Forged Note* (1915), F. Grant Gilmore's *Problem* (1915), Henry Downing's *The American Cavalryman* (1917), and Mary Etta Spencer's *The Resentment* (1920). Johnson's interest in depicting the inner dilemma of his narrator through psychological self-investigation is different from the emphasis on external, public solutions to the problem of the color line found in these novels, which tend to offer simplistic bromides to the racial discourse of the teens. Despite detailing characters who are in various stages of movement, they fall outside the migration novel form because they have no stake in sounding out the complexities of identity associated with leaving one home for another. Instead, they espouse a Horatio Alger-esque moral imperative that argues that diligence and hard work overcome all hardships and that the very virtue of such labor invariably leads to economic and social success, whether the setting is the American frontier west, Africa, or Cuba. Such novels are optimistic, accepting of the myth that America's industrial state offers opportunity for anyone willing to seize it, regardless of race. Thus, in one sense, they downplay the color line by creating blacks in traditionally white roles, a simplistic resolution for the ambiguous state of Johnson's not-white, not-black narrator.

A little-known migration novel of the period, Otis Shackelford's *Lillian Simmons; or, The Conflict of Sections* (1915), takes equally strong stock in the liberating potential of an all-black version of capitalism. Written, according to the preface, to promote intra-racial harmony, Shackelford uses the standard vehicle of a courtship between Lillian Simmons and her southern migrant suitor, Charles Christopher, to explore the conflict between new migrants and their antagonistic northern neighbors. For the most part, the novel is hardly more than a thinly disguised treatise on the race question designed to rally its black readership around a Booker T. Washington–inspired "idea of Negro enterprise, even if it does invite segregation" (*Lillian Simmons* 200). Perhaps the fact that Shackelford's call for "unity of action" within the black population issues from migrant Chicagoans rather than the black south is the book's most important contribution indicating how Washington's philosophy had a strong northern urban toehold even before the great wartime surge of migration.

Johnson departed from his contemporaries by favoring a mode of confession over a more external, less self-interested discourse. The content of that confession was also wholly different. Never before had a black narrator been so startlingly frank about the events leading to the abnegation of his racial birthright, nor about his complicity in that abnegation. Neither had the ample tradition of passing literature offered a precedent for a novel ending in racial neutrality. Until *Autobiography*, stories of passing were about the burdens of racial loyalty. In addition to novels by white writers such as Howells, Twain, Tourgée, and Rebecca Harding Davis, the passing-for-white plot had been well worked out by black writers, such as Webb's *The Garies and Their Friends* (1857), F. E. W. Harper's *Iola*

Leroy; or, Shadows Uplifted (1892), and Chesnutt's *The House Behind the Cedars* (1900). Following Johnson, Walter White in *Flight* (1926), Nella Larsen in *Passing* (1929), and Jessie Fauset in *Plum Bun* (1929) and *Comedy American Style* (1933) would also repeat the standardized stories of this genre. As one critic observes, "Those characters who attempt to cross the color line permanently . . . are either punished through quick demises or soon learn the error of their ways and, chastened, return to the unified black community. The external warning in these novels is clear: the decision to pass for white is dangerous and potentially self-destructive" (Little, "Charles Johnson's Revolutionary Oxherding Tale" 141).

In contrast, the forward-looking *Autobiography* aligns itself more with the future of migration fiction than with previous passing novels. Rather than offering the affirmation of progress through racial allegiance found in a passing novel, it concludes by indicating that the narrator's ascent has left him liminally fixed in an American racial geography where his grand desires of racial advancement and immersion back into his culture must be tempered by "being identified with a people that could with impunity be treated worse than animals" (*Autobiography* 139). In other words, like Dunbar in *The Sport of the Gods,* Johnson is not willing to fictionalize a version of America's racial geography that is significantly more optimistic than the conditions in evidence in the author's own travels around the country. As Johnson observed in a letter to his publisher, his novel is a telling critique "of the conditions between the races as they actually exist today."[19] Taking a position that most later migration novelists would also affirm, he refuses to romanticize migration and consider it as a simplistic panacea to the national racial dilemma. The narrator fully demonstrates his cowardice and favors self-interest over the larger interests of his race, in part because the costs of being black, before and after migration, are too high to pay. Despite the difficulty of that message for many readers to absorb, Johnson offers a version of realistic, hard truth rather than his contemporaries' more palatable fictional expressions aimed at racial uplift.

For his candid self-revelations as well as the weaknesses underscored by those revelations, the narrator has elicited a number of strong responses. The most perceptive of Johnson's critics have astutely demonstrated the man's dubious character. Before Valerie Smith's assessment of the narrator's "temperamental shortcomings" (*Self-Discovery* 64), for example, Stepto showed little sympathy for his blind spots, persuasively arguing that although the text is rooted in numerous antedating black literary tropes and conventions, the narrator neither understands nor embraces anything but a superficial view of African-American culture. This distance between teller and tale "establish[es] the layers of irony that pervade the text" (*From Behind the Veil* 97). As an "ahistorically minded seer of surfaces" (121), the narrator fails to make "true and honest contact" (126) in either the black belt (the South) or "the world of Mammon" (the urban north).

The fullest measure of the narrator's internal spiritual deficiencies lies in his incapacity to move enough below the surface of black folk life to lay a legitimate claim to his black lineage. Stepto's reading demands that we not minimize the self-agency of the man's final station of solitude. The narrator is also responding, however, to a particularly narrow set of cultural options that obstruct each of his previous efforts to find a fixed place of habitation. Each journey from his boyhood onward is begun with some degree of commitment to his black heritage, although that commitment diminishes or disappears as the cost of racial allegiance becomes too high. Measuring the limitations of his psyche within the context of his migrations emphasizes how much the narrator's divided identity remains tied to his inability to overcome the obstacles of his various pre- and postmigration homes.

Johnson positions the narrator's cycle of migration within what may be interpreted as consistently distorted reconfigurations of African-American experiences. Echoed in his various journeys are epochal events, such as the Middle Passage, the slave auction block, the fugitive slave's treacherous journey from slavery to freedom, the arrival on free soil, and the return journey to reconnect with ancestral roots. But in each case, his relation to these events is revisionary. In calling up these events Johnson seems to signify the narrator's failure to emulate his heroic forebears authentically. Evocations in the first and last of the narrator's migrations provide historical and literary touchstones that emphasize his ambiguous connections to family, heritage, community, and home geography.

In the first of the narrator's journeys, from his Georgia birthplace to his Connecticut childhood home, he refracts his recollections of his boyhood south through the lenses of popular literary models. The narrator describes the setting through the forcibly yoked images of plantation romance and slave narrative. Following Dunbar's lead in the opening of *The Sport of the Gods,* he echoes the sensibility of Thomas Nelson Page and fellow nostalgists. The narrator's description issues forth in what Stepto derides as a "torrent of nearly rhapsodic pastoralism" (*From Behind the Veil* 100): His childhood home was a place where "flowers grew in the front yard," a large vegetable garden provided "an endless territory" to entice a "childish fancy," an enclosure housed "a patient cow chewing her cud," and the narrator's white father held him on his knee (*Autobiography* 3). Like the

Hamilton family, however, the narrator's good fortune lasts only as long as his (or, more accurately, his mother's) presence poses no threat to the continuing function of the neo-plantation system. When his mother, who stands in the way of his father marrying "a young lady of another great Southern family" (30), comes to represent a threat by her visible proximity to the event, she and her son are summarily relocated in the North in a symbolic conflation of earlier narratives of imprisonment and liberation.

The critical moment of separation—the beginning of the trek north— is, as Smith has described, a symbolic and parodic recapitulation of the grotesque ritual of family's dissolution at the slave auction block. The moment confirms the conditional nature of the narrator's move to the presumed free soil of the North. It also represents the first stage of the adolescent narrator's estrangement from the source of his cultural roots and from his essential ties to his paternal lineage, "some of the best blood of the South." To placate the narrator and purchase his loyalty, his father drills a hole in the center of a $10 gold piece and gives it to his son: "I have worn that gold piece around my neck the great part of my life, and still possess it, but more than once I have wished that some other way had been found of attaching it to me besides putting a hole through it" (3).

The gesture "demonstrates the mother's and son's continued subordination to the white lover-father" (Smith, *Self-Discovery* 52); it also clarifies the wage basis of the narrator's relationship to his father. The narrator's similarity to his slave forebears is further evident in his childhood recollections and in what he conceals (the specifics of his birthplace, his parents' identities, his name, the lack of detail about his journey north) and what he reveals (his mixed-race parentage, his confusion about his racial identity, and the anguish of his separation from his father). Although the scene may allude to the stage of slave purchase, there are differences that cannot be overlooked. The family separation inverts rather than imitates the trope of being "sold down the river." The mother and son are not separated, and their destination is the North, not the South. The trip is not an escape, but is financed and blessed by the owner/father. Although the coin may indeed represent the narrator's exchange value, it also signifies his filial loss and is a reminder of his connection to and temporary separation from the white side of his lineage. The coin becomes a token of the narrator's ritual initiation into the potential monetary value of a white identity while conversely offering a practical lesson in the material limitations of remaining black. Whatever is to be gained from this ritual must be contemplated within the racial equivocations and uncertainties it engages.

The Narrator's Migratory Identity

Before his final trip north, after he views the lynching by fire, the narrator undertakes other journeys that are equally weighted with ambiguity. When he leaves Connecticut for college following his mother's death and responds to "the peculiar fascination which the South held over my imagination" (*Autobiography* 36), his decision to forego Harvard and matriculate at Atlanta University would seem to anticipate a rediscovery of his ancestry. Instead, he makes a modernized descent that initially carries the symbolic force of a return to southern slavery but soon puts him in the company of "the best class of colored people in Jacksonville" (54). Robbed of his chance to attend college by a black man and forced to make a train trip from Atlanta to Jacksonville doubled up in a "hot" and "suffocating" Pullman linen closet, his description of the "agonies" he suffers in his return south conjure up a personal middle passage. A similar reversal of fortune takes place when he leaves New York for Europe. Forced to flee suddenly when a jealous lover murders his female companion, he parlays his narrow escape into a grand tour of the Continent as the escort of a wealthy white benefactor.

After returning from Europe, and intending to mine the rich musical heritage of American slaves, the narrator's final trek into the South is a personal, if ultimately failed, immersion to create the conditions necessary for realizing a wholly American version of what W. E. B. Du Bois described in *The Souls of Black Folk* as a "better and truer self," something Du Bois viewed as derived from synthesizing both African and American sources. The narrator wants to bridge the gap between the folk sources of his most cherished musical forms and what Dickson Bruce labels the "mainstream cues" (*Black Writing* 260) of his Connecticut childhood. Although these cues may offer him access to a repertoire of piano classics by the great European masters, acceptance into Atlanta University, and an audience for his music in the salons of Europe, they are far removed from such authentic living vessels of southern culture as Singing Johnson and the revival preacher John Brown.

The narrator returns to the South as an ethnologist, a musicologist, an anthropological observer, and a recorder of southern life; he is an outsider rather than a native son. What does it mean for him to observe African-American culture in this way? The real-life experiences of early black collectors of African-American folk material, such as Arthur Huff Fauset and Zora Neale Hurston, as well as Johnson's own three-month teaching stint in the "backwoods of Georgia," which he recounts in *Along This Way,* suggest how tenuous a position the narrator occupies among the people of the South. Having "never seen cotton growing until [he] went to Georgia," Johnson came to his teaching duties uninitiated in rural ways and soon found a common ground in his shared marginality from the encompassing white world that made even him, a member of the African-American "vanguard," connected to other black southerners by "a force stronger than blood." Yet even realizing that "they were me, and I was they," he confesses to "studying them all with a sympathetic objectivity, as though they were something apart" (*Along This Way* 119).

Johnson felt himself to be at once connected and yet detached from the roots of southern culture on many occasions. Such ambiguous feelings exemplify the emotional tensions that inhered in his life-long attempts to promote and legitimize black music and adapt it for the northern stage. As his biographer Eugene Levy explains, "He wanted somehow to maintain the racial identity of the music he was helping to produce, and at the same time 'refine' and 'elevate' it, bringing it into conformity with conventional [European] musical and moral standards" (*James Weldon Johnson* 93). His problematic efforts to reconcile the conflicting implications of populist and elitist impulses tie him to his narrator.

Fauset had to contend with similar issues when he traveled to the Mississippi Delta to collect animal tales in 1925. He gained enough access to black material invisible to the white world to make a valuable reassessment of the tales of Joel Chandler Harris. And yet Fauset, a New Jersey–born school teacher living in Philadelphia, had difficulty penetrating the source of the southern folk experience and found that, among black southerners, his northern origins hurt him more than his race helped. As an Eatonville, Florida, southerner, Hurston would presumably meet fewer obstacles, but her first trip back home from Barnard College, where she was studying anthropology under the firm guidance of Franz Boas, emphasized how difficult the process of reimmersing herself back into her roots became when she traveled there specifically in the role of anthropologist and folklorist. She was able to collect some material, but the trip as she remembered it was a failure because old friends who would have welcomed a returning daughter of Eatonville were reluctant to speak freely to Hurston, the professional northern observer of black life.

Hurston, like Johnson's narrator, recognized that the South indeed held the authentic sources of black expression and black experience. But she made the mistake of trying to explore that experience without giving up her "carefully accented Barnardese." "Pardon me," she recalls saying, in her often-quoted self-parody, "but do you know any folk-tales or folk songs?" (*Dust Tracks* 128). As she wrote of the experience, "O, I got a few items. But compared with what I did later, not enough to make a flea a waltzing jacket."[20]

Hurston's lighthearted account of her failure bears out the narrator's complicated relationship to his roots. As a southerner by birth only, his travel to rural Georgia commences as he "strike[s] out into the interior" on what one critic labels "an imperial incursion" (Sundquist, *Hammers* 12). Like a rural colonizer, he seeks to reap the benefits of the black belt's knowledge without assuming the risks associated with being a part of the southern world he observes. As a black man passing for white, he can listen to smoking-car conversation on the "race question" and obtain a place among the onlookers at the lynching by fire. But the cost of gaining admission to these potent white rituals of southern racial authority comes in his guilt by association, because he makes no outward attempt to judge himself apart from what he witnesses.

Measured by its effect on the narrator and by the sheer immediacy of Johnson's presentation of the horrifying spectacle, the lynching is the climax of the novel. Critical in determining where the narrator's loyalties will lie, the gruesome scene prefigures and causes his final migration north. No doubt the most disturbing and vivid scene of the novel, it also contains some of its most curious moments, particularly in locating the narrator's relationship to his material. He has made his journey ostensibly to look deeply into black culture and uncover the authentic source of his African-American roots, a discovery that will help him use his musical genius to meld European classical and African-American folk musical traditions. But he encounters a quite different yet equally familiar by-product of southern life. Hearing alarming sounds late at night, he leaves his boardinghouse to enter an almost surreal scene in which a mob seeks an unnamed black who has committed an unnamed crime. The narrator joins the crowd and waits. When the victim is finally captured and brought before them, they demand that he be burned alive. Observing the grotesque spectacle, transfixed by the scene, "powerless to take my eyes from what I did not want to see" until "the smell of burnt flesh—human flesh—was in my nostrils" (*Autobiography* 136–37), the narrator hurriedly leaves town, leaves the South, and leaves the black race forever.

In one sense, the scene invites a voyeuristic response similar to a fugitive slave's account of being whipped. Relying on disturbingly graphic detail, its shock value alone makes a compelling argument against the mob's barbaric behavior. To supply the fictional material and accurately measure the terror of what his narrator witnessed, Johnson needed neither to look beyond a narrow escape from his own past nor exaggerate the lynching fever that gripped the South. Although the large number of lynchings of the 1880s and 1890s had diminished by the turn of the century, one hundred a year were still reported after 1900 (Franklin and Moss, Jr., *From Slavery* 282). Even as the numbers gradually dropped, southern whites turned to ever more radical means of using the practice for interracial social control.

A grotesque carnival surrounded the practice of lynching. In cases when the inevitable mob was held in abeyance long enough to prevent a victim from being hanged immediately, the scheduled lynching rapidly transformed into a community celebration. It was heavily promoted via handbills and word of mouth. As time permitted, newspapers supplemented their coverage with advertisements. Conductors offered special train fares. Individuals and families of all ages flocked to the site as if attending a summer church gathering. They arrived early, jockeyed for good views, congregated with friends, on occasion even set out picnics and returned with postcards of the event. Because the lynching itself was a relatively quick affair, ways were found to prolong it. Robert Zangrando has described how the "festive atmosphere" was supplemented by torture, burning, and even dismemberment of the victim, acts that included witnesses cutting off and taking home pieces of fingers, toes, and genitalia as souvenirs (*The NAACP Crusade*). If not the explicit model for Johnson's scene, surely the well-publicized Statesboro, Georgia, lynching in August 1904 embodied the horror the narrator describes. Following the trial of two black men who were found guilty of murdering a white farmer, his wife, and three children, a mob refused to wait for the sentence of hanging to be carried out. They overpowered members of the Savannah militia standing guard over the jail with unloaded guns, dragged the two men outside, and burned them alive. Rather than appeasing the crowd's thirst for revenge, the scene provoked a reign of white terrorism that lasted for several days.

On a less tragic scale, Johnson also narrowly avoided being lynched in 1900 when a group of military police arrested him for walking in Jacksonville, Florida, with a woman who appeared white but who was, in fact, legally black. She was furious about the arrest and charged the major at provost headquarters with full responsibility for the incident, laying on his head "the sins of his fathers and his fathers' fathers" (*Along This Way* 169). Johnson's fate nearly paralleled the anonymous victim of his novel, but for the intervention of his "white" African-American companion. Yet in the author's revision, the narrator remains cloaked behind the safety of whiteness. He not only does not (and cannot) intervene in the fictionalized rendition of what might have been Johnson's tragedy, but he also is, in spite of his passivity, strangely involved, even symbolically implicated, in what he observes.[21]

The narrator announces in the first paragraph that by commencing his tale and "divulging the great secret of [his] life" he is "playing with fire." Feeling the "thrill which accompanies that most fascinating pastime," his statement begins as a simple cliché but becomes, by the novel's climax, a recognition of the high cost of racial betrayal and a tacit acknowledgment of his attraction to the burning—which, in the narrator's occluded vision, reduces the victim to something less than human: "There he stood, a man only in form and stature, every sign of degeneracy stamped upon his countenance. His eyes were dull and vacant, indicating not a single ray of thought" (*Autobiography* 136). The lynching also yokes the narrator to a role beyond mere spectator when the victim is bound and burned alive on a railroad tie.

Throughout the novel, the railroad has served the narrator as a marker of his racial and spatial freedom. On it, he has mimicked superficial versions of a wide array of ritualized migrations—fugitive slaves traveling north to freedom, southern immersions like the one described in Du Bois's *The Souls of Black Folk*, and the staged refusal of the white-skinned Homer Plessy to ride in the Jim Crow car. But unlike those of his forebears, his journeys exhibit no trace of heroism; they expedite instead his convenient retreat into the cowardly posture of racial neutrality. The lynching is the concluding site of the narrator's tentative forays into black culture's ancestral sources, and it transforms him, by different means but with similar alienating results, into the kind of fugitive from his roots who would come to populate the later migration fiction of William Attaway, Wright, and others.

The lynching can be viewed as another kind of initiating moment in the fictional evolution of the Great Migration. Having been left to speculate on the victim's alleged crime, we are invited to view the imagery surrounding the railroad-tie crucifixion as an eerily anticipatory sacrifice for the forthcoming migration's deleterious effects on the white south. Relied upon to perpetuate the hierarchy of segregation upheld by *Plessy v. Ferguson*, the train instead was rapidly becoming (as the narrator's journey attests) the charged conveyance of escape from the vicissitudes of Jim Crow. As the southern victim, left behind as the narrator makes his final trek north, the burning man becomes white southerners' revenge; he is a sacrificial and tragic cost of migration's ongoing search for a livable home.

After considering so much travel, readers are left with the central question of identity. In spite of the narrator's many weaknesses, from what geographic source can his identity come? Whether in Georgia, Connecticut, Florida, or New York, he is ensnared, like the Hamiltons in *The Sport of the Gods*, in the harsh realities of the racial nadir. Whatever he gains from immersing himself in the various versions of black life in the South—ranging from "the best class of colored people in Jacksonville" (*Autobiography* 55) to the "Negro in his relatively primitive state" in the back woods of Georgia (126)—his growth is mitigated by white racism and a "disheartening" (123) lack of black progress. Yet the North is no more promising. The narrator's Connecticut childhood and his entrance into the fast-paced life of the New York club scene are less fixed on racial distinctions and less constrained by racism than would be the case in the South, but they exhibit little connection to any authentic folk culture. This is the same culture that the narrator calls "the treasured heritage of the American Negro" (133) and that Johnson would later identify in *Black Manhattan* as the African-American's "sacred music; the Spirituals; his secular music; the plantation songs, rag-time, blues, jazz, and the work songs; his folk-lore; the Uncle Remus stories and other plantation tales; and his dances" (260).

In Johnson's view, one key to racial progress lay in making the public aware of how greatly American civilization had been augmented by these artistic forms. To this end (and in contrast to his narrator), Johnson's substantial contribution remains most visibly evident as a writer who capitalized on these forms and as a musical collaborator with his brother, Rosamond. It is no surprise that the narrator's grandest aspiration is to follow a similar scheme. He turns down a chance to remain in Europe, choosing instead to return to America and travel into the South: "I made up my mind to go back into the very heart of the South, to live among the people, and drink in my inspiration firsthand. I gloated over the immense amount of material I had to work with, not only modern ragtime, but also the old slave songs—material which no one had yet touched" (*Autobiography* 104).

The narrator's reverse migration has the goal of combining of ascent with immersion. He wants to perform an act of cultural preservation that unites the South and the North by bringing the best of the black belt to the city. Channeling this lofty aspiration through his narrator, Johnson's foresight is striking. Writing several years before the large wartime exodus and a full decade before the studies explaining the Great Migration's causes and effects began to appear, his novel is a constituting critique of the conditions necessary for the black population to make the transition out of the South. What the narrator seeks but fails to achieve is a culture of migration of the kind realized a decade later in the most successful elements of the Harlem Renaissance. It was a spiritual and artistic awakening whose power grew out of congregating a geographically diverse group of African Americans—almost all of them migrants—in a location that enabled rather than inhibited the formation of an African-American-based aesthetic.[22]

2

Migration and the Harlem Renaissance

Georgia opened me. And it may well be said that I received my initial impulse to an individual art from my experience there. For no other section of the country has so stirred me. There one finds soil, soil in the sense the Russians know it,—the soil every art and literature that is to live must be imbedded in.

Jean Toomer

Right now when I look out into the Harlem Streets I feel just like Helga Crane in my novel. Furious at being connected with all these niggers.

Nella Larsen to Dorothy Peterson

City of refuge? City of refuse!

Wallace Thurman

Migration made Harlem the capitol of black America. Observers have long noted how the renaissance that flourished during the 1920s kindled a new black identity—what Alain Locke called "a spiritual coming of age"—but only recently has the extent to which newcomers to Harlem generated this explosion of cultural energy begun to be fully appreciated (Baker, *Modernism*; Bremer, *Urban Intersections* 132–64; Carby, "Policing").

Between 1890 and 1930, New York City's black population increased tenfold, from 33,888 to 327,706, and the majority of the new residents arrived from southern border states. The largest influx corresponded with the World War I labor shortage, which lured more blacks to New York than any other U.S. city even though the service-based economy of Manhattan offered fewer industrial labor opportunities than northern counterparts such as Chicago, Cleveland, and Detroit. But even before the World War I surge, black Manhattan had always been a city of migrants. In 1910 fewer than one-quarter of its 60,534 African Americans had been born in New York state, a proportion that would remain relatively constant throughout the five boroughs over the next two decades.[1]

Before the turn of the century, a relatively stable, small black population lived throughout the poorer working-class sections of New York City. The largest core was clustered around the present-day midtown area, including the sections known as the Tenderloin and San Juan Hill. Mortality rates among the city's African Americans were high, and population growth was attributable to a steadily increasing number of migrants. In addition to rural agricultural workers, they included large numbers of skilled laborers, business people, politicians, and an educated elite whose arrival caused the prewar exodus to be labeled the migration of the "talented tenth." This group, charged with elevating the entire race, was named by W. E. B. Du Bois in his 1903 essay "The Talented Tenth," which appeared in Booker T. Washington's *The Negro Problem,* an anthology airing the often-competing views of seven prominent African Americans. Du Bois contended that no nation was ever civilized by its uneducated masses, relying instead on its exceptional members. Opposing Booker T. Washington's southern strategy of accommodation and economic self-determination, Du Bois's paternal system of racial elevation offered ideal opportunities for the mostly male, college-educated migrants who descended on northern cities.

As the new arrivals strained the housing supplies of black neighborhoods to their limits, the population shifted north, up the West Side into the newer Harlem area, which until around 1900 had been a highly desirable, upper-middle-class, primarily Jewish neighborhood. Responding to the area's obvious appeal, developers had erected large numbers of attractive, well-built homes. When the depression of 1904–5 saw the real estate market plummet, many of Harlem's stylish residences were left vacant. In an effort to minimize their losses, landlords quietly began renting to black tenants. "Harlem," James Weldon Johnson wrote in *Black Manhattan,* "offered the coloured people the first chance in their entire history in New York to live in modern apartment houses" (147). And, despite the concerted resistance of white residents, they seized the opportunity with astonishing swiftness. Following the traditional racial patterns of urban settlement, as blacks trickled into the area their non-black neighbors moved. Property values fell, the market softened, and the trickle rapidly turned into a stream. Landlords responded by increasing their rents and subdividing apartments or by selling out entirely, often to black entrepreneurs such as Philip A. Payton, Jr., whose Afro-American Realty Company made (and later lost) a small fortune by courting black tenants.

Newcomers from throughout the black diaspora, including a large contingent of West Indians from dozens of Caribbean islands, also found their way to Harlem. Although immigration laws of the 1920s severely restricted the flow of Europeans and cut off Asian migration entirely, they had little effect on limiting blacks. By 1930 more than fifty thousand foreign-born Afro-Caribbeans had settled in New York City (Osofsky, *Harlem* 131). As Locke characterized Harlem's diversity, "It has attracted the African, the West Indian, the Negro American; has brought together the Negro of the North and the Negro of the South; the man from the city and the man from the town and village; the peasant, the student, the business man, the professional man, artist, poet, musician, adventurer and worker, preacher and criminal, exploiter and social outcast" (*The New Negro* 6).

Locke's description helps question the extent to which the Great Migration was limited to the rural-industrial working class and calls attention to the class differences among migrating groups. For the first time, the northern African-American middle class, whether politicians or poets, were leaders not of an abstract mass of rural black southerners but of a diverse constituency of urban neighbors (Carby, *Reconstructing* 164). This cultural mix, on the one hand, exacerbated tensions between the entrenched elites of Harlem who lived on "Sugar Hill," the ten-block area of townhouses and apartments that housed Harlem's aristocracy, and the migrants who filled the streets below. On the other hand, while other northern cities attracted mostly rural southern workers, Harlem's heterogeneous blend gave its migrant culture the unique cosmopolitan flavor necessary for a fullscale renaissance.

Harlem rightfully laid its claim to being, in Johnson's words, "the greatest Negro city in the world" ("Making" 635). But two qualifications—both foregrounded in the surge of interest in black literature of the 1920s—temper the misleading impression that it was a monolithic cultural and literary stage. First, the term *Harlem Renaissance* is a convenient, if somewhat misleading, label. It implies that a single location embodied a set of new cultural assumptions when, in fact, it was Harlem's migratory aspect that predicated the existence of a renaissance sensibility. Other American urban centers contributed to Harlem's cultural development, giving the concept of the "New Negro" not a local but a national scope. No one has stated this point better than Sterling Brown, who in 1955 downplayed

Harlem's literary centrality in an essay titled "The New Negro in Literature, 1925–1955": "The New Negro is not to me a group of writers centered in Harlem during the second half of the twenties. Most of the writers were not Harlemites; much of the best writing was not about Harlem, which was the show window, the cashier's till, but no more Negro America than New York is America" (57).

The major literary artists of the Harlem period came of age in the South, the Midwest, or in border cities before gravitating north. Washington, D.C., became an intellectual annex of Harlem. Brown, Locke, Jean Toomer, Rudolph Fisher, Jessie Fauset, and Zora Neale Hurston were among the many writers who had either been raised or had lived in the area. Locke articulated the central tenets of renaissance philosophy and served as an encouraging mentor to many of its writers. His home base was not Harlem, however, but the philosophy department of Howard University, where he was chair.

Brown, Fisher, and Toomer were all born in Washington before taking circuitous paths north. Brown arrived in Harlem after attending Williams College and Harvard University. Fisher moved from Washington to Providence, Rhode Island, where he graduated from high school. He received a degree from Brown University before returning to Washington as a medical student at Howard University. With medical degree in hand, he reached Harlem as a fellow at Columbia University's College of Physicians and Surgeons before settling down as a doctor, musician, and writer. The itinerant Toomer, hailing from a family of southerners, had moved around enough cities and done enough odd jobs, especially during the early 1920s, that he joined Langston Hughes in molding his vision of black-centered identity not out of a single location but from the sum total of his travels. Fauset, who like Locke had been born in Philadelphia, started her teaching career at Washington's M Street (later Dunbar) High School before moving to a Harlem junior high school and then on to DeWitt Clinton High School. Hurston came to Washington's Howard University from Baltimore's Morgan Academy and all-black Eatonville, Florida, before entering Barnard College, where she caught the attention of the renowned anthropologist Franz Boas.

The Utah-born Wallace Thurman arrived in Harlem from Los Angeles, where he had tried to organize a literary group and where he worked in the post office with Arna Bontemps before both men traveled west. Helene Johnson and her cousin Dorothy West moved down from Boston, but not before West had already won several newspaper fiction prizes and had helped publish a small magazine named *The Quill.* Although the black Chicago literary scene was comparatively quiet during the 1920s, it too would spring to life during the depression with the arrival there of Richard Wright, Frank Marshall Davis, Margaret Walker, Gwendolyn Brooks, and others. When Wright moved to Harlem in 1937 he left behind a group of writers whose impressive outpouring of work allowed them to lay claim to their own later renaissance. The talents allowed to flourish among the New Negroes of Harlem had been cultivated in a host of other locations (Singh et al., eds., *Harlem Renaissance* 4).

The second qualification to Harlem's national literary prominence has been perceptively described by Sidney Bremer: "The best publicized 'New Negro' leaders were more often away than in Harlem during the 1920s" (*Urban Intersections* 133). That included Claude McKay, who left in 1922, and Countee Cullen, a local anomaly for having grown up in New York but who had only stayed in Harlem briefly during the 1920s between his studies at Harvard and trips to Paris. Hughes was in and out of Harlem throughout the decade (before later becoming one of the few writers of the period to settle there permanently). The two Johnsons, James Weldon and Charles, along with Bontemps, W. E. B. Du Bois, Nella Larsen, and Arthur Schomburg, all were in and out of Harlem before leaving entirely by the late 1920s (Bremer, *Urban Intersections* 132–35). Brown, a late addition to the Harlem scene, embodied the peripatetic impulses of many writers when he refused to concede Harlem's literary dominance and referred to his periods in New York as "stopovers" (Brown, "The New Negro" 77; Stepto, "Sterling A. Brown"). That everyone arrived from somewhere else and then moved on remains the most unifying characteristic of the dissimilar core of New Negro writers and intellectuals.

Even if few writers made Harlem their permanent home, it remained central to their experience. By the 1919 Armistice signaling the end of World War I, Harlem was the epicenter of black America. If the community needed a birth announcement, it came with the return from Europe of the all-black 369th Regiment. Other key events also might be said to have served a similar function: the 1919 opening of the first all-black production on Broadway, *Shuffle Along;* the March 1924 Civic Club literary banquet that first drew together the renaissance's core of black writers, intellectuals, and white patrons; or the publication in 1925 of *The New Negro,* which had evolved from a "Harlem" edition of *Survey Graphic* that had grown out of a conversation at the Civic Club banquet between Paul Kellogg and Locke (Gilpin, "Charles S. Johnson" 228). But the November 17, 1919, parade was more wide-ranging, inclusive, and more visible to Harlem's black masses than these other events. Thousands had never heard of Locke or Hughes, but everyone knew the 369th.

More to the point, the regiment's return aptly symbolized the paradox of Harlem aspirations and barriers in the 1920s. Having been refused an American command and been put instead under the charge of the French, the "Hell Fighters," as the Germans called them, had proven themselves among the most heroic forces of the European theater. With fighting stamina beyond compare, the 369th had endured more days in the trenches than any other American regiment; it was the first unit of the Allied army to reach the Rhine. The soldiers of the 369th had the unique distinction of having their entire regiment win the prestigious Croix de Guerre for exceptional gallantry. Their parade took them, amid cheering crowds of white and black New Yorkers, through the streets of Manhattan, up Fifth Avenue, through the newly constructed victory arch, and into Harlem. There, led by the music of Lt. James Europe's jazz band, they were welcomed by a spirited black multitude who were made to feel that their own 369th signaled the beginning of a new racial order in America (Franklin and Moss, Jr., *From Slavery* 298–311; Huggins, *Harlem Renaissance* 54–55).

In reality, however, although more fortunate Harlemites were no doubt realizing that goal just as the community was on its way to becoming the exotic uptown playground of white New York, no real social and economic changes had come to the nation that these soldiers fought to protect. They returned to an emerging economic ghetto that was troubled by skyrocketing housing costs, few employment opportunities, and the same racial circumstances that had allowed them to risk their lives for a version of democracy that forced them to live outside its well of opportunity. By the 1930s Harlem would have begun to deteriorate into a slum whose abject living conditions would come to embody the continued disfranchisement of black America. But for the moment, as the 369th marched up Lenox Avenue, it called forth the truest realization of migrant promise, a "city of refuge" signaling racial progress and renewal for blacks of every economic and social level.

In his autobiography *The Big Sea* (1940), Hughes documented the optimism that he had sensed throughout Harlem when he arrived there. Although the impoverished circumstances would sometimes overwhelm Hughes (leading him later to comment, "All of us know that the gay and sparkling life of the so-called Negro Renaissance of the '20s was not so gay and sparkling beneath the surface as it looked"), the awe with which he recalled his 1921 arrival registers the genuine exultation that thousands of other migrants must have felt:

I can never put on paper the thrill of the underground ride to Harlem. I had never been in a subway before and it fascinated me—the noise, the speed, the green lights ahead. At every station I kept watching for the sign: 135th STREET. When I saw it, I held my breath. I came out onto the platform with two heavy bags and looked around. It was still early morning and people were going to work. Hundreds of colored people! I wanted to shake hands with them, speak to them. I hadn't seen any colored people for so long—that is any Negro colored people.

I went up the steps and out into the bright September sunlight. Harlem! I stood there, dropped my bags, took a deep breath and felt happy again. (81)

Despite having been on the move much of his life—he lived in seven cities by the time he was twelve—Hughes felt that he had at last found a home. He would later summarize his long journey in the deftly ironic "Aesthete in Harlem" (1931):

> Strange,
> That in this nigger place,
> I should meet Life face to face
> When for years, I had been seeking
> Life in places gentler speaking
> Until I came to this near street
> And found Life—stepping on my feet!

He had not come to Harlem from the deep rural South, nor was he a typical migrant laborer in search of work. Arriving by ship from Vera Cruz, Mexico, to enroll for what would be a brief stint at Columbia University, Hughes was, if anything, a member of the talented tenth. It is this point that separates the migration experience of most renaissance writers from working-class migrants who constituted the renaissance's veiled chorus and provided the human critical mass necessary to allow it to flourish. Yet Hughes's description highlights the commerce, technology, and vast scale of the city; he recalled the subway as his gateway into a vibrant field of black possibility.

Harlem, which already contained the largest African-American population in the world, offered Hughes and other migrants their first opportunity to live free of white interference. Setting in vast relief the limitations of whatever home they had left behind, Harlem initially seemed to be more than a mere place. It represented a new attitude that embodied not only the sentiments of thousands of migrants but also a whole generation of black writers, artists, dancers, musicians, and intellectuals (as well as white patrons and onlookers) who found a cultural mecca unprecedented throughout the world.

Harlem's Migrant Writers

Despite the imprint of migration indelibly etched on the community of Harlem and the lives of the many writers of its literary culture, the fiction of the 1920s contains surprisingly little emphasis on coming to terms with the impact of the Great Migration. There were, to be sure, Great Migration novels written during the period. The three most apparent examples are Toomer's *Cane* (1923), Walter White's *Flight* (1926), and Larsen's *Quicksand* (1928).

Cane is hardly a conventional inclusion in the migration form—a point punctuated by the long debate over *Cane*'s formal status as a novel—but central to its concerns is the split relation between the South and North. *Flight* and *Quicksand* structure their narratives around journeys into and out of Harlem. (Thurman's *The Blacker the Berry* [1929] follows a similar pattern but is not, in the precise sense, a Great Migration novel because its protagonist, like Thurman himself, migrates from the West Coast.) Generally, however, in keeping with these examples, when Harlem writers featured migration as a part of their plots they regarded the experience within the localized, personal quests of individual characters and positioned the dilemma of replacing one home with another in the context of more extensive examinations of class and color identity. Such emphases were fully in keeping with the personal concerns of the writers as well as with the general enthusiasms of readers, publishers, and the larger public more interested in surveying the exoticism of Harlem than with mining the roots of a new urban culture.

Harlem writers saw themselves as having little in common with their working-class neighbors, so it is not surprising that there were few works like Fisher's "City of Refuge," whose rural North Carolina-born protagonist King Solomon Gillis could hardly have been more different from the physician who created him. Because the story was published in *The New Negro,* Locke may have been thinking about Fisher and Gillis when, in the same volume, he observed about Fisher's generation that "the young Negro writers dig deep into the racy peasant undersoil of the race life" (51).

Despite the lyrical appeal of his earthen metaphor, Locke's romantic elevation of the common folk was not an altogether accurate characterization of either his anthology or Harlem literature.[2] Overall, the era was more interested in capturing artistic force from a psychology of highest achievement. Animated by the bohemian sensibilities of a middle-class artistic community and devoted to personal discovery, Harlem's self-conscious black aesthetic championed black accomplishment, pride, and advancement in a distinctly urban setting. Where its writers came from seemed only a minor prelude to the exciting prospect of where the new urban culture was headed.

In reality, however, few of the young writers were as distant from their migrant neighbors as they may have liked. If they spent their nights rubbing elbows with Harlem celebrities and rich whites, their days were marked by more practical pursuits. No matter their education or background, they faced the same economic challenges as everyone else in Harlem and were forced to accept patronage and work at a range of menial and low-paying jobs to make ends meet. Hughes waited tables, and Cullen worked as a busboy. Thurman was a managing editor of the labor-oriented *Messenger,* the sole black reader for the Macaulay publishing house, and head of the board that organized the short-lived literary magazine *Fire!!* Despite holding the most enviable and prestigious literary position among Harlem writers, he still had to support himself by writing adult movie scripts and selling "true confessions" to tabloids under such pseudonyms as Ethel Belle Mandrake and Patrick Casey (Hughes, *The Big Sea* 233–34). Even the heralded rent parties of the period, which helped fuel Harlem's reputation as uptown New York's exotic party capital, were, more tellingly, pointed expressions of the tenuous economic circumstances in which all but a very few were forced to live.

Nonetheless, the movement of the southern black masses into Harlem went largely unexplored in fiction. Instead, Locke's *The New Negro* joined such novels as Fauset's *There Is Confusion* (1924), McKay's *Home to Harlem* (1928), Fisher's *Walls of Jericho* (1928), and Thurman's *Infants of the Spring* (1932) in bringing to life the hum and buzz of Harlem's spirited, almost-human personality. Fauset, Thurman, and Fisher found compelling literary material in critiquing the bohemian social habits of Harlem's new bourgeoisie. Both Fauset and Thurman—despite employing a dizzying number of characters, many of them witty replicas of their real-life satirical targets—focused on a relatively narrow portion of Harlem society, with minimal critical success. Fisher added more breadth to *Walls of Jericho* by including one of the few fictional members of the Harlem intelligentsia, Fred Merrit, to express compassion for the migrant lower-classes. Yet Fisher's focus remains on Merrit, and the distance between his world and that of his less fortunate neighbors is made so prominent, especially in the latter group's use of dialect, that Fisher's sympathies for ordinary migrant culture seem strained.

The payoff for these novelists came in demonstrating that although their middle-class characters were worthy of satire, the best among them possessed essentially the same assimilationist goals and values as their white counterparts and were exemplary models of racial uplift, deserving of praise from such older members of the black intellectual community as W. E. B. Du Bois and Benjamin Brawley.

McKay's *Home to Harlem* chronicled an entirely different, lower-class setting. One of the renaissance's most controversial works, the novel was more criticized and more popular than any except *Nigger Heaven* (1926), the notorious paean to black exoticism by Carl Van Vechten, a white patron and mentor of black causes. Throughout *Home to Harlem,* McKay's protagonist, Jake Brown, is physically and spiritually liberated by the urban setting's vitality: "Harlem! Harlem! Little thicker, little darker and noisier and smellier, but Harlem just the same. . . . Going, going, going Harlem! Going up . . . Lawdy! Harlem bigger, Harlem better . . . and sweeter!" (25–26).

That was not, however, the Harlem that Du Bois wanted represented in renaissance fiction. When he reviewed the novel (together with Larsen's *Quicksand*) in the June 1928 *Crisis,* he told readers that *"Home to Harlem* for the most part nauseates me, and after the dirtier parts of its filth I feel distinctly like taking a bath." His fulmination betrays his horror at seeing the sordid side of Harlem night life put on display for all of white America to witness. If art, as Du Bois maintained, was potent racial propaganda, McKay's emphasis on "drunkenness, fighting, and sexual promiscuity" was a direct affront to the black struggle for social equality ("The Browsing Reader" 202). But by completely dismissing McKay's accomplishment, Du Bois also indicated his detachment from the everyday affairs of the struggling masses his cherished talented tenth was to elevate. More recently, the major criticism directed at *Home to Harlem* has shifted from the class divisions implicit in Du Bois's charges to gender considerations that recognize its one-dimensional representation of women, who, in Nathan Huggins's words, exist as "mere instruments for male behavior" (*Harlem Renaissance* 126).

The novel's contemporary opponents were challenged on multiple fronts when *Home to Harlem* won several literary awards. It became the first novel by a Harlem writer to reach the bestseller list. It also received enthusiastic support in reviews written by whites, who praised it for its engaging style, careful reproduction of an interesting variety of dialects, and realistic and joyous depiction of a heretofore under-represented class of people.

The response to the novel was somewhat divided along racial lines. Its controversial reception was also owing to its multifaceted view of the

Harlem landscape and the broad range of its male characterization. Instead of appealing to Du Bois's artistic philosophy of racial uplift and addressing the narrow concerns of upwardly mobile blacks, McKay rendered the generally sympathetic Jake through a dynamic, unapologetically masculine vision of working-class, folk primitivism.[3] As a sensual man of instinct who moves with assurance through Harlem's cabaret scene, Jake is contrasted by a Haitian intellectual, Ray. The dour and alienated writer is never able to come to terms with Harlem's complicated combination of fertile artistic potential and spiritual and physical blight. Fearful of becoming "a contented hog in the pigpen of Harlem," Ray refuses an opportunity to marry, choosing instead to flee America and the white values it represents by signing on as a mess boy on a ship bound for Europe. Between the internal contemplations and episodic adventures of both men, McKay explores the full spectrum of competing approaches to black male existence.

Du Bois's views notwithstanding, *Home to Harlem* is only one element of McKay's considerable overall achievement. Although the novel is not a part of the migration novel form, it covers similar ground by replacing the South with the Caribbean as McKay's genus loci and thus offering a noteworthy complement to the domestic migration novel, which would find potent expression in later Afro-Caribbean migration novels such as Paule Marshall's *Brown Girl, Brownstones* (1959). McKay's success, especially as a poet, derived in a large degree from his willingness to look back sympathetically at his Caribbean origins and draw on the total of his experiences and education, both before and after he traveled to the United States. No one during the 1920s more successfully made a career of exploring the dichotomy between city and country than McKay. He contrasted the idyllic, preindustrial quality of life in the tropics that typifies many of the island poems of his collection *Harlem Shadows* (1922) with the "harsh, the ugly city" characterized in "The Tired Worker." In exploring the dilemma of black identity as it is tied into reclaiming a racial past, McKay addressed a central issue of the renaissance in its full magnitude.

As a reflection of Harlem literature of the 1920s, McKay's work leads to a critical observation about the renaissance's attention to the Great Migration. Almost without exception, the Harlem writers who, like McKay, looked beyond local concerns and debates and drew artistic inspiration from their pre-Harlem origins produced the most critically praised literature of the period. This includes Toomer's *Cane,* the multigenre writings of Hughes, and, later, Brown's poetry and Hurston's folklore and fiction. Regardless of where they resided, these writers used the South as the historical and emotional anchor of their imaginations. Because the term

New Negro was understood to be synonymous with the "black elite," and because many within that elite expressed a loathing for the new urban masses with whom they came to be affiliated, Harlem's literary reputation, ironically, hinged not on finding distance between these antagonistic groups but in tapping directly into their shared past. The reputation of the Harlem Renaissance's literature ultimately rested on its migrant origins.

Jean Toomer equaled McKay's achievement in *Cane,* a lyrical pastiche of sketches, stories, poetry, and closet drama, by exploring a similar opposition between the soilbound culture of the South and the urban worlds to which so many southerners were moving. More than any literary work that preceded it, *Cane* elevated the black South above stereotypes. Toomer conveyed a measured blend of the humanity and cruelty of rural black life, particularly among women, through his talent for drawing out the beauty of even the most oppressive surroundings. It was Toomer's friend Waldo Frank who best summed up the transcendent lyricism of the work: "For Toomer, the Southland is not a problem to be solved; it is a field of loveliness to be sung: the Georgia Negro is not a downtrodden soul to be uplifted; he is material for gorgeous painting" (Toomer, *Cane* 139).[4]

Strictly speaking, the degree to which *Cane* allows itself to be read as migration fiction lies in whether it can be considered a novel at all, or whether it is, as Darwin Turner has argued, a singular, indefinable literary achievement that a fellow critic described as poetry and prose "whipped together in a kind of frappé" (Bontemps, "The Negro Renaissance" 25). The basis of unity in the novel does not come from conventional causal relationships, from character development, or the mode's usual chronological progression (Reilly, "Search" 197). Rather, its novelistic unity is achieved by its use of geography as a structuring device. The associational, modernistic narrative follows an overriding migratory pattern. It moves from the six vignettes about Georgia women and the ten transitional poems in the first section to the second section's imagistic rendering of Washington, D.C., "a crude-boned, soft-skinned wedge of nigger life breathing its loafer air" (Toomer, *Cane* 41). The third section follows with a drama about Toomer's alter-ego Ralph Kabnis, about whom Toomer wrote in a letter to Frank, "Kabnis is *me*" (Rusch, *Jean Toomer Reader* 25). He is a northerner who, in coming South to teach school, finds himself filled with "loneliness, dumbness, awful, intangible oppression" as he is forced to confront his ancestral connections to the Georgia soil, which reduces him to "an atom of dust in agony on a hillside" (Toomer, *Cane* 85).

The book's southern landscape, "the soft, listless cadence of Georgia's South" (17), is rendered in an ever-building accretion of images—cane fields, pine forest, liquor stills, cotton stalks, red soil, saw mills, smoke, fire, and the ubiquitous "purple haze" of dusk—which are all part of the spontaneous, sensual, sometimes violent day-to-day rhythms of rural black folk who live outside the cycle of modern progress. The North, in contrast, is a paralyzing landscape of smooth asphalt, back alleys, basements, dead houses, police, chorus girls, and false prophets. Its central image is the theater, where "the director will herd you, my full-lipped, distant beauties, and tame you, and blunt your sharp thrusts in loosely suggestive movements appropriate to Broadway" (52). Dorris, the most promising of these "beauties," finds that she cannot break free of the stage's world of artifice, where personality and authenticity are dulled by marketplace demands, despite a southern consciousness grounded in notions of "canebrake loves and mangrove feastings" (55), fleeting domestic fantasies of children and a home, and despite her futile effort to be an individual apart from the chorus line's mass of "dancing ponies" (53).

She makes a genuine effort to challenge the urban pressures that repress the kind of free-flowing sexuality so evident among the Georgia women described in Part 1. In comparison, the anonymous woman in "Calling Jesus" in Part 2 is alienated from everything, including her own soul, which is "like a little thrust-tailed dog, that follows her, whimpering" (58). The woman forces that dog to stay in the vestibule at night, where it shivers while she sleeps. The dog "symbolizes the essence of the Southern Negro and what he has lost in the city. Only when the dog's mistress forgets in sleep 'the streets and alleys, and the large house where she goes to be of nights,' is she receptive to the Soul of her Negro heritage" (MacKethan, "Jean Toomer's *Cane*" 233).

The contrasting geographies are drawn together by the presence first of the intermittent narrator and then Kabnis, both of whom are northern outsiders attempting to tie themselves into the nurturing geography of their southern past. While walking along the Georgia Pike in "Fern" the narrator realizes that "when one is on the soil of one's ancestors, most anything can come to one" (19). In spite of a local reputation for being "prejudiced" and "stuck-up," the narrator tests this realization by trying to reach out to one of the town curiosities, Fernie May Rosen. Fern's appeal is radiated through her eyes: "They were strange eyes. In this, that they sought nothing—that is *nothing* that was obvious and tangible and *that one could see*" (16, my emphasis). Instead of forging a meaningful association, the narrator finds himself succumbing to her sexual appeal and objectifying and alienating her, just as other men have repeatedly done. Having angered Fern's neighbors, the narrator leaves town on the train that crosses the road beside her house. In one of *Cane*'s most enduring symbolic images, he looks out his window as the train heads north and sees her sitting on her porch, "eyes vaguely focused on the sunset" (19). Juxtaposing separation and connection, movement and stasis, technology and nature, this fleeting moment both condenses the numerous differences between the narrator and his ancestral culture and emphasizes Toomer's understanding of the difficulty of forging a meaningful union between the two.

To the extent that *Cane* may be read as a meditation on Toomer's own journey to Sparta, Georgia, where he was employed for a few months as a substitute teacher in a small industrial academy, it joins Du Bois's *The Souls of Black Folk,* Johnson's *The Autobiography of an Ex-Coloured Man,* and David Bradley's *The Chaneysville Incident* (1981) in trying to reconcile the educated black northerner's wish for technological, economic, and educational progress and the need to accept his racial past through traveling into the simpler, more rustic black belt. Each of these works testifies to the challenge of making this journey, of drawing not only on the regenerative power of southern soil, folk songs, blues music, and folk religion but also coming to terms with slavery and all it represents. Like trying to comprehend Fern's eyes, which fool men into thinking "that she was easy" (16), the South cannot be possessed simply be stepping onto its soil. In questioning Toomer's success in completing his own journey in *Cane,* Du Bois noted in a review that "Toomer does not impress me as one who knows his Georgia but he does know human beings" (Toomer, *Cane* 171). The observation might, ironically, be a more accurate assessment of Du Bois's relation to his own distant southern roots. Toomer, despite the heightened sensation of belonging he felt during his residence in Sparta, still willingly addressed his sense of separateness from its culture through the ruminations of his thinly veiled self-portrait, Ralph Kabnis, whose psychic punishment is to remain "suspended a few feet above the soil whose touch would resurrect him" (98).

This visual image of liminality typifies Toomer's characterization of the ambiguous relation between the South and North. For all of its allusive poetry, expressive characterization, thematic unity, and original mode of representation, *Cane* repeats the migration novel form's conventionally equivocal view of the geographic options available to African Americans. It concludes with the double-edged image of Carrie Kate, the unspoiled little sister of Kabnis's friend Fred Halsey, reaching out to Kabnis and, Christ-like, drawing the fever from his body. Carrie Kate embodies a potent combination of innocence and power. As the symbolic agent of Kabnis's potential salvation, she substantiates Toomer's view of the South as

a landscape that is essentially feminine. Her gesture allows Kabnis to begin ascending from the subsoil of Halsey's basement as the morning sun
slowly illuminates the scene. Kabnis has entered the basement to escape
an imagined lynching party and join Halsey and his friends in a night of
debauchery with two women, Cora and Stella. Instead, he finds the basement transformed into a ritual site of ancestral recovery wherein he attempts to reclaim his poetic voice, which has been reduced to "misshap-
en, split-gut, tortured, twisted words" (111). The basement is the symbolic
womb from which the voiceless and alienated postmigration New Negro,
Kabnis, seems about to be reborn. To this end, the scene projects optimism
about the fecund south's power to inject life into a disaffected culture of
transplanted northern artists. Through his protagonist's awakening consciousness, Toomer tells a young generation of New Negro writers, Kabnis's real-life counterparts, from where he feels their artistic inspiration
must come.

On the other hand, despite this expression of regeneration and potential rebirth, Kabnis, the "cut off" northerner, trudges upstairs, perhaps
having ascended too soon without taking proper heed of the scene around
him. He only tentatively moves beyond his earlier repudiation of the blind
Father John, the aging "symbol, flesh, and spirit of the past" who remains
hidden in the basement. "An' besides," Kabnis says, "he aint my past. My
ancestors were Southern blue-bloods" (108). Like the graphically represented arcs that begin each section of *Cane*, Kabnis's story concludes in
the process of him possibly completing his journey—hauling the dead coals
of his past upstairs to reignite them—but indeterminate about the ultimate
success of the effort.

The difficulty of Kabnis's rebirth is punctuated by the presence of Ralph
Ellison's narrator, three decades later, similarly sitting below-ground at the
conclusion of *Invisible Man*. In keeping with the demographic changes
brought on by the Great Migration, Ellison's staging ground moved from
Toomer's rural Georgia to the streets, basements, subways, and sewers of
Harlem. There his narrator concludes his story, having retreated into his
imagination, reflecting on comparable dilemmas about the geographic
sources of identity and, like Kabnis, still on the threshold of reemerging
into the world. The parallel to Ellison is an important one. *Cane*, like *Invisible Man*, dramatically documents how geography structures African-
American consciousness and how migration is thus as much a psychological as a geographic movement. The events of both stories are repeatedly
subsumed by the consciousness, feeling, and intuitive experiences of the
characters and the rich, fluid imagery that floats around them (Toomer,

Cane 196–201). *Cane* is often considered the first major literary work of the Harlem Renaissance. Its experimental form, incorporation of folk images and forms into the thread of its narrative, and emphasis on the battle between seeing and invisibility make it more stylistically and thematically akin to *Invisible Man* than to contemporary Harlem novels, however.

Cane, among the earliest published works to be associated with the Harlem writers, makes only passing reference to Harlem; in fact, Toomer never lived there. He favored the downtown atmosphere of Greenwich Village. Ironically, his reputation as a renaissance artist has come to rely on recognizing the brilliance a novel that is not about Harlem. Only a year after *Cane*'s publication, Toomer abandoned his interest in exploring the black aspect of his past and began a long affiliation with the psychological and philosophical ideas of Georges I. Gurdjieff, an eastern mystic whose emphasis on discovering the core of human essence strongly appealed to Toomer and occupied the latter part of his career. Among Toomer's writings, and within the Harlem Renaissance and among other migration novels, *Cane* remains a singular achievement.

Migration Novel Offshoots

Langston Hughes, in contrast, turned time and again to the same ground that Toomer covered in *Cane*. Among Harlem writers who had American roots, only Hughes joined Claude McKay in making a career out of examining the urban scene through the filter of his own past. Before Brown's impressive poetic debut with *Southern Road* (1932), no one except Hughes thematized his premigration origins with anything resembling the nostalgic longing for home that McKay showed for his native land throughout his poetry and in his third and final novel, *Banana Bottom* (1933). Although Hughes never wrote a migration novel as such, he incorporated his connection to his roots into his work so thoroughly that he emerges as the premiere migration poet of the century. His migrant sensibility found proper expression in the *Nation* in June 1926 in what remains the most enduring *ars poetica* of the period, "The Negro Artist and the Racial Mountain": "Until America has completely absorbed the Negro and until segregation and racial self-consciousness have entirely disappeared, the true work of art from the Negro artist is bound, if it have any color and distinctiveness at all, to reflect his racial background and his racial environment" (692).

More than any of the novels of his contemporaries, Hughes's poetry yoked the theme of Harlem as a vibrant urban landscape to the southern rootedness of blues and jazz. Incorporating these vernacular aural modes into lyrical verse allowed him to evoke in writing the humor and beauty as well as the pain and hardships of everyday life in the city.[5] In bringing a migrant's sensibility to his urban poetry, Hughes forged just the kind of affirmative cultural alliance between the South and North, high and low, that had eluded *Cane's* Ralph Kabnis and the narrator in *The Autobiography of an Ex-Coloured Man*—and that even now remains the engrossing quest of migrant fiction. In celebrating the man and woman furthest down, Hughes alone among his Harlem peers found a successful way to merge northern ascent with southern immersion. Because everyday Harlem was powered by the energy of this fusion, when the renaissance's fiction writers tended to favor middle-class subjects or look only into the more exotic pockets of Harlem for their material they failed to evoke the urban scene with anything approaching the complexity of Hughes's poetry. His work thus not only realizes the Great Migration's powerful potential as a source of art but also tempers the more pessimistic tone of the depression-era migration fiction that would follow.

Hughes's vision of Harlem as a synthesis of the urban and the folk was brilliantly spelled out in his *Weary Blues* (1926) and *Fine Clothes to the Jew* (1927), a hotly debated collection that Arnold Rampersad calls "one of the more astonishing books of verse ever published in the United States" (*Life* 141). Nonetheless, the influence of the man who the former radical turned arch-conservative George Schuyler praised as "the poet of the modern Negro proletariat" (Rampersad, *Life* 140) remained small compared to sensational portraits of the Harlem found in the best-selling novels *Home to Harlem* and *Nigger Heaven,* both of which "explored the cabaret Harlem, of joyful, erotic, and musical exuberance, that exercised a dominant influence on the literary use of Harlem by black and non-black authors alike . . . and has resonated in the literary idea of Harlem ever since" (De Jongh, *Vicious Modernism* 26).

When Harlem novelists followed Hughes's and Toomer's poetic cues and looked down home, their unromantic, ambivalent characterizations of their protagonists' origins led to mixed results. For example, Cullen, a poet, attempted to portray a working-class Texan in his only novel, *One Way to Heaven* (1932). But his characterization of Sam Lucas, a one-armed religious conversion artist, is a labored examination of black religion and class issues, and it illustrates how complicated it was for the adopted Harlem minister's son to write convincingly about a population about whom he knew very little. White's *Flight,* Larsen's *Quicksand,* and Thurman's *The Blacker the Berry* filter the conventional migrant's search for a home through stories about the difficulty of overcoming class and color consciousness within the black middle class. But each of these migration novels downplays the effect of geography on identity in favor of emphasizing the renaissance's internal debate over the politics of skin color.

Portraying the South as a terrain of moral enslavement (a condemnation more traditionally reserved for the urban North), *Flight* is the story of a light-skinned New Orleans Creole, Mimi Dauqin, who is driven from her home for becoming pregnant by a man who refuses to marry her. Not willing to submit to an abortion, Mimi delivers the baby, whom she names Jean, but suffers the wrath of the community for her carnal misdeed. Forced to sever connections to the South, she leaves her child in an orphanage and goes north, living in several cities before finally gravitating to Harlem on the advice of her aunt. After a troublesome visitor from New Orleans exposes Mimi's past, Harlem society expels her from its social circles. To escape the torment of being ostracized, she crosses the color line, starts working as a dressmaker on Fifth Avenue, and soon marries a wealthy white man.

Mimi has made a respectable class and color transition as a result of migrating, and her successful ascent appears complete. But White, who had blue eyes and light skin and could have easily passed for white himself but never did, is not appealing for cultural amalgamation. Nor is he willing to create a heroine whose success is predicated on denying her sexuality in exchange for the material prosperity of a new urban culture. Rather, White makes clear that Mimi's act of passing, much like the act of migrating, forces her to forsake the most authentic and satisfying source of her identity. As a passing migrant, she is doubly suspended from her roots. As a mother, no amount of economic comfort overshadows her longing for her son.

To solve this dilemma, White settles for a simplistic treatment of the passing theme in *Flight*'s conclusion. In accord with the typical ending of passing fiction, blood overrides money as Mimi's pain in denying her heritage leads her back into the fold of the black community. The "call of Harlem" (200) proves too great, her married life too stifling, and her child's future too uncertain. She leaves her husband, reclaims her black identity, and with young Jean takes to the life of single-parenthood, exuberant in her newfound freedom: "'Free! Free! Free!' she whispered exultantly as with firm tread she went down the steps. 'Petit Jean—my own people— and happiness!' was the song in her heart as she happily strode through the dawn" (300). Mimi has been reunited with her son and the black world, but the novel's hollow conclusion undercuts White's complex rendering of her environment early in the book.

As one of the early part of the century's two most detailed examinations of the intersection between cultural dualism and geographic identity, *Flight* yields to a temptation avoided by its more subtle predecessor, *The Autobiography of an Ex-Coloured Man*. White inscribes an unambiguous happy ending, taking for granted the presence of a viable postmigration northern setting that will accommodate Mimi. He thus turns away from the complex issues of racial solidarity and gender oppression by negating the overarching presence of a cruel, oppressive social world, concluding the novel instead in an artificial environment united around racial passion and female determination. This is not to say that such emotions could not or did not exist, particularly in the middle-class setting where the novel closes. White, however, provides little evidence that Mimi's and her son's lives will improve, other than her own vague sense that they will. She is penniless, unable to acknowledge many of her friends, alienated from the shallow yet sympathetic white community, and unable to bridge the schism between herself and her black neighbors.

Succumbing to the urge to read beyond the novel's final pages and wonder how Mimi will turn vague concepts such as freedom and happiness into food and rent money suggests that White's tidy conclusion only weakly fulfills the need to affirm his call for racial loyalty. Although *Flight* is something of a flawed minor note in the migration novel tradition—one reviewer characterized it as "demonstrating a factual truth but not an artistic one" and others called it "entirely disappointing" and "notably dull and stereotyped"—it well illustrates how complicated the formation of female identity becomes when the presence of class division, gender exploitation, and racial preference further complicates the effect of changing geography on a character's consciousness.[6]

Thurman's *The Blacker the Berry* approaches the subject of skin color from a different angle and a different setting. It is one of the few novels following a west-to-east movement. Emma Lou Morgan is born into a Boise, Idaho, family of such all-consuming color-consciousness that she feels "there is no place in the world for a girl as black as she" (26). Having inherited the very dark skin of her father, Emma Lou is, from her earliest days, disdained by her mother's family, whose motto is "whiter and whiter every generation" (19). In a debasing inversion of the image of the northbound freedom train, her grandparents explain their move to Boise from Kansas as an escape from "those hordes of hungry, ragged, ignorant black folk arriving from the South in such great numbers, packed like so many stampeding cattle in dirty, manure-littered box cars" (15). To rid themselves of their embarrassingly dark progeny, the family encourages

Emma Lou to enroll in the University of Southern California, which, they hope, has a student body possessed of a wide enough range of hues that she will be allowed entrance into a social circle of mulattoes.

Even more color-prejudiced than Boise, Los Angeles proves a grand failure, and Emma Lou leaves after two years. She settles in Harlem, where her sense of inferiority and self-hatred is further confirmed. She is refused an apartment in a mulatto neighborhood and cannot find a job because male employers prefer lighter-skinned women. She eventually lands work as a school teacher but gives up her job to move in with and care for Alva, a hustler whose relationship with her seems predicated on scorning her color as much as she does. He finally rejects her, which allows Thurman to append a hopeful ending onto what is otherwise a bleak novel. Finding wisdom in the words of her friend Campbell Kitchen, Emma Lou realizes that "everyone must find salvation within one's self" (256). She concludes that "she had ever been eager to shift the entire blame on others" and realizes that she must "accept her black skin as being real and unchangeable" (256–57).

In his conclusion, Thurman follows White's *Flight* in transferring the burden of Emma Lou's happiness from her external to her internal world, which similarly allows for an optimistic, if hollow, solution to her problems. Thurman seems convinced that the intra-racial hatred, manifested by the black community's fixation on color, is present no matter where a dark-skinned African American tries to live. The novel's strength lies in its protagonist's internal struggle to overcome her self-loathing. This internal struggle is evinced outwardly in Emma's migratory quest to find a community whose repudiation of intra-racial color prejudice contrasts her family's color obsession. Thurman, whose own very dark skin allows obvious biographical parallels, calls forth a painful awareness of how damaging the black middle-class's preoccupation with color is to its goals of racial advancement. He concludes that the problem of color prejudice is not likely to dissipate, no matter how much supposed progress the New Negro of the 1920s claimed to have made.

To transcend the limitations of this prejudice, it is necessary to settle down and try to find acceptance from within. When considered within the context of other migration novels, however, this prospect is not a hopeful one. Overall, *The Blacker the Berry* verifies the difficulty of achieving a sustaining internal identity within the new urban environment absent a mental framework of support drawn from a family or cultural past. Placing his overt plea for black solidarity in a unique west-to-east migratory trajectory, Thurman also reaffirms the migration novel form's understanding of the intrinsic relation among kinship, community, and postmigration success.

Quicksand and *Their Eyes Were Watching God*

This same message is carried over into Nella Larsen's *Quicksand,* one of the notable fictional achievements of the era. Published the same year as McKay's *Home to Harlem, Quicksand* is the bleakest analysis of migration since Dunbar's *The Sport of the Gods.* Although entirely different in tone and in the range of its coverage, *Quicksand* resembles *The Sport of the Gods* beyond mere superficialities. Structured around tensions between country and city but discarding the traditional dichotomy between pastoral innocence and urban corruption, both novels begin and end in southern locations that undermine any elevated conceptions of folk culture. Where Dunbar challenges the conventions of the plantation tradition, Larsen, as Carby has observed, critiques the form of southern romance (*Reconstructing* 173–75). Larsen imagines no place that Helga Crane can find "peace and contentment" (43). Following Helga's migration to "teeming black Harlem" (43), Larsen extols the vitality of New York's cosmopolitan environs. It is a "gorgeous panarama," a landscape filled with theaters, art galleries, restaurants, expensive cars, high fashion, and furs. But these temptations of consumer culture, well out of Helga's reach, tantalize rather than satisfy her. Recalling Dunbar's ambivalent representation of city life, Larsen's heroine is soon overwhelmed by the many ways in which the urban setting strains her social relations.

Other similarities extend beyond the authors' shared suspicion of the wisdom of northward migration. Both novels trace the inevitable decline of characters whose false sense of superiority alienates them from the supporting presence of their own racial community. Like the Hamilton family, Helga Crane's downfall comes from the absence of a usable past. With neither real nor surrogate family to sustain and guide her, she is unable to imbed herself within a stabilizing, unified, progressive community. Toward the end of the novel, Helga Crane quite unexpectedly abandons the Harlem that has come to be represented by Anne Grey and Robert Anderson. In an aborted fantasy of southern immersion, she instead marries the Reverend Pleasant Green, "a fattish yellow man," but finds that the stilted version of domestic life in the small Alabama town where she goes to live "use[s] her up." The temporary fulfillment Helga finds in her new role of wife and mother is negated by her loss of mobility. Weighed down by illness, fatigue, and domestic burdens, she will be destroyed, ironically, because she cannot, as she has always done, flee from the family affiliations she has spent her life trying to forge. In pairing domestic stasis with slow death, Larsen concludes the novel having shut down all avenues of escape from the oppressive forces confronting Helga.

Larsen's view of rural folk life is harsh, even by the standards of the highest-brow renaissance writers. The Alabama town of sharecroppers is circumscribed by poverty, devoid of any aesthetic outlets, enslaved by the mundane expectations of utilitarian sensibilities, and driven by an oppressive religious fervor. Although Larsen's characterization is worlds apart from the insular middle-class society of Harlem to which she worked so hard to belong, she still brought a migrant's sensibility to bear on her work. She formed her views of the South during a year at Fisk University in Tennessee (when she was briefly and unhappily married to a Fisk professor) and, later, during two frustrating years spent as a nurse in Tuskegee, Alabama. In addition, both her father-in-law and her husband spent time ministering in the South, although her biographer Thadious Davis reports that her in-laws, who took pride in their attachments to the black church, were insulted by her condescending portrayal of the southern minister and his loyal flock (*Nella Larsen* 280).

Sharing Dunbar's skepticism about any American setting, whether Harlem or the rural South, liberating her heroine from her race- and gender-imposed marginality, Larsen betrays a profoundly felt sadness about the capacity of these settings to negate the promise of the talented, educated Helga Crane, who, like the author, would seem to possess all the requisite qualifications for success. In motion from one unsatisfying set of social arrangements to another, Helga is in perpetual search of a means to negotiate the various forces and emotions that divide her. As long as she keeps moving between Chicago, Naxos, Harlem, Copenhagen, and finally to rural Alabama, her frustrated quest to fill her inner void remains tentatively alive via ongoing changes of place and people that present her with new options. Helga's migration is connected less with the physical and economic liberation conventionally found in other works of fiction than with the drive to be emancipated from her inner turmoil.

Quicksand has more psychological depth than *The Sport of the Gods, Flight, The Blacker the Berry,* or even the fiction of Jessie Fauset—the contemporary to whom Larsen is most often compared. Larsen ties her heroine's ongoing sense of emptiness and her eventual downfall into a combination of personal and environmental factors. It is a subtle character study of how the rootless Helga mediates among a range of contradictory impulses. *Quicksand* has, from its publication, been recognized as one of the Harlem Renaissance's major achievements. Du Bois and Locke wrote positive reviews, praising the novel, in Locke's words, as "a social document of importance, and as well, a living, moving picture of a type not often in the foreground of Negro fiction."[7] Early critics such as Hugh Gloster and J. Saunders Redding emphasized Helga's cultural dualism by identifying her as a conventional "tragic mulatto" caught between the worlds of her Danish mother and black father. More recently, black feminists such as Carby, Davis, Deborah McDowell, and Hortense Thornton have shifted critical attention toward "the more urgent problem of female sexual identity." They critique the sexism that underlies the gulf between Helga's desire for social respectability and longing for sexual fulfillment. Like her urban contemporaries who became famous as blues singers, Helga cannot, given the limitations imposed on black women during the 1920s, satisfy both desires (McDowell, "Conversations" xiii–xvii).

Other factors also divide Helga: competing career and domestic ambitions, an internal conflict over aesthetic and sensual desires, a longing to blend into upper-middle-class black society, and the need for both individual autonomy and self-expression. With such oppositions driving the narrative, *Quicksand* speaks to many of the period's central debates, particularly about the role of black women in the expanding postmigration environment. The novel is an equally forceful examination of the limitations of American racial geography. Thematized around the migration novel form's central impulse, the difficult search for a livable home, it looks beyond the vitality and gaiety often associated with the era of the New Negro and concludes that Helga's geographic options are hardly better than the ones Dunbar had described two decades earlier in *The Sport of the Gods*.

As if in answer to Larsen and her Harlem Renaissance colleagues, in *Their Eyes Were Watching God* (1937), Zora Neale Hurston provides a striking rejoinder to earlier representations of the South. As a fascinating variant on the migration novel form, the story that Hurston composed far from Harlem on the island of Haiti in a seven-week spurt of energy at the end of 1936 is decidedly not about migration. By completely ignoring the presence of the North at a time when its effect on African-American life in the South loomed ever-larger, Hurston's novel represents an almost willful desire to negate the existence of the movement that had propelled her into the middle of Harlem culture more than a decade earlier.[8]

Hurston was the only major Harlem literary figure of the period who had roots in the Deep South. Although as a Barnard student she exhibited few connections to the rural working-class migrants who flooded the city, her fiction was very much of a piece with the migrating masses. It dramatically repudiated the tenets of what she lambasted as the *"so-called* Negro Renaissance" (my emphasis), which Robert Hemenway positions as an alternative to Hurston's vision: "Hurston was the closest [to the peasant South], and her person and her fiction exhibited the knowledge that the black masses had triumphed over their racist environment, not by becoming white and emulating bourgeois values, not by engaging in a sophisticated program of political propaganda, but by turning inward to create the blues, the folktale, the spiritual, the hyperbolic lie, the ironic joke" (*Zora Neale Hurston* 51).

Their Eyes Were Watching God ignores the North as a setting. Instead, Hurston imaginatively reinvents a fantasized alternative to the Great Migration by creating a communal setting of shared, egalitarian, agricultural labor. Janie and Tea Cake, her adored third husband, prosper down in the "muck" precisely because it represents a mythic space that opposes an ethos of postmigration life represented by the male-centered, hierarchical values of Janie's first two husbands, Logan Killicks and the "citified" Joe Starks. Both men measure their worth by competitive ownership, including the individuality and autonomy of their wife. Killicks finds meaning in solitary accomplishment and work; Starks, in mercantile competition and social dominance. They embody unsatisfactory southern versions of the driving force behind northern urban capitalism. In the failure of Killicks and Starks to enrich Janie's vision of herself lies Hurston's negation of the transformative potential of migration, especially for women.

Hurston had already issued a fictional warning about the North's encroachment on the rural South four years earlier in "The Gilded Six-Bits," a story whose popularity led to the contract for her first novel, *Jonah's Gourd Vine* (1934). Published in *Story Magazine* in 1933, Hurston's best-known short work made roughly the same point about the North as *Their Eyes Were Watching God*. Beginning in the southern setting most familiar to Hurston, "a Negro yard around a Negro house in a Negro settlement," the story revolves around whether the migrant northerner Otis Slemmons, from Chicago and other "spots and places," will come between Missie May and her husband, Joe, who, until Otis comes on the scene, share an idyllic marriage in the "happy" location of Eatonville, Florida. Every Saturday morning, Joe and Missie play out a ritual in which he throws nine silver dollars in the door for her to pick up. Slemmons, seemingly in possession of the riches of the North "wid his mouth full of gold teethes" and a $10 gold coin on his watch chain, intrudes on this scene of domestic bliss. He tantalizes Joe with what appears to pockets full of gold six-bits and then uses the same money to seduce Missie May, even though the six-bits turn out to be gilded slugs.

Hurston attaches the symbolic weight of the story to each man's set of coins. Joe's silver pieces are more authentic and ultimately hold more value as instruments of exchange than Slemmons's slugs. But their highest value is as an affirmation of Joe's love for his wife in the context of the playful folk ritual that energizes their relationship. Slemmons employs his coins as cash tokens designed to "purchase" the affections of Missie May. He seeks to supplant the premigration, relation-based bond between Missie May and Joe with an alluring but ultimately counterfeit postmigration connection fused by false currency. Like Janie Crawford, however, who earns her right to be with Tea Cake by rejecting Logan Killicks and outlasting Joe Starks, Missie May and Joe Banks weather the threat that Slemmons represents.

In the moral universe that Hurston constructs, the couple emerges even more prosperous than before Slemmons's arrival. By the final scene, the couple's money game, as the flirtatious initial stage of lovemaking, has given them a baby boy. Because his features make it clear that he is Joe's and not Slemmons's progeny, the baby represents the continuation of family and community and thereby underscores the enduring values of immersion. Hurston's ironic conclusion both morally rewards Joe and repositions his encounter with Slemmons in terms acceptable to maintaining his reputation in the community. Joe seizes the opportunity to tell a shop owner a revised version of Slemmons's visit. This time, he casts himself as a hero who sees through the northerner's con and saves the innocent people of Eatonville from the alluring temptations of the crafty migrant. In this reconstituted version, Hurston allows her southerner the fantasy of negating the intrusive and unwelcome cash nexus of the North that has violated the harmony of his marriage. Joe thus earns the right to return to Missie May and their new son, where, in a subtle indication that there remains a profitable return in remaining down home, the coins he throws against her front door have grown in number from nine to fifteen.

It might well be argued that Hurston's fictional erasure of the Great Migration during the 1930s was an artistic attempt to cope with Harlem's rapid decline and the formidable set of national problems that the depression created. In pointing out the false patina of northern opportunity, "The Gilded Six-Bits" countered any lingering hopes that the northern exodus might offer a solution to the horrific economic conditions gripping the South. Living hand-to-mouth in a perpetually downward-spiraling cycle of debt, the rural folk who populated Hurston's fictional world were the hardest hit of all American workers. By the early 1930s landless black farmers were earning an average income of only $295 a year.

As industry after industry invoked a last-hired-first-fired policy to terminate black male employees, cities were equally stressed. New York, Cleveland, Detroit, and Chicago could no longer accommodate the steady influx of southerners. Even the small but once-prosperous black-owned businesses that catered to inner-city constituencies quickly descended into bankruptcy. When unemployed workers found it necessary to widen their search for jobs, more than half of all migration during the period occurred from city to city. Relief statistics told perhaps the grimmest story. Southerners, whether black or white, no longer moved to cities for jobs but for federally subsidized, locally administered public welfare.[9] By the mid-1930s half of all urban black families received relief; the figure for white families was just above one in ten. Eighty percent of the black residents of some southern cities, such as Norfolk and Charlotte, were on the relief rolls (Goldfield and Brownell, *Urban America* 317).[10]

The depression drove a quick and fatal blow through Harlem's artistic community. The Harlem Renaissance, migration's finest cultural achievement, was transformed almost overnight from an emblem of racial uplift and accomplishment to the leveled plane of an artistic ghetto. Hughes wrote that "we were no longer in vogue, anyway, we Negroes. . . . Colored actors began to go hungry, publishers politely rejected new manuscripts, and patrons found other uses for their money" (*The Big Sea* 334). According to some of the renaissance's old guard, even if economic aid had been available there was no emerging community of deserving young writers in Harlem to claim it. Dorothy West, editor of *Challenge* magazine, recalled trying to find new material worth accepting: "We were disappointed in the contributions that came in from the new voices. There was little we wanted to print. Bad writing is unbelievably bad. We felt somewhat crazily that the audience must be spoofing and they didn't really mean us to take their stuff for prose or poetry" (*Challenge* 39).

In spite of its aspirations for making a permanent transformation, Harlem's literary community receded from public view. No one stepped forward to take up its charge. The writers' waning influence was symptomatic of the larger conflict between the well-established northern middle class and the new population of migrants, whose influence and power was on the increase. African-American life in Harlem and other northern cities came to be shaped by a vast culture of migrants, poor but in place, rather than a relatively small orbit of writers, intellectuals, and artists.

Migration fiction registered this shift. The renaissance's core of writers, propelled by the vision of racial pride spelled out in Locke's manifesto *The New Negro,* was supplanted by a younger generation of artists who came of age in different places and under different circumstances. The majority of Harlem writers, having disregarded their migrant neighbors and embraced the commercially appealing topics of passing, primitivism, intraracial color prejudice, and urban cabaret life too vigorously, ensured for themselves a legacy of fleeting period pieces and, unsurprisingly, offered those who followed little to emulate. The new generation of writers—fueled by the depression economy, personal deprivation, and a strong sense of displacement—put migration at the center, not the periphery, of its artistic imagination. The gritty middle-American industrial center Chicago, rather than Harlem, became their home base. At the center of the group was a young migrant from Mississippi, Richard Wright, who turned to a terrifying new vocabulary of sociological detail, documentary realism, and violent black agency to summarize the conditions of black urban America. In the divide between him and his Harlem predecessors, the next generation of migrant novelists found dramatic new ways to register the difficulty of finding a home.

3

The Fugitive Migrant Novel's Critique of Ascent

No-one can know much about the Negro race . . . until he has become acquainted with the masses of the peoples as they are in the black belt counties of the South. They are strong, vigorous, kindly and industrious people; simple minded, wholesome and good as God made them. They are very different from the people of the cities. As yet they have been very little affected with either disease or vice. The boys and girls that come from the country are usually earnest and ambitious. The young folk from the cities on the other hand are very likely to be indifferent and frivolous, and disposed to live by their wits. I noticed the difference as soon as I entered a school where a majority of the students were drawn from the sophisticated classes in the cities. Fortunately the great majority of the race still live in the country and if they can be educated there, where they can grow up slowly and naturally, and be kept out of the cities where they will be forced along at a pace that will make them superficial and trifling, the race problem will eventually solve itself.

Robert Park to Booker T. Washington, May 29, 1913

I can remember when young fellows like him had first to commit a crime, or be accused of one, before they tried such a thing. Instead of leaving in the light of morning, they went in the dark of night.

Ralph Ellison

Before reaching a train station, many sharecroppers virtually had to escape from the plantation. Often held perpetually in debt by landlords who juggled accounts and made certain that

> a tenant's crop never brought more money than the landlord
> had advanced over the previous year, sharecroppers could not
> simply walk out on their obligations. Nearly all tenants were
> likely to be in debt to a landlord or merchant until "settlement
> time" at the end of the year. Whether or not a creditor kept
> books honestly, the departure of a debtor before the harvest
> was likely to leave a crop worthless in the field and an
> uncollectible debt secured by that same crop.
>
> James Grossman

In a climate of failed economic progress and dried-up literary support, the form of the Great Migration novel reached its fully developed form in the 1930s and early 1940s. Exhibiting notably harsh views of migration, George Washington Lee's *River George* (1937), Richard Wright's *Native Son* (1940), William Attaway's *Blood on the Forge* (1941), Curtis Lucas's *The Flour Is Dusty* (1943), and Carl Offord's *The White Face* (1943) constitute a "fugitive migrant" impulse. They contrast any display of fondness for southern pastoral nostalgia, including the reenshrinement of a model plantation South following the publication and screening of Margaret Mitchell's *Gone with the Wind* and the fiction and folkloric studies of Zora Neale Hurston. Fugitive migrant novels also undermine the utopian connotations derived from popular images of the North as the biblical land of Canaan. Unable to imagine any inhabitable geography (symbolic or real), they offer the migration form's severest critique of ascent as a mechanism to achieve racial and cultural advancement.

In each of these novels by male authors, the questing migrant breaks a law or social contract of the community and takes flight as a fugitive. Having refused to endure a whipping or some other form of violence from an adversary, such as an overseer, the migrant lashes back at his attacker, almost kills him, and avoids retribution by heading to the purportedly safer ground of the North. The primary motive behind the fugitive's migration is his desire for physical and spiritual freedom as a heroic response to violent white oppression. His principal quest is one of identity. Rather than facing the inward, psychological traumas resulting from the ambiguities of dual bloodlines, as in *The Autobiography of an Ex-Coloured Man, Flight,* and *Quicksand,* the fugitive seeks agency in worlds configured by disquieting external realities of the kind that offered such a range of material to the period's naturalist writers.

The fugitive migrant, following on the quest of the fugitive slave, is driven by the search for a nonmarginal place in which to reside and prosper. Also like nineteenth-century slave narratives, the fugitive migrant novel initially projects the existence of a north free of racial encumbrances. The fugitive's vision of a New Canaan disappears, however, as he confronts a multitude of obstacles that forestall his ability to pass out of his suspended state. Finally, having been forced to sever his ties to the kinspeople of his native land, able to return only with fatal consequences, and incapable of fashioning a postmigration identity within an urban counterprojection of the black south, the fugitive's freedom-finding efforts fail.

The narrative concludes by confirming the absence of a fixed site of habitation. It also concludes by affirming that the condition of kineticism—itself a negation of the inhabitable fixed location that serves as migration's goal—is a marker of continuing African-American geographic enslavement. Unable to prosper in the South or acculturate in the North, the fugitive migrant must either keep moving (like Chinatown and Melody in *Blood on the Forge* and, provisionally, Jim Harrell in *The Flour is Dusty*) or die (like Bigger Thomas in *Native Son*, Big Mat in *Blood on the Forge*, Aaron George in *River George*, and Chris Wood in *The White Face*).

The most fully registered conclusion of fugitive migrant fiction is its frustration with America's racial landscape. The sources driving this frustration can be apprehended within a set of cultural and literary circumstances surrounding the two pivotal texts of the fugitive impulse, Wright's *Native Son* and Attaway's less well known *Blood on the Forge*. They constitute the best exemplars of the fugitive migrant novel's powerful protest against the geographic limitations of the postmigration north. The wellsprings of this protest are located within Wright and Attaway's own experiences with migration, within the successes and failures of the contemporary analytic philosophies of black experience associated with the Chicago Renaissance of the 1930s and 1940s, and, finally, within the fugitive migrant novel's intertextual responses to its principal antecedent, the antebellum slave autobiography, whose chronicle of escape from bondage established a cultural and literary line of descent for the fugitive migrant's abiding drive toward freedom.

Native Son, Blood on the Forge, and the Chicago Renaissance

Native Son is the most pronounced example of what one contemporary reviewer, summing up the black novelists of the age, called the "spirit of defeat" that permeated their fiction. This fiction is in keeping with the central intellectual imperatives of an era that Robert Bone and others have convincingly established as a Chicago Renaissance.[1] As a casualty of a technologically advancing age, Bigger Thomas derives his explanatory force from what has been labeled the "pejorative tradition" in racial sociology associated with Robert Park's Chicago School of sociology, which calls on "the use of social pathologists' data to describe black communities as disorganized and culturally nonadaptive" (Szwed, "Politics" 159).

Among many things, the novel is, after all, the story of Bigger's tragic migration. From his initial confrontation with a giant rat that he is forced to kill in his family's one-room tenement in South Chicago through the final moment, when the steel door of the jail clangs shut behind Boris Max as the lawyer leaves Bigger to await his execution, *Native Son* moves unrelentingly toward the conclusion that the Great Migration failed black America. Where other fictions of migration—including even those by Wright himself, such as "Big Boy Leaves Home"—retain a small if ambiguous measure of faith in northern migration, *Native Son* concedes only a faint realm of hope for Bigger and his fellow migrants within the expressive and transformative capacities of murder and violence. As a summary statement of the fugitive impulse, the novel obliterates the liberating capabilities of immersion and ascent.

From the moment in March 1940 when Wright jarred the American reading public awake with *Native Son,* his unapologetic portrait of Bigger Thomas, this angry, terrified and terrifying young man has come to represent the archetypal urban racial misfit. His set of environmental responses simultaneously brought home to depression America the volatile mindset of disadvantaged northern migrant slum-dwellers and offered a prophetic forecast of the equally potent social forces that would drive the urban unrest of the civil rights era and beyond. There is no more revealing vantage point from which to comprehend the proliferation of such civil disturbances as the 1992 Los Angeles riots than the Thomas family's one-room Chicago tenement. Through his creation of Bigger, Wright provided a comprehensive picture of a caged victim of white oppression. This same version of Bigger was then coopted by that same society and reduced to a convenient emblem of blame for everything that remains wrong with cities.

Yet in Wright's description of the creation of *Native Son,* which he spelled out in Harlem for a Schomburg Library audience shortly after the novel's release and which was later published as the now-famous article "How Bigger Was Born," Bigger began as a creation not of the city but of the Jim Crow south. "The birth of Bigger Thomas," he noted, "goes back to my childhood, and there was not just one Bigger, but many of them, more than I could count and more than you suspect." He detailed aspects of five real-life Biggers, all of whom were modeled on especially rebellious men he had known in the "locked-in Black Belts" of Dixie. Each had found different ways to flout the laws and customs of Jim Crow, and for their defiance each eventually paid a similarly high price: "They were shot, hanged, maimed, lynched, and generally hounded until they were either dead or their spirits broken" (Baker, ed., *Twentieth-Century* 24–25).

And yet inasmuch as the Biggers came from the fabric of southern life, Wright maintained that he could not think seriously of writing about them until he went to live in Chicago, where, "free of the daily pressure of the Dixie environment," he gained the perspective and the intellectual and ideological grounding necessary to create African-American literature's most notorious outsider. Without migration there would be no Bigger Thomas.

Bigger's actions are framed within a conventional migration sequence well in keeping with the works of Wright's fellow fugitive migrant authors. Although in real distance the trip is but a few miles, to Bigger it represents a change of culture akin to entering a foreign country. His purported reason in setting out north for the Daltons' home is the promise of a job, which his relief worker-labor agent has demanded that he accept under the threat of cutting off his family's relief money. More indirectly, he leaves because his fear of white people prevents him from robbing Blum, a store owner, and leads him instead to pull a knife on his friend Gus. A permutation of the push and pull factors that set the majority of other migrants in motion frame Bigger's short journey. His labor exodus distances him physically from Chicago's South Side culture, from which he has already been psychologically alienated.

After arriving at the Dalton home, his initial terror soon gives way to a sense of unexpected good fortune as he relishes in the trappings of a seemingly successful ascent: discretionary income, access to transportation, a private room (with two radiators), and all the food he can eat. For all his seeming progress, however, the environment he inhabits indicates that little of substance has changed. He is relegated to a private ghetto, a segregated room well below the Dalton family, where he faces piles of garbage outside his door and must forsake his family and community for the domestic responsibility of literally keeping the Daltons' home fires burning. From this typical post-migration arrangement, his downfall is set in motion because of his inability to recodify his symbolic north in anything other than the terms of his symbolic south. He unknowingly smothers Mary Dalton rather than reveal his proximity to her drunken and sexually volatile form because he is trapped within a code of racial etiquette that was first internalized in Mississippi and then reinforced in his South Side Chicago neighborhood.

From the snow-lined city streets and the squalid Thomas apartment to the rigidly demarcated Dalton home and the Cook County Jail cell that both protects and confines Bigger, Wright fashions the spatial geography of Chicago into a symbolic map mirroring his version of America's racial configuration as a whole. As he explained in "How Bigger Was Born," Chicago is "the pivot of the Eastern, Western, Northern, and Southern poles of the nation" (Baker, ed., *Twentieth-Century* 39). Real street names, addresses, building descriptions, transportation routes, and various local businesses as well as topical references to cinema, city politics, journalism, and advertising delineate the racial coordinates of the country's most segregated, centrally situated, and geographically bifurcated microcosm of pre- and postmigration America.

In every instance, the localized detail emphasizes Bigger's estrangement. Hostile to his family, friends, and any situation that "exacted something of him" (Baker, ed., *Twentieth-Century* 44), he finds self-affirmation through rebellion, rejecting any claim of community as a native son of the black belt. What he embraces instead is a fragmented version of white success—symbolized by his desire to fly and mapped out in the game he and Gus play called "white"—which he can only superficially comprehend through bits and pieces of political posters, distant skywriters, and movies. That he remains so thoroughly alienated from his real and his imaginary worlds is a measure of his marginality. That his double-consciousness imprisons rather than helps liberate him signals Wright's overt hostility to the viability of southern folk culture.

To put the matter within the larger scheme of migration fiction, Bigger's downfall is inevitable precisely because his native culture offers so little in the way of usable models that his failure is assured once he leaves. He resides in a kinetic topography (adding an additional layer of irony to the novel's title) where the only behavior that gives him a sense of purpose also sets him in flight. Wright imagines the black characters who have contact with Bigger—his mother, siblings, friends, Bessie, the Reverend Hammond—not as personalities capable of shaping the contours of their environment but as pawns manipulated by and reacting to a larger dominating presence. All of them remain strangely distant from the sustaining institutions and folkways of black communities. Even the parodically devout Hammond's black dialect and heavy-handed posture of religious acquiescence recall debased remnants of the black southern church's empowering forces. Bigger's consciousness is shaped by kitchen tenements, restaurants, taverns, poolhalls, white-owned grocery stores and bakeries, and the streets. There are no visible church buildings, no neighborhood organizations or clubs, and little evidence of musical culture or family life beyond Bigger's own—nothing that provides, in James Baldwin's words, "any sense of Negro life as a continuing and complex group reality" (*Notes of a Native Son*, 39).

The root of Bigger's alienation is Wright's southern boyhood. Like his protagonist, Wright formed his view of the world through the eyes of a migrant. As a perpetual wanderer, he spent his life putting physical distance between himself and the South in an effort to become emancipated from its severe limitations. Yet despite his best efforts, no matter where he moved the region remained the most enduring psychic frame through which to interpret his surroundings. Born on a farm outside Natchez overlooking the Mississippi River, Wright spent a rootless childhood moving between Mississippi, Memphis, and Arkansas, where, abandoned by his father when he was six, he was shuffled between his chronically ailing mother, an orphanage, his relatives, and his fanatically religious grandmother. After living in various sharecroppers' shacks, rooming houses, and apartments, Wright left Memphis for Chicago in 1927 at the age of fifteen and commenced his quest for a means of overcoming his caste oppression, his lack of access to education, his abiding poverty and hunger, and the deficiencies of his family life. In Chicago he spent the formative years of his writing career as a part of the Federal Writers' Project, heavily influenced by Robert Park's School of Sociology at the University of Chicago. In 1937 he left Chicago for New York. After spending a decade there, he expatriated permanently to Paris, where Jean Paul Sartre and Simone de Beauvoir, among others, provided Wright a philosophy in existentialism that positioned his migratory impulses in the context of a more global search for a means of combating the modern disease of social and spiritual isolation.[2]

Wright's lifelong rootlessness is heavily documented in his autobiography *Black Boy* (1945), which, along with the more recently published continuation of that autobiography, *American Hunger* (1977), provides the fullest account of what migration meant to him.[3] Viewing his departure from Memphis in terms paralleling the heroic liberation of a fugitive slave, Wright concludes *Black Boy* in an upbeat tone, heading north "full of the hazy notion that life could be lived with dignity, that the personalities of others should not be violated, that men should be able to confront other men without fear or shame, and that if men were lucky in their living on earth they might win some redeeming meaning for their having struggled and suffered here beneath the stars" (285).

The Chicago that comes into view at the beginning of *American Hunger,* however, undercuts *Black Boy*'s hopeful conclusion. The city evokes the fragmented urban landscape of T. S. Eliot's "unreal city" in *The Wasteland* and Carl Sandburg's "City of the Big Shoulders" in "Chicago." Both writers played critical genealogical roles in Wright's early development as a writer.[4] Wright's initial impression anticipates the physical and psychic landscape that Bigger Thomas will inhabit: "My first glimpse of the flat black stretches of Chicago depressed and dismayed me, mocked all my fantasies. Chicago seemed an unreal city whose mythical houses were built of slabs of black coal wreathed in palls of gray smoke, houses whose foundations were sinking slowly into the dank prairie. Flashes of steam showed intermittently on the wide horizon, gleaming translucently in the winter sun. The din of the city entered my consciousness, entered to remain for years to come" (*Later Works* 249).

Radiating throughout *Native Son,* Wright's view of Chicago in *American Hunger* represents migration as a mass experience of atomization that necessitates the search for a new mode of community, culturally divested of the South. Immediately following Wright's opening description, his sketches of his relatives' rough adjustments to city life suggest that the city has a similarly alienating effect on everyone (Maxwell, "Down-Home" 7). When transforming this collective experience into fiction, Wright positions Bigger's rage and frustration as an inevitable response to predetermined social forces that grew, as he notes in "How Bigger Was Born," out of a "civilization" that "contained no spiritual sustenance, [and] no culture which could hold and claim his allegiance and faith" (Baker, ed., *Twentieth-Century* 32).

Summarized by its bleak naturalism and modernist undertones, the setting of *Native Son* mocks any pretensions of smooth adjustment to postmigration life. By giving full measure to the fury of the new northern migrant culture, Wright, together with the like-minded core of writers suitably labeled the "Wright school," offered a stark contrast to the less eruptive urbanization of the black bourgeoisie as it had been detailed, for example, by Nella Larsen and Jessie Fauset. Included in this school were migrant novelists such as Aldon Bland and Offord. Emerging as the bleakest of the period's conventional migration novels, Offord's *The White Face* directly, if less successfully, followed Wright's lead in yoking the fate of a naive black southerner to political structures and social forces that operate on a magnitude well beyond his ability to comprehend them.[5]

Bernard Bell has described *Native Son* and the literature orbiting around it as "informed by the belief that character and human history can be completely explained by biological and socioeconomic facts" that "stress the violence and pathological personalities that result from racial oppression and economic exploitation" (*The Afro-American Novel* 167). Political in intent and demoralizing in effect, the canvas of social realism inferred from this description accurately portrays *Native Son* and the other migrant novels of the period as characteristic of the broad strokes of a premodernist nineteenth-century realism but equally marked by fragmented, alienating—distinctly modernist—urban landscapes.

Wright and Chicago Sociology

When Wright turned to social realism in the wake of participating in the Great Migration, he did so as a devoted pupil of the Chicago School of urban sociologists, which provided a sophisticated academic model for him to account for the disturbing psychological and social dislocations brought on by the exodus. Indeed, *Native Son* is Wright's case study of Chicago theories. Although Wright was never an official student at the University of Chicago, he had numerous connections with its sociology faculty. The Wright family's caseworker was Mary Wirth, the wife of Louis Wirth, one of the faculty's principal investigators in a massive urban study that included Chicago's black South Side.

Wright also became good friends with Wirth's research associate, Horace Cayton. When Cayton teamed with St. Claire Drake to write *Black Metropolis* (1945), a comprehensive study of black urban life and one of the most enduring and influential products of the school, the two prominent scholars asked Wright to write an introduction. Part autobiography, part philosophy, and part trenchant social analysis, the introduction reproduced the wide-ranging and eclectic view of black urban acculturation that Wright had successfully incorporated in *Twelve Million Black Voices* (1941), his black folk history of the epic transition from rural south to urban north. "I did not know what my story was," he recalled, "and it was not until I stumbled upon science that I discovered some of the meanings of the environment that battered and taunted me. I encountered the work of men who were studying the Negro community, amassing facts about urban Negro life, and I found that sincere art and honest science were not far apart, that each could enrich the other" (*Black Metropolis* xvii–xviii). He then explicitly connected his first novel and the information found in the study: "If, in reading my novel, *Native Son*, you doubted the reality of Bigger Thomas, then examine the delinquency rates cited in the book; if, in reading my autobiography, *Black Boy*, you doubted the picture of family life shown there, then study the figures on family disorganization given here" (*Black Metropolis* xxi).

Represented in the work of Robert Park and his many associates and students, such as Ernest W. Burgess, Robert Redfield, E. Franklin Frazier, Cayton, and Wirth, the Chicago School viewed the black adjustment to northern cities not as a failure of individual conditioning or genetic deficiencies but as an ill-fated yet rational group response to a combination of environmental pressure and deficit culture. By correlating his work to the findings of a well-respected university department, Wright legitimized his controversial politics and translated the somewhat abstract theories of the Chicago School to an artistic venue more palatable for mass consumption.

One of the Chicago School's sociological innovations was to suggest that the city be treated in much the same way as it had been by late-nineteenth-century naturalist writers, namely as a natural laboratory. The methodological results of this innovation are in evidence in the school's early manifesto, Park and Burgess's *Introduction to the Science of Sociology* (1921). In this and subsequent volumes, the researchers used new methods in urban sociology to enter the national discourse on race. Their aim was to dismantle biologically based justifications for racial hierarchies by relying on scientific methodology and apparently neutral data. As the central figure of the Chicago School, Park's cyclical view of race relations dominated the sociology of race for more than a quarter of a century. A summary of the cycle suggests how Park's theory influenced Wright's interpretation of the new black urban milieu and its premigration roots in the folk culture of the black south:

> The race-relations cycle proceeds in four stages—contact, conflict, accommodation, and assimilation—in the course of which there unfolds a great cultural and social drama. Each act of this drama is dictated by laws of history and culture, Park writes, and the sequence cannot be halted or diverted. The first stage, contact, occurs, when two races meet on a "racial frontier" and are obliged to interact. Conflict arises when the races compete for valuable resources. The conflict is resolved by accommodation, in which a stable but asymmetrical and unequal social order is established. Finally, accommodation gives way to assimilation, when the two races merge culturally and, ultimately, physically. In the end, society becomes homogeneous. (Lyman, *The Black American* 27–28)

Migration plays a fundamental role in this evolutionary progression toward a utopian city-state. Leaving their peasant societies behind, it is the "multiplicity of subcultures," writes Robert Bone, who arrive in the city and break down the existing "old sacred cultures" before replacing them. The inevitable casualties along the way who fail to make the adjustment— the Bigger Thomases who populate the terrain of depression-era urban naturalism—are merely, in this view, the unfortunate by-products of the overall cost of progress. The building blocks of Park's urban theory are founded on the distinction, advanced in the writings of Ferdinand Tönnies, between *Gemeinschaft* and *Gesellschaft,* or between the communal ties of a peasant society and the associational, voluntary set of human relations that characterize urban-industrial settings.[6] These distinctions imply a Darwinian bias that views human history "in broadly evolutionary terms: the progression from simple to complex, naive to sophisticated, rural to urban, static to dynamic" (Matthews, *Quest* 131). As the motor of social change, the city in its best sense serves as a liberating catalyst, disengaging its inhabitants from the limitations of their past communal traditions and releasing their individual energies in the secularized, less constricting setting.[7]

As early as 1913, while still working as emissary, public relations agent, and ghostwriter for Booker T. Washington, Park was already refuting the residual traces of racial Darwinism left over from the post–Reconstruction racial nadir.[8] He replaced biological explanations of racial difference with cultural ones and helped lead the way in countering the long-held popular view that the hierarchies of racial inheritance were unalterable. "The chief obstacle to the assimilation of the Negro and the Oriental," he asserted in an early article on racial assimilation, "are not mental but physical traits."[9] It was partly urban black America's inability to hide its "racial uniform"—in contrast to white immigrants—that impeded its progress. Behind this contention lies one of the prominent and recurring themes of Park's essays, a theme that would serve Wright as something of a summary statement for *Native Son*. Park maintained that the African American "has had his separateness thrust upon him because of his exclusion and forcible isolation from white society" (Lal, *Romance* 547).

This point was obviously well validated by Wright's personal experience and gained its potency from the conclusions he drew from it. Park and his fellow Chicagoans correctly claimed that excluding blacks from the privileges of mainstream culture led to racial conflict, the very inevitability of which was an indication not of social dysfunction but of black aspiration, progress, and ongoing resistance to white dominance. Park noted that racial conflict was more likely to happen in cities, where social conventions were less fixed and the prescribed status of minority groups was less constrained than in the rural south. He was also among the earliest sociologists to follow Franz Boas's lead in recognizing the necessity of black migrants retaining their southern cultural roots, a process that the city's deplorable physical conditions and multiethnic drive toward assimilation severely challenged. For Wright, the importance of Park's empirically based theories cannot be overstated. He used the authority of a Ph.D. in the social sciences to assert that not only was Bigger's extreme behavior predictable within the contours of a macro-sociological model, but it was also—given what Park called the "obstinate and irrational resistance to the Negro's claims' by whites"—a rightful, inescapable precursor to urban acculturation (Park, "Bases of Race Prejudice" 300).[10]

For a more comprehensive political ideology than the Chicago School provided, Wright turned to the Marxism of the American Communist Party, whose appeal was tied in to its view of the southern black belt as an oppressed nation in need of liberation (Draper, *American Communism* 311–16). Wright's communism lies outside the scope of this study, but its strong presence in Chicago during the early 1930s joined with Chicago sociology to highlight the range of European-derived intellectual options that greeted a young migrant writer bent on rapid self-education.

Wright was not alone in his desire to novelize the documentary sources of his artistic imagination. A group of writers who allied themselves in various ways with the sociological zeitgeist of Chicago during the 1930s came to constitute a Chicago renaissance of equal proportion to the one that had occurred in Harlem a decade earlier. Although the Harlem Renaissance was directly obligated to the experience of migration, it had paid surprisingly little attention to either migration's effects or liabilities. In contrast, the Chicago Renaissance, following Wright's potent example in *Native Son,* repudiated familiar and retrospective images of rural southern folk life, and looked instead "toward the future, toward the necessary adaptations and adjustments, toward the risks and adventures and existential dilemmas of modern life" (Bone, "Richard Wright" 467).

The Parkian model also validated a problematic edge to Wright's fiction (and protest fiction in general) that has led a host of readers, beginning with Hurston and Baldwin, to condemn the basis of Wright's approach. It was Hurston's well-known review of Wright's collection of four stories, *Uncle Tom's Children* (1938), that set the tone for much ensuing criticism of Wright and led Henry Louis Gates, Jr., to refer to the quarrel between the two writers as a defining conflict of "the great divide in black literature" (*Signifying Monkey* 182). Noting that "there is lavish killing here," Hurston chastised Wright for reducing the black south to a site of masculine violence and hatred (Hurston, "Stories of Conflict" 32). This view, she suggested, was in keeping with his affiliation with the Communist Party, an entity she strongly opposed. Hurston's frustrated response to Wright no doubt can be read as a rejoinder to a review of *Their Eyes Were Watching God* that he had written several months earlier for *The New Masses* and in which Wright lampooned the "quaint" novel's "minstrel technique."[11] Whether locating it in the South or the North, Wright's (and the Chicago School's) emphasis on black suffering was anathema to Hurston's racial politics, which were grounded in individual pride.

The Chicago School gave credence to the lives of black slum-dwellers and legitimated their frustrations by elevating the ill-effects of deficit culture to a position of dominance. But it did so at the cost of stigmatizing them. Chicago's urban ethnographers shifted their research emphasis away from the individual psyche and toward the circumstances that had produced that individual. By doing so they placed an abnormally high emphasis on what Oscar Lewis, an anthropologist, came to call the "culture of poverty," Kenneth Clark termed "the pathology of the ghetto," and the infamous Moynihan Report would later label the "tangle of pathology" that characterized black urban families.

The heated debates surrounding these gloomy labels, which emphasize the deteriorating social fabric of slums, have identified several problems with the respective models. They fail to account for individual modulations within the collective black experience, underestimate the white effect on deterring black progress, and make an obsession of casting blacks, such as Bigger Thomas, in the dehumanizing role of victim.[12] In Baldwin's often-repeated criticism of Bigger, the character is a one-dimensional social entity devoid of a range of human emotions: "All of Bigger's life is controlled, defined by his hatred and his fear. And later, his fear drives him to murder and his hatred to rape; he dies, having come, through this violence, we are told, for the first time, to a kind of life, having for the first time redeemed his manhood" (*Notes of a Native Son* 22).[13]

As Wright's example suggests, migration novels are particularly sensitive to the limitations of the American racial setting. Only by drawing upon a much more viable southern past measured in a wider range of possibility were writers such as Hurston and, to a lesser extent, Baldwin able to contrast Wright's dramatically pessimistic literary portrait of African-American migration. In the meantime, Wright's naturalistic vision of a migrant wasteland remained the depression's most familiar image of urban blackness.

Sharecroppers and Slaves: *Blood on the Forge*

Following *Native Son,* Attaway's *Blood on the Forge* is one of the central works of Great Migration literature and a model of the fugitive migrant form. Written toward the end of the depression and published in 1941, the novel is set at the height of the World War I migration. By explaining the novel's action in terms of the social pathology of the pre- and postmigration settings, Attaway provides an especially focused account of the causes and effects of the mass exodus. The environmental determinism and broadly framed historical materialism propelling his characters suggest *Blood on the Forge*'s affinity with Wright's *Native Son,* whose much-acclaimed publication just a year earlier helps explain why the underappreciated *Blood on the Forge* received less than the attention it was due (Margolies, "Introduction" vi–xviii).

The similarities between *Blood on the Forge* and *Native Son* are by no means coincidental. Like Wright, Attaway lived in Chicago during the depression, and the men knew each other as members of the Illinois Writers' Project. Like Wright, Attaway drew upon the powerful model of literary naturalism of the kind fostered within the intellectual climate of the Chicago Renaissance. Although Attaway's connection to the University of Chicago's School of Sociology is less traceable and less direct than Wright's, his delineation of the Moss brothers' displacement from their peasant roots is as thoroughly Parkian as anything Wright composed. Following his own sociological construction, Attaway used a one-family peasant culture as a forceful vehicle of protest against the growth of industrialization and its deleterious effects on the family's individual personalities and on its organic unity.

Attaway's literary application of the reigning theories of migrant atomization offers a broad cultural framework that gives contemporary accounting to *Blood on the Forge*'s place within the fugitive migrant form. His obligation to the narrative strategies and resonant images of nineteenth-century slave narratives provides an equally evident intertextual antecedent out of which the more historically rooted literary motifs of the fugitive migrant emanate. In its evocation of the slave narrative as a means of transcending the immediate temporal and geographic situations of its characters, *Blood on the Forge* provides a rich text for summarizing the fugitive migrant novel's debt to the earlier African-American autobiographical form.

In accord with his fellow Chicago writers of the 1930s, Attaway's imaginative world was characteristically sociological. In contrast to Wright, however, whose past, as outlined in *Black Boy* and its continuation *American Hunger*, starkly parallels his view of black life as a casualty of environmental deprivation and the pathological forces of American racism, Attaway's comparably comfortable childhood exhibited few connections to those of his characters other than the fact that he also was a product of migration. The son of a physician and a school teacher, Attaway was born in 1911 to one of Greenville, Mississippi's prominent black families. Unwilling to let their children grow up in the Jim Crow south, the Attaways moved to Chicago when William was six. As he described the motives for the move in the *Daily Worker*, "My father . . . had a notion that Negro kids brought up in the South unconsciously accept the whites' estimate of them, and they never get to know what it is to be a human among humans. He brought us north hoping we wouldn't absorb these false Southern ideas." Planning a career as an auto mechanic, Attaway finished high school at a vocational school, but at his father's urging he entered the University of Illinois. When his father died, he left college and traveled aimlessly for several years, working as a seaman, a labor organizer, a salesman, and at other odd jobs. As he recalled the period, "In Chicago, I had all the advantages that a self-made man imagines are good for an only son. But after my father's death I rebelled and spent my time hoboing" (Sims, *Lives of Mississippi Authors* 15).[14]

Gravitating back to his early love of writing, Attaway eventually returned to complete his degree at the University of Illinois in 1936, but not before coming under the formative influence of the Illinois Writers' Project, which furthered the literary ambitions of the Chicago Renaissance in much the same way the University of Chicago advanced its sociological ends. The WPA-sponsored unit, under the directorship of John T. Frederick, a professor of English at Northwestern University, provided much needed support for a dazzling array of writers who included Saul Bellow, Nelson Algren, Jack Conroy, Studs Terkel, Margaret Walker, Willard Motley, Frank Yerby, and Arna Bontemps as well as Wright, who was rapidly earning a strong reputation in Chicago's progressive literary circles.

Details of Attaway's friendship with Wright are sketchy, but judging by their similarities it is likely that the men found much to admire in each other from the time they first worked together at the Wells Street IWP office in late 1935 to help prepare a guidebook to Illinois. They shared common political viewpoints, an equally heightened sense of marginality, a distrust of formalized education, a thirst for knowledge wrought of experience, an interest in exploring that knowledge through writing, and, most important, common roots in Jim Crow Mississippi. An incident retold in the

Daily Worker illustrates Attaway's admiration for Wright and hints at their shared disaffection for the effete literary climate from which Attaway broke away at the University of Illinois:

> Bill heard [Wright] and invited him to speak to the college literary society on writing. When Wright showed up that night, he faced an audience of formal clothes and gowns, lots of fancy trimmings. He didn't know whether to go ahead but Bill urged him and he pulled out the manuscript of his "Big Boy Leaves Home," one of the short novels in his "Uncle Tom's Children." "He started to read that swell story," said Bill, "and, when he got to the second paragraph, half the audience had fled. Dick went on, set on giving it to them, and at the end, the room was empty of the literary set and only Dick and I were there."

Attaway's first novel, *Let Me Breathe Thunder* (1939), received mixed reviews. It offered a proletarian vision well in keeping with Wright and his WPA associates. Drawing heavily from his experience riding the rails during his hoboing days, Attaway focused on two white migrant farm workers whose wanderlust kept them—borrowing the popular Jack Conroy novel title—"disinherited" from conventional society. In favoring the faint possibilities offered by a kinetic, rootless existence over the static, drawn-out death of labor exploitation, *Let Me Breathe Thunder* repeated the prominent theme of Wright's "swell story" that sent the university crowd fleeing for safety.

Blood on the Forge is also told from the vantage point of the dispossessed. Commencing in the red-clay hills of Kentucky, the novel concerns the Moss family—Chinatown, Melody, Big Mat, and his wife, Hattie—all of whom have long been victims of the sharecropping system. As the depleted soil on their small patch of farmland produces a little less each year, the family falls further behind in a perpetually accelerating cycle of debt. The Moss brothers' migration is set in motion quite suddenly when a labor agent appears at their home and encourages them to accept his invitation to go north. The timing of his offer fortuitously allows Big Mat Moss to escape being lynched after he has refused to endure a whipping (the keynote incident of the fugitive migrant experience). In a compressed depiction of the train ride north, Attaway brilliantly summarizes the psychological and physical torture of the journey inside a sealed boxcar and simultaneously recognizes the mythic and symbolic attributes of this historically charged vehicle of migration. Once the Mosses arrive in the North, they find the industrial climate there so severe that even the brothers' cohesiveness rooted in the harsh work ethic of the sharecropping system prove no match for the life-negating forces of the factory complex.

By this point in the evolution of Great Migration literature, Attaway's general conclusion is as familiar as it is despairing. However pernicious the racial and environmental conditions of the South may be for a black population bent on escape, their exodus to the industrial centers of the North will exact new and equally lethal tolls. The dehumanizing conditions of the Allegheny steel mills destroy the brothers' physical bodies, rob them of their sanity, and undermine their family unity, which, until they traveled north, was both their primary defense against southern racism and an affirmation of the African-American ideal of community. Countering all visions of hope and prosperity that might be gleaned from technological advances, Attaway portrays the postmigration setting as a wasteland laid bare by the unchecked desire to exploit the land without thought to human or natural costs.

Although Attaway may well have summarized the trajectory of many southern-born blacks, his presentation was too pessimistic for Ralph Ellison, whose move from the Southwest to the South to the North was similar to those of both Attaway and Wright. When Ellison reviewed the novel for *Negro Quarterly* in the spring of 1942, his assessment betrays hints of the literary values that were later in evidence in *Invisible Man*. Among these was his call for migrant characters who possessed enough self-awareness to remake their experience in their new northern environment in their own terms:

> Conceptually, Attaway grasped the destruction of the folk, but missed its rebirth on a higher level. The writer did not see that while the folk individual was being liquidated in the crucible of steel, he was also undergoing a fusion of new elements. Nor did Attaway see that the individual which emerged, blended of old and new, was better fitted for the problems of the industrial environment. As a result the author is so struck by the despair of his material that he fails to see any ground for hope in his material. Yet hope is there. (Ellison, "Transition" 90–91).[15]

Expressing more confidence in the liberatory potential of migration than Attaway and his fugitive counterparts, Ellison already recognized in this apprentice stage of his career that the future of African-American advancement lay in retaining a conscious attachment to the folk south, which he firmly believed was not only possible but also necessary given the obstacles of urban life. Both the seeds of his repudiation of the fugitive position and his break with the leftist politics of the Wright school can be detected within his comprehension of how this "blend" of both old and new "better fitted" the migrant for the city. Even in the late 1930s and early 1940s, when he was writing for *The New Masses,* Ellison internalized neither the sectarian Marxism nor the literary naturalism of his fellow writers. From the beginning, as Larry Neal writes, "His work appears always to have been striving for penetration into those areas of black lifestyle that exist below the mere depiction of external oppression" (Benston, *Speaking* 107). As he moved outside the strict contours of Wright's deterministic world, his effort signaled, in his words, his attempt to "participate *as a writer* in the struggle for human freedom" (Ellison, *Shadow and Act* 113, emphasis in the original).

In contrast, Attaway's concerns throughout *Blood on the Forge* run parallel to those of his fellow Chicago writers and academics. He shared their interest in the postindustrial adjustment pangs of what Robert Park had described throughout his career as the South's "new world peasant class." Attaway converted personal experience and the extensive research on this area into a dramatic narrative of protest and used the forum of the novel to measure the depth of social discontent that migration fostered. His intellectual orbit, interested in giving voice to the traumas of urban adjustment and undermining the seductive lure of western technology, provided an alliance that concurred with his despairing approach to postmigration life.

The picture that Attaway paints of the Mosses, his one-family "peasant society" in premigration Kentucky, however, is hardly in keeping with Park's willingness to contrast the pathologies of urban life with what the sociologist termed the "primal innocence" of a rural existence, a view of southern black culture that Park inherited from his study of "primitivist" modes in Germany and from his fieldwork in the rural south under the philosophic guidance of Booker T. Washington. *Blood on the Forge*'s portrait of sharecropping resembles a more severe version of the setting Wright laid out in his short story "Almos' a Man" (1939). Both texts juxtapose the static circularity of sharecropping with the linear but far less certain kineticism of flight. Before Dave Saunders jumps on the Illinois Central, gun in hand and bound "somewhere where he could be a man," Wright gradually reveals the frustration, boredom, and lack of respect that lead to the boy's accidental shooting of Jenny the mule and ironically free him from the chains of the plow. Attaway opens *Blood on the Forge* with a similar interruption of the repetitive plowing cycle, punctuating that interruption with a notably grotesque image. Part one of the five-part novel begins in medias res four weeks after the Moss brothers' mother drops dead behind her plow and is dragged over the ground by a mule "trained never to balk in the middle of a row" (6). The overused, rocky, and ruined soil mangles her so severely that "she didn't look like their maw anymore."

The gruesome incident provides a telling opening metaphor for the naturalistic drama acted out between the Moss family and their human and environmental adversaries. They are people of the soil, inextricably linked to each other and to the rhythms of their surroundings. Like the land on which they try to hack out a meager existence, they are being exhausted and have little hope for regeneration. Hattie's seventh miscarriage will later add to the couple's barren marriage and confirms that the family appears destined to die off as surely as the sterile and depleted farm. The mother's death firmly establishes that the land is, in Big Mat's words, "bigger 'n any white man" (36) and has its own ways of extracting the cost of its abuse.

The novel's first section lays out the way in which Attaway's sharecroppers derive small measures of meaning in their lives from the virtues of work and family. The Moss family's line of defense is to retreat within itself, looking to the bonds of family unity as a way of rising above subjugation. Each member of the family has a different means of enduring the family's collective hardships, and each contributes a separate, essential part to its survival.[16] The eldest brother, Big Mat, despite a grim religious faith and ever-brooding presence, makes the most elemental contribution by serving as the family provider. He also plays the heroic role of protector and serves in this capacity as the literary antecedent to a number of strong slave forebears. Hattie, despite her barrenness, assumes the traditional domestic role of keeper of the home.

Chinatown, the youngest brother, counters Big Mat by adding a much needed pleasure-principal to the family. Personified by a freewheeling folk energy, Chinatown's closest literary cousin is Tea Cake, Janie Crawford's irrepressible companion in *Their Eyes Were Watching God*. As hedonistic as his world will allow, Chinatown is cheerfully playful, irresponsible, and indolent. His identity is embodied within his prized possession, a shiny gold tooth: "Without that tooth, I ain't nobody" (41). The tooth's value has increased because he "work for that tooth when all I wants to do is laze in the sun." Chided for letting his brothers labor in the fields for him, he responds in his typically guileless way, "I lazy, and they smart . . . I lazy and hungry—they smart and hungry" (4).

Melody, the middle and most complex brother, is a blues figure and uses his music to buffer the pain of his world. His rendition of "Hungry Blues" embodies his ability to harness its negative energy:

> Done scratched at the hills,
>   But the 'taters refused to grow. . . .
> Done scratched at the hill,
>   But the 'taters refuse to grow. . . .
> Mister Bossman, Mister Bossman,
>   Lemme mark in the book once mo'. . . .   (3)

Melody's capacity to transform the twin oppressions of peonage and dead land into an evocative sharecropper's lament points to the redemptive power of his suffering and suggests why the musician, as a folk bluesman, represents the best hope among the brothers for persevering in the limited confines of his world. At the novel's end, even though his music has dried up, he alone walks away from the steel mill with all his faculties intact.

The family's unity reflects the admiration and affection Attaway shared with Park for rural black life, which Park, the lifelong academic, curiously praised as "places untouched by the influence of Tuskegee" (Matthews, *Quest* 74–76). But Attaway parted company with the Chicago sociologist over the day-to-day lives and futures of these exploited workers. Never having to endure the down side of race and class exclusion himself, Park found the moral virtue and the simplicity of black folk life attractive. He held on to the Washingtonian belief (alluded to in the headnote to this chapter) that through keeping rural blacks out of cities and educating them so that "they can grow up slowly and naturally" at home in the South, the "race problem will eventually solve itself." Despite the strong note of naive paternalism behind that assertion, however, Park was also enough of a realist to recognize that cities held attractions too strong to resist. In a spirit of evolutionary fatalism, sharecroppers would inevitably yield to the lure of western technology, regardless of whether they were better off on the farm, and gravitate like lemmings to urban centers, where the slow and steady process of acculturation (and the attendant racial conflict) would grind forward.

Like Wright's Dave Saunders, Attaway well understood the appeal of leaving the preindustrial caste system of the South. But like Wright himself, Attaway drew from a more personal well of impressions on the Jim Crow south than Park and seems to have found little essential virtue or moral privilege in being born on the bottom rung of America's economic ladder. In this light, *Blood on the Forge* convincingly challenges any sociological fondness for an ideology of primitivism that seeks to bestow faith in sentimentalizing the "simpler" life of southern sharecroppers. It offers no romantic images of this existence, no avenues for escaping its cultural isolation, no means of cultural advancement, and no merit in the working lives of black southerners that provides them with enough power to overcome the historical burden of racism.

Fugitive Slaves and Fugitive Migrants

Within African-American cultural history, Attaway's characterization of Melody Moss confirms not only his recognition of the affirmative capacity of the blues but also his awareness of the expressive possibilities of tapping the rich vein of his cultural roots. Attaway's most pronounced obligation to the authority of tradition appears in the way that *Blood on the Forge* returns to the ritual ground of slave life as it may be inferred from the published accounts of escaped slaves. Although few slave narratives were in print for Attaway (or any writer of this period) to read, it is of little relevance either to argue or attempt to show that he had access to specific works. The argument is at best speculative and probably unresolvable. The oral folk conduits through which much African-American material traveled would make any fixed textual referents merely singular written manifestations of a much larger and more complex system of indebtedness. More to the point, the connections, wherever they appear, attest to an ongoing cultural atmosphere in the age of migration, especially during the economic hard times of the depression, in which the themes of slave autobiographies and the historical phenomenon of slavery find an applicable resonance.

Reading *Blood on the Forge,* or any migrant novel, through the slave narrative confirms common ground that allows generalizations about their affinities. Although the relationship between the two forms is easily discernible throughout African-American written literature, the immeasurably large impact of these nineteenth-century autobiographies on more recent autobiography, poetry, and fiction has, with a few notable exceptions, only recently begun to be appreciated fully.[17] The reasons for this are tied to a gamut of issues that are no less ideologically complicated than other extra-literary realities of American racial life. But as a staging ground to migration novels, a partial explanation can be found in the fact that slave narratives were long read as a formulaic rather than artistic form that yielded to rather than resisted classification. For this reason slave autobiographies, bowing under the weight of modernist critical values, were not so long ago perceived as little more than a second-class genre.

Nowhere is the significant progress of African-American literary and historical studies more notable than in the turnabout of opinion on slave narratives. For years most scholars held onto a moderated version of the southern historian Ulrich B. Phillips's assertion that the stories slaves published once they reached freedom were no more than fictionalized, anti-Confederate propaganda. They were also derivative, historically unauthentic, and of little consequence to the corpus of twentieth-century black texts. Marion Starling, despite providing the first comprehensive survey of the genre, wrote that the chief importance of the "sub-literary" slave narrative lay in its "genetic relationship to the popular slave novels of the 1850s," such as Harriet Beecher Stowe's *Uncle Tom's Cabin*. Following a similar line in his seminal *The Slave Community,* the prominent slave historian John Blassingame dismissed Harriet Jacobs's *Incidents in the Life of a Slave Girl* as "too orderly" and "too melodramatic" to be credible.[18] After all, so the formalist logic went, one can hardly place high value on a genre that is inherently orthodox and conventional rather than personal and original, especially when its texts are frequently encased in a hostile white discursive frame of elaborate written authentication demanding that readers penetrate a rhetorical mode favoring propaganda and persuasion over the factual and lyrical recounting of a true life story.

Even Ralph Ellison, whose *Invisible Man* is fully intertwined within the narrative structure of these earlier stories of vertical migration, said in a 1978 interview,

> I think too much has been made of the slave narrative, as an influence on contemporary writing. Experience tends to mold itself into certain repetitive patterns, and one of the reasons we exchange experiences is in order to discover the repetitions and coincidences which amount to a common group experience. . . . I wouldn't have had to read a single slave narrative in order to create the narrative pattern of *Invisible Man*. It emerges from the experience of my own sense of literary form, out of my sense of experience as shaped by history and my familiarity with literature. (Davis and Gates, Jr., eds., *Slave's Narrative* xviii–xix)

Ellison's objection, although resting on the assertion that he did not consciously set out to imitate the earlier form, highlights the slave narrative's importance in his work by acknowledging its undeniable presence, not explicitly but as a system of narrative patterns inhabiting later black literature and residing within the much larger cultural space of African-American life. Ellison's point must be mediated through his statement "I had no need of slave narratives" to grasp the significance of "the movement from South to North" (xix).

It is no surprise that the author—long concerned with establishing himself within a more universal lineage and, at the time he made this statement in 1978, still feeling the effects of strident nationalistic denunciations of *Invisible Man*—would balk at limiting himself to so seemingly narrow a literary legacy as the slave narrative. But his perception, nonetheless, rests on his assumption that by the time he wrote the movement was an essential enough common point of reference to be comprehended indirectly as a major part of African-American life, if not experienced directly. "All this is not to put down the slave narrative," Ellison concludes, "but to say that it did not influence my novel as a *conscious* functional form" (Gates and Davis, eds. *Slave's Narrative* xx, emphasis added). As Gates and Davis adroitly offer in summation, "Ellison's final word on the subject inserts 'consciousness' as a substitute for intention, which is one reason critics qualify any author's account of their own origins."

Perceptions such as Ellison's (which even at the time of his interview were opposed by a small core of slave narrative supporters led by Arna Bontemps) have been replaced by the recognition that slave autobiographies are the heart and soul of the written black self, that these narratives provide the richest collection of historical information about an enslaved culture in human history, and that twentieth-century African-American literature may be read as a sweeping, grand response to the call issued and the foundation built by the first-person narratives of black former slaves. In spite of the manifold attempts by white abolitionists, editors, and amanuenses to seize ex-slaves' stories for their own designs, they nevertheless wrote themselves into the human community. In a large-scale autobiographical quest for voice, fugitive slave narrators seized an identity, in the face of white culture's ongoing resistance, by using their "written life" to authenticate the details of their "lived life" (MacKethan, "Black Boy" 123). They also issued calls for a means of finding order and community expression in what were otherwise inexpressibly painful and heroic individual accounts of African-American experience.

Twentieth-century migration novelists—through direct borrowing, revision, and various other kinds of structural, thematic, and formal reconfigurations—have responded to antedating slave narratives by continually reinterpreting present experience through the African-American slave past. The intertextual encounter between the slave and the fugitive migrant implies much more than the grafting of one text onto another. The network of relations signified by the link helps further whatever claims need still be made about the sui generis nature of the African-American literary tradition—more so because the connections exhibited in the lesser-known novels of, for example, Attaway, Lee, Offord, and Lucus point to a diachronic continuity that transcends any select group of major canonical black texts.

To be sure, the earlier autobiographies and personal chronicles tended to emphasize a more affirmative set of results than, for example, the Moss family's decline. Martha K. Cobb summarizes the slave narrator as a "defined hero who goes through a series of tribulations before he achieves his shining goal, freedom, the central theme in works of this genre" (Sekora and Turner, *Art of Slave Narrative* 36). Sidonie Smith joins many critics, however, in noting that the narrative is also "the story of failure to find real freedom and acceptance within American society, a disturbing sequel to the successful story of the radical break away from southern society" (*Where I'm Bound* 24). Just as the escaped slave's freedom in the North proved again and again to be illusory (a realization that often necessitated another, more liberating stage of migration to Canada or England), the fugitive migrant naively begins his journey convinced that his exodus will make him free. When William Andrews summarizes the equivocal results of exchanging the world of the road in favor of settling on apparently free soil for mid-nineteenth-century autobiographers, the observation remains strikingly applicable to the quest of black migrants a century later. The route of the exile "both confirms and refutes the Afro-American transcendental ideal that maintained that one could break out of a realm of racist perversity to discover, beyond the margin, a Canaan-land of freedom, fairness, and brotherhood with whites. The persistently hopeful liminal figures in this group of black autobiographers could never quite 'get over,' for every time they thought they had crossed Jordan into campground, they found themselves deceived by a mirage and sojourning still in the same old desert" (*To Tell a Free Story* 188).

The fugitive slave narrative, delineating a version of what Phyllis Klotman calls the "running man" tradition in American literature (*Another Man Gone*), has been described as a "master plan" (to include all the phrase's intentional irony) that sets into relief the conventionality of its language, structure, and character. James Olney's case for the "overwhelming *sameness*" of the narratives is convincing enough that he can list recipe-fashion all the essential elements in any narrative. Although he is concerned with the apparatus of the narrative, front cover to back—including engraved portraits, authenticating testimonials, and a "bewildering variety of documents" such as poetic epigraphs, sermons, and antislavery speeches situated before, after, and in the middle of the narrative—the fictionalized migrant inherits the most detailed version of this legacy from the actual text of the slave narrative, what may be termed the episode. Olney has listed the twelve recurring, episodic features that made the "heterogeneous, hetero*generic* elements in slave narratives come to be so regular, so constant, so indispensable to the mode" ("'I Was Born'" 152, emphasis in the original). His list provides a useful starting point for uncovering the roots of many of the scenes associated with the fugitive migrant:

- description of a cruel master, mistress, or overseer, details of first observed whipping and numerous subsequent whippings
- an account of one extraordinarily strong, hardworking slave—often "pure African"—who, because there is no reason for it, refuses to be whipped
- record of the barriers raised against slave literacy and the overwhelming difficulties encountered in learning to read and write
- description of the amounts and kinds of food and clothing given to slaves, the work required of them, the pattern of a day, a week, a year
- description of patrols, of failed attempt(s) to escape, of pursuit by men and dogs
- description of successful attempt(s) to escape, lying by during the day, travelling by night guided by the North Star
- taking of a new last name . . . to accord with new social identity as a free man
- reflections on slavery. ("'I Was Born'" 153)[19]

Read within the frame of Olney's criteria, Attaway's *Blood on the Forge* recreates the atmosphere of slave narratives thoroughly enough to establish a persuasive relationship between the third-person novel and its first-person autobiographical precursors. The intertextuality—or, more appropriate to the cultural origins of the texts, the call and response pattern—evident in the Attaway's depiction of character, setting, and structure can be elucidated through scenes from the well-known published narratives of William Wells Brown, Olaudah Equiano, and Henry Box Brown.[20]

Recalling his pre-freedom days, Brown, in one of the most memorable scenes from his *Narrative of William Wells Brown, a Fugitive Slave. Written by Himself* (1847), tells of the fate of Randall, "a man of great strength and power . . . [who] was considered the most valuable and able-bodied slave on the plantation" (181). Randall's distinction comes from his pronouncement "that no white man should ever whip him—that he would die first" (181). Taking this as a challenge, Randall's "tyrannical and cruel" overseer, Mr. Cook, soon finds sufficient fault with his slave to order him to the barn for punishment. When Randall refuses, Cook solicits the help of three companions to try and subdue him. When "one after another" Randall lays each out on the ground, one of them manages to shoot him. He is then beaten severely and returned to the field, attached to a weighted ball and chain, where, in his incapacitated state, he is required to perform the same share of labor as his fellow workers.

Like Frederick Douglass's careful rhetorical maneuvers in detailing his encounter with Covey the slave-breaker, Brown uses the Randall episode to denounce the institution of slavery from several angles. He sounds an alarm to his northern readers over the slave owner's casual disregard for slave humanity, he calls attention to the institution's severity by showing how it destroys even the most physically powerful of slaves, and, more subtly, he implies that treating slaves in such a way makes poor economic sense. Brown's sympathy for the plight of Randall—who, measured solely by his labor output, drops in utility from "most valuable" to average—underscores the obvious weakness of a system that sacrifices the productivity of its ablest worker in order to reaffirm the mere fact of its existing hierarchy.

Within the similarly exploitive set of relations that bind the sharecropping system, Attaway presents what appears to be a more satisfying rewrite of Randall's story, but it also includes some notable discrepancies. Big Mat Moss, a paradigmatic slave ancestor, plays the role of chief antagonist whose refusal to be whipped similarly reconstitutes the southern plantation as a site of individually heroic resistance. Deploying the character trope that Olney identifies as the "pure African," Attaway describes Big Mat, able to out-labor three other men, as stronger and "blacker than his half brother." As a child, he suffered the insults of the white sharecroppers' children, who told him his "father must have been a lump of charcoal." His resemblance to the portrait of the formulaic slave is fortified by Attaway's willingness to put aside his suspicions of formal religion and position Big Mat's actions within a religiously based, biblically grounded ideology of survival, the slave community's chief protection against despair and a practical storehouse of wisdom and appropriate behavior.

The parallel scene, as Attaway novelizes it, begins as Big Mat goes about his work of butchering seven hogs. The role of "Mr. Cook" of this setting is played by two men, Mr. Johnston, who is Big Mat's overseer, and his riding boss. Johnston approaches him and tempts his hunger by commenting what "damn good eatin'" the blood sausages will be. He at first refuses to let Big Mat take home even the entrails, remarking, "It ain't my fault your folks ain't got nothin' to eat," before instructing him to "throw the rest of the [guts] back to the other hogs" (*Blood* 15). When Johnston later relents and allows Big Mat to take some entrails home (mainly as a bribe to keep him from being tempted by a northern labor agent), the gesture is so paltry that it assures that black laborer and beast feed on the same leftovers.

In this compressed moment, Attaway dramatizes a critical difference between slavery and sharecropping, which in turn points up a damning irony of emancipation. The peonage system binds the family legally to the white plantation by debt, but because none of its members are "property" they lose whatever minimal protection such status afforded slaves. If Attaway's characterization and setting are posed against the canonical slave image that Wells Brown provides, the atmosphere of psychological torture may be traced as far back as *The Interesting Narrative of the Life of Olaudah Equiano, or Gustavus Vassa, the African. Written by Himself* (1789). Equiano's description, coming from his account of the Middle Passage between his African homeland and Barbados, plays off similar oppositions between hunger and satiation, scarcity and surfeit: "One day [my captors] had taken a number of fishes; and when they had killed and satisfied themselves with as many as they thought fit, to our astonishment who were on the deck, rather than give any of them to us to eat, as we expected, they tossed the remaining fish into the sea again, although we begged and prayed for some as well as we could, but in vain" (36). Attaway's rewrite builds on this scene and exploits its fullest dimensions, not by recapitulating the horrible victimization of the Africans but by subtly altering the discursive space from a scene of outright abuse to a scene of psychological control wherein Big Mat must prepare the food that is promised to him and then denied.

After firmly establishing the tension between Big Mat and Johnston, Attaway moves into the climactic scene of heated conflict between the sharecropper and his riding boss. Attaway joins Equiano, Douglass, Jacobs, Solomon Northup, John Brown, and a host of other slaves in rendering a version of what is surely the most brutal, enduring, and widely protested trope of enslavement, the spectacle of the whip. References to floggings, beatings, and other physical tortures are recounted in nearly every narrative. The accounts range from extended, explicit, and detailed descriptions of the "driver's lash" to casual references implying the practice was common enough to be a customary part of daily plantation life. One of the early defenders of the slave narrative's authenticity, Charles Nichols, writes, "All the narrators report that they were whipped at some time during their enslavement, and many displayed their scarred and striped backs to amazed audiences at abolitionist meetings" (*Many Thousand Gone* 63). Attaway, along with his fellow migrant authors Lee, Offord, and Lucus, collectively seizes the trope's connotations of painful physical exploitation and, recognizing migration's liberatory potential, infuses it with a different set of meanings. The whipping scene, beginning as an act to subjugate the worker, not only temporarily reverses the role of victim and oppressor but also becomes the initiating moment of freedom.

Lee's *River George* was the earliest fugitive migrant novel to frame its protagonist's migration around a whipping. Published in 1937, the same year as *Their Eyes Were Watching God,* the novel marks a transition from the concerns of the Harlem Renaissance to those of Chicago. Like Hurston, Lee writes admiringly about black sharecroppers, a relatively invisible segment of the literary population (with the notable exceptions of George Wylie Henderson's underread gem *Ollie Miss*). Lee pays homage to the bonds of southern kinship, to the heroic possibilities of common people, and to the unadorned simplicity of black folk culture. At the same time, he anticipates Wright's frustration with the southern black population's inability to effect substantive change on its own behalf. In Lee's view, without modernized farming techniques and large-scale educational reform, no amount of romanticized attachment to an ideology of pastoral, agrarian triumph will interrupt the South's never-ending cycle of exploitation.

Lee's protagonist is Aaron George, who, like Attaway's Mat Moss, Chris Woods in *The White Face,* and the title character of George Wylie Henderson's *Jule,* replicates versions of the hardworking, dark-skinned sharecropper-slave typologized in Olney's schema of the slave narrative. *River George*'s defining scene as a fugitive migrant novel occurs when Aaron's riding boss, Mr. Turner, produces a leather strap to whip him. Aaron turns the lash back on his boss, who, "injected with little flashes of fear" and "smoldering with hate," has no defense against his powerful adversary. Summarizing the heroic resistance of all fugitive migrants, Aaron announces triumphantly, "'You ain't gonna whip nobody right now'" (110). As a revenge, he is set up to discover his girlfriend in the arms of a "mean-spirited, mean-souled white man" who has forced Ada to be his mistress. When Aaron attacks his adversary, accidentally shoots him, and narrowly eludes a lynch mob by escaping north, he repeats a familiar pattern that yokes sex, violence, and a triangulated love relationship.

Frederick Douglass's recollection of hiding in a closet as a small boy after watching his bare-backed Aunt Hester being whipped for visiting Lloyd's Ned, a fellow slave, offers the most wrenching narrative legacy ordered around positioning the black male response to white dominance as an interracial blood feud over who would lay claim to the objectified black woman's body. A decade before the publication of *River George,* Jean Toomer improvised on the same conflict in "Blood Burning Moon," the short story in *Cane* in which Tom Burwell, the black lover of Louisa, is burned alive to the light of a full moon after slashing the throat of Bob Stone, his white rival for the young woman's affections. Other similarly plotted examples to follow included Wright's "Long Black Song," the third story from his collection *Uncle Tom's Children,* and Henderson's *Jule,* the migration novel that follows as a sequel to *Ollie Miss.* Although the scene that Lee depicts lacks the narrative immediacy of Douglass's or Toomer's accounts of white violence, it nonetheless underwrites a comparable version of gender and race exploitation.

Lucas's *The Flour Is Dusty* (1943) offers a skewed rewrite of the same confrontation to illustrate the extent to which the dramatic moment of confrontation and the trope of the fugitive migrant permeates the fiction of the era. Less well-known than Lucas's later novel *Third Ward Newark* (1946), *The Flour Is Dusty* is not much more than an awkwardly executed detective novel published to a few unfavorable reviews. Having little in common with other fugitive texts after the first few scenes, the novel's principal conflict early on lies between the young Jim Harrell and his father, a joyless, hardworking sharecropper in rural Georgia. Following in the long tradition of freedom-seekers, Jim's primary means of combating his father's exploitation is literacy. Afraid that education will ruin his son as a fieldworker, the elder Harrell has beaten Jim after catching him reading. Banished to the field, he plots ways to liberate himself and find the strength to emulate his hero, Frederick Douglass. Replaying a thinly disguised version of the Douglass-Covey fight, Jim attacks his father after being hit, surprisingly overpowers him, and, believing his father is dead, flees north to Atlantic City.[21] Little of interest follows, as Jim tries to exonerate himself from a murder in Atlantic City that he did not commit. Ultimately he solves the murder, marries the daughter of the victim, and is happily reunited with his father. Despite Lucas's attempt to inscribe within his formulaic detective story a somewhat superficial connection to African-American themes and historical figures, *The Flour Is Dusty* exhibits little of the narrative power of other fugitive migrant authors.

In contrast, the pivotal whipping scene of *Blood on the Forge* is filled with narrative tension. When Big Mat reminds the riding boss that "'us used to play together when your folks was sharecroppin' next to mine,'" his insult lands Big Mat a whipping across the face. At first numb to the quirt's power, he springs to action when the riding boss insults his dead mother: "The riding boss fell to the ground, blood streaming from his smashed face. He struggled to get to his feet. A heavy foot caught him in the side of his neck. His head hung over his shoulder at an odd angle. . . . Then he saw the uneven movement of the red throat, the fluttering blood bubbles at the nose. The riding boss would live to lead a lynch mob against him" (28). As he walks away, a "great calm settled on him" (29). By paralleling Big Mat's confrontation with the simultaneous appearance of a "jackleg" recruiting southern black labor for northern steel mills, Attaway compresses the push and pull forces of migration into a unified dramatic explanation for the brother's departure on a northbound train.

The first section concludes with an image of loss and broken community that typifies the beginning of the fugitive migrant's journey. Not allowed to transport women with them, the brothers hastily leave as Hattie stands "barefoot . . . in the doorway." It was common for migrant families to go North in waves. But even though Big Mat promises he will send for Hattie, the industrial world for which they are bound mitigates the necessity of "attached women" by consciously replacing marriage and family with prostitution and work-related camaraderie as the operative relationships. As a wife, Hattie poses a threat to the labor process. She potentially subsumes the competing needs of the factory for those of the family unit, and her presence will undermine the fragile illusion of "equality" among the black and white male workers. As women of any race entered the labor scene, the behavioral codes of the color bar became more overtly antagonistic (Hamilton, "Work and Culture" 149). Furthermore, migration scholars have agreed that black men and women had divergent motives for migrating north, and once they arrived they encountered radically different social and economic situations. Black women faced far greater economic discrimination and were less likely to find employment than their male counterparts. Even when they were able to find work, it was, compared to others in the labor force, the least desirable and least remunerative (Clark Hine in Trotter, Jr., *The Great Migration* 130).

Given such historical realities, it is no surprise that Hattie, once the brothers are in Pennsylvania, rapidly disappears from the text. When Attaway sends only his male characters north, he replicates the migration patterns of many sharecropping families. He also avoids addressing the difficult, even oppositional, role of women in the migration process. By leaving all but superficial references to southern black women behind, Attaway, like many male migrants in search of work, perceives the process as almost devoid of gender implications and prefers to focus on the brothers' family disintegration within the tripartite dynamic of class, race, and region.

Part two continues to follow the pattern of slave narratives. It is a compressed transitional section telling of the brothers' trip north in a sealed boxcar, an object of conveyance that offers a vibrant field of symbolic interpretation.[22] Evoking a host of comparable black ritual journeys of liberation and enslavement in a few short pages, Attaway foreshadows the ambiguous potential of the brothers' ascent. On one hand, he echoes Equiano's gruesome accounts of the Middle Passage. Recalling the slave ship's assault on human senses, Equiano endured "fearful noise," the "stench of the hold," the "pestilential" impact of his surroundings, the "heat of the climate," and the "filth of the necessary tubs" (*Interesting Life* 35). His plaintive longing for family, the terror of knowing so little about his captors, and his lack of any knowledge about what lay ahead added an additional level of internal pain. Attaway similarly intermingles the sensory with the psychological in the way he characterizes the discomfort of the ride and the feeling of uncertainty that it forces on the brothers. Holding on to the lingering image of the previous butchering scene, the brothers are "bunched up like hogs headed for market." "They were headed into the unknown and there was no sun, they forgot even that they had eyes in their heads." The "pounding of the wheels shaking" echoes so loudly that nothing can be heard above that "piercing scream." The air is "fetid with man smell and nervous sweat." "Warm urine began to flow into the corner" where Big Mat sits. The experience is "enough to make them all brittle" (*Blood* 38–42).

Paralleling these evocations of simple discomfort with the more charged implications of the Middle Passage compounds the horror by portending the end of the journey and the industrial slavery that lies ahead. On the other hand, the narrative and geographic movement of the section are reminiscent of a journey to freedom like that of Henry Box Brown (*The Narrative of Henry Box Brown* [1849]). Brown's story is one of the more amazing and unique escape accounts ever recorded. It is also one of only a handful of narratives such as William and Ellen Craft's and James W. C. Pennington's that provides details of an escape from slavery. Brown retells how he had a two-by-three-foot wooden box built and, in the box, he literally mailed himself north (a witty pun on "male" not lost on Brown) to Philadelphia and freedom. Most of the time he was jammed in the box and rested in a "dreadful position" upside down on his head, arriving so contorted that he narrowly avoided permanent injuries.

Vassa's trip across the Atlantic exchanged images of freedom, kinship, and tribal heritage for slavery, anonymity, and an erasure of his history. Brown's—and likewise the Moss brothers'—self-imposed entombment inverts this pattern. They confine themselves in order to be free, moving from the static, slow death of the southern farm through mobile self-imprisonment and, finally, after a time of recovery, into a period of illusionary freedom and stasis. By the time the brothers arrive at the bare hills of the Alleghenies, Attaway, in one of the novel's notable achievements, has set the localized, personal trauma of the ride into striking relief and elevated the experience to a higher level. He evokes the migrations of thousands of fellow slaves and sharecroppers over the years who, like the Moss brothers, went north carrying only their cultural and communal connections with each other, the common experience of their exploitation, and a vague sense of faith in bettering their lives.

Part three leaves the fertile, symbolic ground of southern slave life and continues Attaway's naturalistic parable in Allegheny County, Pennsylvania. Portraying the brothers' helplessness in the face of industrial progress, it initiates them into the stark realities of life in a factory town. A summation of what is in store for the brothers, and the clearest statement of one of the novel's principal themes, ironically comes through the ramblings of Smothers, the crippled, supposedly mad, black prophet of the bunkhouse:

> It's wrong to tear up the ground and melt it up in the furnace. Ground don't like it. It's the hell-and-devil kind of work. Guy ain't satisfied with usin' the stuff that was put here for him to use—stuff of top of the earth. Now he got to git busy and melt up the ground itself. Ground don't like it, I tells you. Now they'll be folks laugh when I say the ground got feelin'. But I knows what it is I'm talking' about. All the time I listen real hard and git scared when the iron blast holler to git loose, an' them big redhead blooms screamin' like the very heart o' the earth caught between them rollers. It jest ain't right. (*Blood* 53)

Although the harrowing details describing the transition from farm to blast furnace alone are enough to dramatize working in the steel mill, Attaway compounds the horror through the use of a commentator, whose remarks are italicized and who speaks as an omniscient fellow migrant, summarizing the impressions of the new migrant population. Recording details of the factory environment, what it describes as the *"ugly smoking hell out of a backwoods preacher's sermon"* (45), the angry voice periodically interjects to interpret the northern setting through the psychological veil of southern experience:

> *We have been tricked away from our poor, good-as-bad-ground-and-bad-white-men-will-let-'em-be hills. What men in their right minds would leave off tending green growing things to tend iron monsters.* (44)

> *Yes, them red-clay hills was what we call stripped ground, but there was growing things everywhere and crab-apple trees bunched—stunted but beautiful in the sun.* (44)

> *We can't see where nothin' grows around here but rusty iron towers and brick stacks, walled up like somebody's liable to try and steal them. Where are the trees?* (45)

*The sun on the red hillsides baked a man, but it was only a short walk to the
bottoms and the mud that oozed up between his toes like a cool drink to hot
black feet, steppin' easy, mindful of the cottonmouth.* (46).

*What do we count for against machines that lift tons easy as a guy takes a spoon-
ful of gravy to his mouth? . . . What does that make a man?* (56)

Such passages engage the dialectic of ascent and immersion, similarly juxtaposing a negative representation of the North with a more favorable view
of the South. Manifesting the consciousnesses of Chinatown, Melody, and
Big Mat, the over-voice calls up images of loss and separation. By coun-
terposing the pastoral language of "green growing things" and "apple
trees" with "iron monsters," Attaway maintains the locus of the migrants'
collective psyche within their southern setting. The brothers are overwhelmed by environmental, socioeconomic, and biological forces beyond
their comprehension, and each futilely attempts to make the hills of his
southern home a touchstone through which he comprehends his new
world. The examples are telling in their superficiality. The small engines
that move steel on the river are "mules," a word that "sounded like home."
The heat of the pit where they work reminds them of the Kentucky mid-
day sun. Even letting water while standing out in the open is a "touch of
the past," reminding Chinatown and Melody how back on the farm this
"made a feller feel free—space around him and the warm water running
in the weeds" (51–52). Attaway is pessimistic about the survival of southern black peasants in the new industrial world. These pathetically insuffi-
cient modes of sense-making stress his recognition of how unprepared his
characters are for the northern factory.

But in a subtle point well in keeping with a conclusion drawn first by
Dunbar in *The Sport of the Gods* and repeated in ensuing migration novels, the brothers' downfall cannot be explained entirely by the harsh realities of geographic determinism. Chinatown, Melody, and Big Mat retain
these limited associations to their past, but their mistake is to discard the
more authentic, viable, and important connections to folk culture that are
not only necessary to support them but also determine the success or failure of their ascent.

By the fourth and fifth sections of the book, the brothers have abandoned all ties to Kentucky. The most damaging difference in their lives is
the change in their relationship to each other, as petty feuds and jealousy
replace the familial cohesiveness that once nurtured them. Each individual changes as well. Chinatown's gold tooth, worn in the South "like a
badge" (84), loses its power to bolster him. Melody's folk blues do not

sound right in the mill, and, after experimenting with a less plaintive, lu-gubrious sound, the musician who could once "hear music in a snore" (98) puts away his guitar. Big Mat, after learning of Hattie's miscarriage, dis-cards his plans to bring her to join him and turns his affections to Anna, a fifteen-year-old prostitute. His inner preaching voice deserts him. Even his love of honest toil, which has given him enough stature among his fellow workers that they name him "Black Irish," gradually disappears amid his obsession for Anna and his growing love of violence to assert his manhood. In the short space of a few months the sustaining folk virtues of music, marriage, family, and honest labor have been corrupted or rendered inad-equate in the brothers' northern home.

Following in the path of Dunbar's Hamilton family, the brothers' de-feat comes, in part, from their inability to become what Stepto terms "trib-ally literate." Failing to understand the importance of retaining the usable parts of their past, they misread the necessary codes of acculturation in their new surroundings. The tragic result is documented in the novel's cli-mactic scene. When Big Mat is duped into being deputized to help break up an impending strike, his drastic transformation is complete. Rather than comprehending the strike's struggle for authority through the well of his own marginalized experience, drawing on the wisdom of immersion to guide him, he yields to the temptation of modeling himself after the very figure who oppresses him the most. In what will be his only moment of supreme, self-willed power, he becomes a "riding boss" with enough mas-tery to feel "big as God Almighty" (231). And like the riding boss he had once "beaten down," his destruction at the hands of the strikers comes from placing too much faith in the authority of his position of dominance.

Big Mat's death and the final scene of the novel, in which Melody and the now-blind Chinatown continue their migration by leaving for Pitts-burgh, suggest a tragic end for the brothers. Wishing they could return to Kentucky, they travel not south but further north. Viewed in the context of the development of migration novels from Dunbar through Wright, however, the conclusion of *Blood on the Forge,* in contrast to *The Sport of the Gods* and *Native Son,* seems to provide a small window of oppor-tunity for future southern black migrants. And in so doing it indirectly alludes to what will be for the communal migrant novelist the conditions necessary for successful acculturation. Both earlier novels concluded with images of stasis. Berry and Fannie Hamilton retreat as far back into the illusionary benevolence of southern paternalism as their circumstances will allow and thus end in the same place they began. Bigger Thomas, having found nothing in his past he could import north and having merely exchanged one prison cell at the novel's beginning for another one at its end, awaits his execution having made no progress at all. In contrast, by implicating Big Mat in his own downfall, Attaway concedes the possibility of an alternative story, that of a migrant who goes north and makes a more fortunate set of choices about what to cull from his past, which then provides for him at least a tentative purchase toward successful urban acculturation. Finally, as long as the two remaining brothers, like their fugitive slave ancestors, possess the power to keep moving from one place to another, and as long as the novel concludes with them pushing forward in search of something different from the circumstances that oppress them, they have the capacity to seek and imagine a place of freedom.

4

The Communal Migrant's Recuperation of Immersion

> The idea of community itself depends upon both language and story: a community is a group of people who tell a shared story in a shared language.
>
> James Boyd White

> This really was Harlem, and now all the stories which I had heard of the city-within-a-city leaped alive in my mind. The vet had been right: For me this was not a city of realities, but of dreams; perhaps because I had always thought of my life as being confined to the South. And now as I struggled through the lines of people a new world of possibility suggested itself to me faintly, like a small voice that was barely audible in the roar of city sounds.
>
> Ralph Ellison

> "You're just one generation away from the South, you know. You'll find," he added, kindly, "the people will be willing to talk to you . . . if they don't feel that you look down on them just because you're from the North."
>
> James Baldwin

The next stage of migration novels addresses the inseparable relationship between self- and community-identity. While continuing the search for the conditions that make the North inhabitable for African-American migrants, the novelists' general emphasis shifts from the fugitive's theme of flight to one of quest. Waters Turpin's *O'Canaan!* (1939), George Wylie Henderson's *Jule* (1946), Dorothy West's *The Living Is Easy* (1948), Aldon Bland's

Behold a Cry (1947), Ralph Ellison's *Invisible Man* (1952), and James Baldwin's *Go Tell It on the Mountain* (1953) together constitute a more optimistic, more nuanced perspective on migration than their fugitive migrant forerunners. The shift reflects the one taking place between the depression and the postwar decade in African-American literary culture generally. Signified more specifically in Ellison's transformation from a radical young protégé of Richard Wright reviewing for *The New Masses* to the celebrated author of *Invisible Man,* the shift incorporates new modes of representation that rejected Wright's 1930s' brand of naturalism with its overcommitment to ideology, naive politics, and formulas of protest in favor of more universal, mythic, and psychological terms of social analysis (cf. Scruggs, *Sweet Home* 41).

The breakthrough in form was, to some degree, long overdue among migration novels. Raymond Williams has tied such innovations in form directly into the "fact of immigration to the metropolis, and it cannot too often be emphasized how many of the major innovators were, in this precise sense, immigrants." Although he relies entirely on British literary sources to explore the key cultural factors that make modernism an urban enterprise, Williams might well be referring to Ellison's migrant narrator when he describes the migrant urban community: "Liberated or breaking from their national or provincial cultures, placed in quite new relations to those other native languages or native visual traditions, encountering meanwhile a novel and dynamic common environment from which many of the older forms were obviously distant, the artists and writers and thinkers of this phase found the only community available to them: a community of the medium; of their own practices" (*Politics of Modernism* 45).

The common assumption that binds novels of this chapter together is that each explores how relational ties, especially those drawn from the communal folk sources of the South, are the most effective means of resisting the harsh obstacles of urban acculturation. The underlying quest theme of this group impulse frames the conditions necessary—however difficult to attain—for realizing the possibilities of "communal ascent," the recuperation of immersion's communal values into the more liberated postmigration setting. What I will consider, particularly within the more extended discussions of West and Ellison, are the various ways in which postdepression migration authors envision these community-building efforts within the context of a new urban setting.

By using the word *community,* I mean to include not only a novel's emphasis on the interrelation of characters but also those characters' link to similar values, common traditions, and a shared past.[1] The literary exploration of the potential of community finds strong precedent among this century's African-American writers. In his fine study of community's successive conditions, Michael Cooke writes that one kind of community, kinship, "has become a major option or even program of black literature in recent years" (*Afro-American Literature* 110). "Kinship" can refer to an ancestral lineage, as it is mapped out by Toni Morrison in *Song of Solomon* and Rita Dove in *Thomas and Beulah;* it can refer to "making generations," the unrealized desire of Gayle Jones's sterile narrator in *Corregidora;* it can place high value on the primacy of communal connections of the kind developed in Gloria Naylor's *Women of Brewster Place* and Marita Golden's *Long Distance Life;* or it can mean a system of interwoven textual organization, such as the Faulkner-esque, multiple-voiced narration of Ernest Gaines's *A Gathering of Old Men* or Naylor's *Mama Day.* These writers—adding to Cooke's own examples of John A. Williams, William Melvin Kelly, Michael Harper, and Eldridge Cleaver—all suggest that, as of late, "kinship has come to the fore" (110–11). From Cooke's use of the term as a stage in the African-American writer's gradual move from the self-veiling of Charles Chesnutt, James Weldon Johnson, and Nella Larsen to the achievement of intimacy in contemporary writers such as Alice Walker and Robert Hayden, it can be noted that kinship, however manifested, is an ur-value of Afrocentric culture.

The configurations of preexisting African life, together with the shared experiences of African removal, slavery, and racial oppression, have, for African Americans, repeatedly turned the effort of constituting an identity into a group dilemma. Drawing from the community-building impulses of, for example, the Harlem and Chicago renaissances, Garveyism, and other expressions of nationalism and incipient nation-building—including the Great Migration—black writers have made convincing cases for the importance of community as a value system, a mode of behavior, a means of self-definition, and a strategy to combat racial marginalization.

Within the form of the Great Migration novel throughout the early part of this century the myriad efforts at constructing the kind of kinship to which Cooke refers—both as collective avenues of resistance and as rituals of urban immersion—found little ground on which to thrive within the oppositional climate of racial and geographic exclusion. The most personal and highly charged account of growing up in this narrow cultural space is undoubtedly Richard Wright's autobiography, *Black Boy* (1945). He creates a southern world so convincingly devoid of both human and historical connections that his childhood has, particularly for white readers, come not only to exemplify but also somehow to "explain" the position of blacks in American life in the South. And, not surprisingly, although Ralph Ellison bristled in his brilliant "Richard Wright's Blues" at the failure of such readers and critics to locate as wide a spectrum of human response and emotion in African-American life as they accord everyone else, he also recognized "the full extent to which the Southern community renders the fulfillment of human destiny impossible" (*Shadow and Act* 80–81).

The early decades of the migration novel form suggest that Ellison's point extends beyond the South to the American community as a whole. Migration writers, from Paul Laurence Dunbar to Nella Larsen to Wright, had much difficulty in locating what has been labeled a usable geography in which their tentative matrices of kinship could thrive. The novels of Ellison and his fellow communal migrant writers represent attempts to envision the conditions necessary for such urban spaces to exist. Where they are successful, the city is not opposed to the migrant's origins but is related harmoniously to a real and an imagined migrant past.

The written quest for an operative psychological, cultural, and geographic space is in no way limited to African-American writers. The first prominent studies of the city in canonical American literature—Blanche Gelfant's *The American City Novel* (1954), Morton White and Lucia White's *The Intellectual versus the City* (1962), and David Weimer's *The City as Metaphor* (1966)—all stressed, in Gelfant's words, "man searching for a complete self in an urban world where personal integration or completeness seems to have become impossible" (23). More recent scholarship on American city literature—for example, James Machor's *Pastoral Cities* (1987) and Sidney Bremer's *Urban Intersections* (1992)—has moved well beyond representing the city as mere "bete noire" (White, *Intellectual* 2), "miraculous" locale, or "extension of the psyche" (Weimer, *City as Metaphor* 7–9). Although the result has been "to expand, not further dichotomize, our literary resources for urban life and culture" (Bremer, *Urban Intersections* 17), Machor has identified an enduring artistic response to the urban setting grounded in the paradox of "American writers over the past two hundred years increasingly [making] urban life the focus of their imaginative explorations" and these same writers' sense "that a more meaningful life is possible closer to nature beyond the constraining, complex, and corrupt city" (*Pastoral Cities* 3).

Within this fluid opposition, both Machor and Bremer have established an increasingly varied and complex set of responses in locating a meaning-filled domain within the city's multiple depictions, yet developing a coherent self within any representation of urban life has remained elusive. Trying to articulate this lack of coherence has been a central aesthetic and formal challenge for mainstream modernist writers. But as Craig Werner has pointed out, Euro-American modernists "experience their situation as individual and, to some extent, ahistorical, while Afro-American modernists generally perceive a communal dilemma deriving from historical and political forces" ("Bigger's Blues" 121). Although this is a necessarily reductive introduction into Werner's more subtle appraisal of Richard Wright's modernism, it nonetheless calls forth the radically different artistic derivatives underlying black and white writers' imaginations. The concrete realities of slavery and segregation can scarcely be compared, for example, to one of the more commonly cited touchstones of the modern self, the homefront spiritual anxiety that World War I produced (cf. Fussell, *The Great War and Modern Memory*).

If the existential undertones of white modernism draw upon an embraced sense of historical discontinuity—a fracturing of the past that substitutes a highly personal self-conscious and subconscious perception of reality for what can roughly be termed "tradition"—African-American writers have rarely had the luxury, in a perpetual climate of racial exclusion, of reconstituting themselves in such individual, even solipsistic, terms. Their ability to do so has relied on finding provisional ways, like William Melvin Kelly's Tucker Caliban in *Different Drummer* and Rutherford Calhoun in Charles Johnson's *Middle Passage,* to remove themselves temporarily from the enthrallments of immediate history and personal community. Moreover, insofar as black writers have expressed the need to articulate a collective and profound sense of cultural dislocation, they have always been both modern and communal.[2]

When W. E. B. Du Bois described the doubly conscious position of blacks in America in 1903, he summed up a century-old mindset analogous to the modern temper's "multiplicity of consciousness" referred to, for example, by Malcolm Bradbury and James McFarlane (30). He also positioned his desire to "merge [the African-American] double self into a better and truer self" into a broadly Hegelian framework of unified communal consciousness in which black identity emanated from collective sources, what Du Bois labels the "two warring ideals" residing within America and within the "older self" of a transnational Africa (*Souls* 365).[3]

Whatever its sources, the claim for community, as it is manifested through representations of family, kinship, and shared history, is so copiously documented throughout African-American literature as to be almost self-evident. In their stories, black migrants emphatically position community as an ideal, expressing it as the need to be embedded in rather than resistant to their new cultural geography. This communal impulse, although in evidence throughout migration fiction, emerges, as the following novels display, as a dominant trope by the 1940s and early 1950s. Seen through the framework of the migration novel form, the success of traveling North depends on sustaining rather than severing the threads of community. Migration emerges, finally, not so much as a physical move between places as a process of substituting one set of social relations for another.

Communal Migrant Expressions

Turpin's *O'Canaan!* (1935), Henderson's *Jule* (1946), Bland's *Behold a Cry* (1947), and Baldwin's *Go Tell It on the Mountain* (1953) illustrate the varied possibilities of migration fiction focusing on the attainment and loss of family and community. Despite differences in style, range, and effect, what stands out in these novels is the similar moral basis by which they critique the traditional north-south dichotomy. Their migration-based thematic structures demonstrate the debilitating effect of cities on rural consciousness while affirming southern community as the emotional, cultural, and artistic anchor of black urban life.

The earliest three of these novels conventionally revolve around characters who escape the vicissitudes of southern oppression only to find themselves challenged by the city's economic barriers and entrapped by its promiscuity, gambling, lack of religion, and general distance from the values of their premigration homes. Turpin's Joe Benson, Henderson's Jule, and Bland's Ed Tyler all arrive in the North, where they ignore for a time the down-home lessons of virtue and forbearance and succumb to the usual array of urban temptations, for which they are punished in one way or another. Joe and Jule finally achieve small victories over their environment, despite many setbacks along the way, by coming to value relational ties ahead of the more alluring trappings of material prosperity. In contrast, Ed so thoroughly negates every trace of his southernness that by the novel's end he has been reduced to yet another small-time urban denizen ejected from a barroom dice game. By the novel's conclusion, however, Bland has posed Ed's thoroughly unassimilated wife, Phom, as a sympathetic and enduring alternative to the lecherous Ed and thereby predicated the existence of a positive urban black future on Phom's retention of her southern identity.

The work of Waters Turpin has not been widely read despite his broad-ranging career as a novelist, poet, textbook writer, journal editor, playwright, critic, and long-time Morgan State University English professor. *O'Canaan!* was the second of his three novels, and like *These Low*

Grounds (1937) and *The Rootless* (1957) it emphasizes everyday heroism in the face of racial adversity. With the exception of *O'Canaan!* Turpin showed little interest in southern folk culture. As a setting for his writing, he favored the region around his birthplace on Maryland's peninsular eastern shore. Focusing on the area's black pioneers, *These Low Grounds* details the struggles of three generations of the Prince family to ascend from their slave roots. Despite a grand scale that some critics, including Ellison, saw as too far-reaching, the novel vaulted Turpin to temporary literary prominence and paved the way for his novel about pioneers of another kind, *O'Canaan!* Turpin had recognized the importance of the Great Migration and felt it to be a subject worthy of his far-reaching fictional designs. Having spent time neither in the Deep South nor Chicago, however, he had to come by his material secondhand. A field trip to Chicago in 1936 while he was still at work on *These Low Grounds* allowed him to meet and talk to a number of recently arrived southerners and conduct some informal field research at Chicago's Urban League (Hollis, "Waters Turpin" 291). He apparently did not conduct a similar excursion to the South. The result is a short, early section in *O'Canaan!* set in Three Forks, Mississippi, that has little of the documentary authenticity underpinning his expansive portrait of South Chicago.

Joe Benson leaves the South because of crop failure and white oppression. Expanding on the biblical reference of the title, Turpin elevates the Bensons' exodus to the level of black epic. Despite the considerable effect that the 1916–18 migrant stream had on Harlem's artistic community of the 1920s, Turpin (who lived in Harlem for a short time in the early 1930s while attending Columbia University) was the first novelist to focus on this pivotal wartime period of the Great Migration. The rise and fall of the Bensons' personal, family, and business fortunes are set against a home-front perspective on the war, the Chicago Riot of 1919, the Great Crash of 1929, the Harlem Renaissance, and the depression. Focusing on squalid tenements, storefront businesses, steel mills, hospitals, gambling dens, and a host of other work and home settings, Turpin's domain is reminiscent of the broad strokes of the nineteenth-century writers who sought to frame singular characters within the burgeoning panorama of industrialization. Like his Victorian precursors, he shows little faith in the ability of provincial outsiders to cope with their new environment. Turpin's narrator summarizes one of the novel's principal themes by yoking the Bensons' flight north to failed dreams of an entire generation of migrants: "The North was the land of promise to them. They had been called—industry needed them—a war was going on! They were forced to live in the filthiest kind of environment and scorned because they couldn't rise like yeast in a few years. Now look at them! Living in hovels, swelling the crime and charity lists. They were welcome once, but industry doesn't need them any more. It's used them, no it's through with them! It wishes to God they'd all go drown themselves in the lake!" (*O'Canaan!* 293)

Within its sweeping aspirations, however, *O'Canaan!* is primarily a domestic family saga. Joe Benson, a born leader with a strapping physique and robust constitution, is a patriarch trying to provide for his family. As one of the strongest, most resourceful characters in African-American literature, he is called upon to overcome Herculean obstacles. When he steps off the train to behold Chicago for the first time, the "call of the bustling, fabulously rich, industrial North" (19) appears to offer just the kind of setting in which he and his family can prosper. He begins a business whose success represents a perfect union of southern community and northern commerce. He turns nostalgia into profit by selling food and merchandise that remind his customers of their down-home roots.

But as Joe gains in wealth, power, and respect, his economic ascent is tainted by an insatiable greed that turns him to bootlegging and numbers-running. His moral decline parallels the disintegration of his family. One son, Sol, is killed in the Chicago riot (after having safely returned from the seemingly more dangerous soil of wartime Europe). Joe Jr. becomes a pimp before contracting syphilis and dying. After bottoming out her bank account, Joe's wife, Christine, has an affair with a gigolo under the disapproving eyes of her children. Defeated by the city, she uses Joe Jr.'s death as an excuse to return south to bury him "where he ought to be" (191). Her decision to remain in Mississippi allows for a halfhearted commentary on the unaffordably high cost of material wealth and social prestige.

The mythic possibilities of Turpin's Chicago are at best ambiguous. For someone of Joe's capacious aspirations and talents, the city is, for a time, just the kind of land of opportunity where free will reigns and where the North is, indeed, the plentiful land of Canaan. If such optimism is unique among African-American novels published during the depression, its affirmative possibilities are undercut by Turpin's sense of the innate corruptibility of his characters, regardless of their environment. He constructs the foundation of successful assimilation on the support network of family but offers no character whose development is not marked by moral and spiritual decline. By the novel's conclusion, when Joe has suffered heart seizures and walks away from Essie and Paul, the daughter and husband who represent hope for the next generation, Joe is a "heroic figure vanishing into the distance." His "peasant's trudge" (310) is one of an enduring southerner whose body has been broken by the city but whose exuberant spirit remains undaunted. In the face of such tentative optimism, the bonds of family are solidified not by prosperity but by misfortune and oppression.

Henderson's *Jule* is a family migration saga of a different kind. It celebrates the unity, wisdom, and quiet dignity of southern peasants before they come north. The novel continues a narrative set in rural Alabama. It is a story that Henderson began in *Ollie Miss* (1935), his underpraised first work noted for its sympathetic interpretation of rural life, authentic use of black dialect, and portrayal of its title character, a resourceful, independent female protagonist. *Jule* picks up after Ollie Miss has been abandoned by Jule's father to raise her child on her own. Within an established rural-to-urban structure, *Jule* does little to extend the boundaries of the migration novel form. In an effort to reflect the simple speech and naive sensibilities of its rural speakers, the novel employs what a contemporary reviewer derided as a "primer style" whose "results are often monotony, exasperation and unnecessary explanation (Nelson, "George Wylie Henderson" 100). The result is, in one critic's view, "one of the glaring failures among novels about black life published during the [1940s]."⁴

To dismiss the novel on formal grounds alone, however, fails to account for its important presence as an alternative to the decade's protest literature. Although the novel is a coming-of-age story that relies on the typical overturning of pastoral conventions found in the fugitive migrant novel form to portray its protagonist's fall from innocence, it joins Hurston's *Their Eyes Were Watching God* and Arna Bontemps *Black Thunder* in providing a strong rejoinder to the Wright school's polemical repudiation of southern black experience. Where migrant novelists such as Attaway, Lucas, and Offord followed Wright's lead in writing about alienated individuals trapped in urban cycles of violence and economic and racial exploitation, Henderson drew on his experiences as an Alabama-born latecomer to the Harlem Renaissance to set down a more uplifting, if equally familiar, tale. Tied into the central thematic structure of migration fiction, his title character avoids becoming a victim of the city by retaining the work ethic, morals, and communal ties of his Alabama folk roots.

Set in the impoverished but happy community of Hannon, Alabama, Jule's Edenic childhood is interrupted by a brutal confrontation drawn straight from the pages of slave history. A mean-spirited white employer named Boyken Keye, spurred by competition for Jule's young girlfriend, Bertha Mae, turns a gun on Jule. After Jule easily overcomes the middle-aged illiterate brute, he is forced to jump a freight train to avoid the white community's inevitable retaliation. On arriving in Harlem, he initially shows none of the usual enthusiasm about the famous city, whose fabled lamp post on West 135th Street means nothing to a hungry, penniless fugitive.

Jule soon finds work and gradually makes friends among the community's black elite and, for a time, is awakened to the allure of liquor, sex, and Harlem night life. Following the lead of George Washington Lee and Turpin, Henderson turns Harlem into a staging ground of moral debate. Jule's interaction with members of the black bourgeoisie allows Henderson to make superficial commentary on Harlem's obsession with color and class-consciousness, primitivism, white patronage, and other issues that had been commonly addressed during the 1920s. *Jule* is alone among novels of the 1940s in its dramatic restaging of these topics more than a decade after the vogue for the New Negro disappeared from fashion. Only by drawing on the virtues of his upbringing is Jule able to make the necessary adjustments to ward off Harlem's temptations. He keeps a steady job, goes to night school, and assures his success when he obtains his union card with the help of a sympathetic white printer. None of these tokens of ascent, however, signify his successful assimilation until he restages his pastoral beginnings. He travels home for his mother's funeral and convinces Bertha Mae to return to Harlem with him.

Bland's *Behold a Cry* commences in South Chicago during the same postwar period as *O'Canaan!* The novel records the deteriorating marriage and family life of Ed and Phom Tyler after Phom and their two boys come north to join Ed. Through a pastiche of random dialogue, sounds, and images, Bland captures the lively, liberating street life that has quickly transformed Ed from a lowly migrant into a licentious urban dandy. When he finally sends for his family and meets them at the train, he is "disgraced by their fresh-from-the-country appearance" (12–13). The straightforward plot follows Ed's restless move from one relationship to another as Phom competes with her more sophisticated, urbane rivals for Ed's affections. Bland attributes the family's breakup as much to weaknesses in Ed's character as to the hardships of trying to adjust to Chicago. In the novel's conclusion, when Ed runs off with his upstairs border, Cleo, his departure is predictable. Phom has realized much earlier that the southern boy who married her and went north with vague promises to make a better life for the family bears no resemblance to the grim, mean-spirited man who shared her Chicago home. In her eyes, "The old Ed was broken to bits" (52). Conversely, Ed can never reconcile why the country woman he married cannot transform herself, chameleonlike, into one of the streetwise, attractive women who seem to populate every corner of the city.

Bland problematically frames his narrative around the stereotypical opposition between the predatory black male, free and on the loose, set against the long-suffering, static, black female who must endure the basic fact that it "ain't no fun being a woman" (47). Rigidly defined by their relationships with males, Bland's women seem, at first, incapable of existing without men. Phom spends all her time trapped within the walls of her tiny home, waiting patiently for Ed to come home, dependent on his random largess. Although Ed's first mistress, Mamie, is economically self-sufficient, she, too, spends her days alone, accomplishing nothing until she powders and bathes herself in preparation for Ed's return. When Cleo becomes Ed's mistress, her fate is the same. Bland complicates his reductive representation of black womanhood, however, in the way he portrays Phom, who grows stronger and more independent as she gradually comes to rely on other women for support and community. One of the novel's most meaningful moments comes when the lonely and frustrated young mother recognizes that she has a friend and sympathetic ally in Clara, a sensitive neighbor who understands that Phom's peculiar, stoic nature is the result of growing up in the South.

Despite Bland's more multidimensional representation of Ed and his world, the author's final sympathies lie with Phom. Having completely erased his southern origins, Ed concludes his ascent trapped in the futile—decidedly urban—cycle of unsatisfying affairs and social climbing, while the future of better-adjusted migrants remains secure in Phom's "queer mixture . . . of kindness and sympathy combined with an elusive hint of toughness" (228–29). As Ed leaves once and for all, Phom is liberated by another, more powerful kind of cycle, the life-renewing seasons of her pastoral past: "All-cleansing, all purifying, the spring rains came, loosening the years' accumulation of grime, making way for the lushness of summer. In the noiseless cycle of the universe came the new rhythm of growth. Life everywhere and forever washed in the ever-renewing strength of hope" (229).

Baldwin's *Go Tell It on the Mountain* represents the geography of Harlem as the site of a far more potent ritual of purification involving the spiritual redemption of John Grimes. Structurally, that ritual is compressed into the events of a single day, John's fourteenth birthday. But in Joycean fashion, its implications extend far beyond John's personal struggle to overcome the individualistic authority of his dictatorial minister-father. On a larger level, the quest is excavated not only through the personal stories of Gabriel, Elizabeth, and Florence, who are united by their shared participation in the Great Migration, but also through the communal structures that have developed in response to their shared migration. Cutting to the heart of the relationship between the folk roots of the fundamentalist black church and the urban ghetto, the novel's enduring achievement is to demonstrate how church and family—the major black institutions to have descended intact from slavery—remain central to the lives of Harlem's first-generation migrants. The problem, as it is framed not only in the monologues and flashbacks detailed in the "Prayers of the Saints" but also as it is brilliantly laid out in autobiographical terms in Baldwin's essay "The Fire Next Time," is that the church's hold over the lives of its members is constantly challenged by the secular city. How, Baldwin wondered throughout his career, does one mediate the opposition between church and street, between the "soul's salvation" and the "wine-stained and urine-splashed hallways" where the body housing that soul is forced to reside (*Price* 339, 343).

The "Threshing-Floor" section becomes the novel's staging ground for addressing this dilemma. The setting itself—the "dusty space before the altar" where John "coughed and sobbed" as his conversion begins (194)—draws the same parallels between moral and physical geography that Baldwin establishes earlier inside John's home, "where dirt was in the walls and the floorboards, and triumphed beneath the sink where roaches spawned; was in the fine ridges of the pots and pans, scoured daily, burnt black on the bottom, hanging above the stove; was in the wall against which they hung, and revealed itself where the paint had cracked and leaned outward in stiff squares and fragments, the paper-thin underside webbed with black" (21–22). In these terms, John's spiritual triumph relies not only on personal transformation but also on cleansing the "unbelieving streets" (200), which, as he emerges into the early-morning air of Harlem in the novel's concluding scene, have been converted, in John's mind, from "some gray country of the dead" into a landscape that is "exhausted and clean, and new" (215).

The authenticity of John's transformation is tested as he and Elisha discuss the cost of salvation: "The silence was cracked, suddenly, by an ambulance siren, and a crying bell" (218). Urgent, foreboding, and hinting at crisis and unseen pain, the siren's intrusion is momentary but significant. Like so many earlier occasions in migration fiction, slum reality threatens to neutralize the potential for communion. However—and here Baldwin triumphantly repudiates the wholesale dismissal of the North by his fugitive migrant forebears—"the ambulance raced past them," their conversation revives, and the bond between the two is secure. Baldwin concludes in the communal migrant's domain, having confirmed that John's conversion has moved him from a profound sense of spiritual, cultural, and sexual isolation into a community of fellow saints where the sorrows and burdens of the northern ghetto are shared by a "multitude" of family and friends (203).

Searching for the Southern Folk Ideal: *The Living Is Easy*

West's *The Living Is Easy* is the richest portrait of migration told from the perspective of a black woman. Published in 1948, it looks back to the Harlem novels of the 1920s by drawing much of its energy from a satiric portrait of the black middle class, which she labels as Boston's "counterfeit bourgeoisie." The novel indicts black society artificially modeled on false white values and celebrates black folk life situated within a feminized, communal matrix.

Having read the novel primarily through its middle-class veil, critics have paradoxically aligned it with the very subject that it mocks. Tagging *The Living Is Easy* as middle-class fiction puts it in a position that has frequently borne the critical and cultural burden of being anti-black. The roots of this sentiment can in part be traced from white readers' biases toward "exotic" and "sociological" black literature exemplified both by Wright and the nationalistic celebrations of black identity of the 1960s and 1970s. West, as she has been perceived, has been excluded from dominant black literary categories, such as the Wright school of naturalism and the black aesthetic movement. At most, she rests on the margins of a critical remapping that has come to privilege African American-based folk values, linguistic tropes, and "pregeneric myths," to use Robert Stepto's terminology (*From Behind the Veil* ix). Reconsidering *The Living Is Easy* in the context of the migration novel form, particularly as West lays out a female communal migrant's position, allows her novel to reside squarely within these current African-American critical imperatives.

Despite her invisibility, West's entire literary career merits significant notice. The careers of one- or two-novel writers are often devalued for their lack of productivity, but by the time *The Living Is Easy* was published in 1948 West was a long-respected member of the African-American literary community. More than forty of her short stories had been published, and she had edited two of the most important black literary journals of the 1930s: *Challenge* and *New Challenge*. She remains one of the few living legacies of the Harlem Renaissance and has proved a willing and patient oral source of information about the era (Guinier, "Interview"; McDowell, "Conversations"; Newson, "Interview"). And yet West's fiction has received scarce critical notice, even while the writings of her contemporaries, such as Jessie Fauset, Nella Larsen, Ann Petry, and Marita Bonner Occomy, find new life among contemporary readers. In the 1970s, West's obscurity might have been accounted for in the context of the invisibility and institutional indifference that engulfed all black women writers and critics. When Barbara Christian, a professor at the University of California, Berkeley, began her career, for example, *Their Eyes Were Watching God* was out of print, and Toni Morrison and Alice Walker were known but to a few readers, most of them women.

The nascent boundaries of a critical perspective answering the needs of black women had nothing resembling a much-needed manifesto until Barbara Smith's *Toward a Black Feminist Criticism* (1977). Since then, however, interest in black women's writing has experienced a phoenix-like surge, which Christian and Nellie McKay have charted to similar ends.[5] West's works have not received any but passing notice in the pioneering black feminist literary studies such as Christian's *Black Women Novelists: The Development of a Tradition, 1892–1976;* Marjorie Pryse and Hortense Spillers's collection *Conjuring: Black Women, Fiction, and Literary Tradition;* and Hazel Carby's *Reconstructing Womanhood: The Emergence of the Afro-American Woman Novelist;* nor has it been noted in surveys such as Bernard Bell's *The Afro-American Novel and Its Tradition.* Despite her central and active role in the literary activities of the Harlem Renaissance, West is curiously absent both as a source and as a player in studies focusing on the period.[6]

West's fiction has failed to find a critical ground on which to rest even within the recent general studies that are charting the contours of African-American literature's distinct tradition. But as Lawrence Hogue argues, this tradition is no more "natural" than are Euro-American literary theories and canons, all of which are formed through specific ideological critical pressures rooted in the production of literature: "To fail to examine this process [of production] is to be entrapped into believing that these images and representations are reflections of the Afro-American social reality rather than productions of it" (*Discourse and the Other* 22). West does not need a reconfigured ritual ground to accommodate her. Rather, she needs to be reconsidered within the limitations of the social and literary circumstances that conditioned, and ultimately silenced, her voice. Examining West's use of migration in *The Living Is Easy* provides a means for reviving her critical reputation and placing her in a central, pioneering position in feminist and African-American discourse.

The successes of West's early career seem decidedly at odds with her present critical marginality. Mary Louise Pratt has offered a theoretical intervention useful to West's case. She condemns reader response at the beginning of the 1980s as a "bourgeois esthetics"—a consumer-oriented, dehistoricized formalism masking as a reader-oriented theory. Critics should undertake "exploring the specifics of reception as a socially and ideologically determined process and coming to grips with the question of artistic production" ("Interpretive Strategies" 205). To consider production is important because it takes a writer such as West out of a cultural vacuum and situates her inside a complex field of influences that "inspirit"—to use Michael Awkward's term—and also limit. Pratt notes that just as reception is determined by "shared norms" and interpretive communities, "production takes place and is determined by productive communities or norms of production" (206). Because discursive formations potentially limit as much as empower, production can fail to take place because of such norms as well. West's virtual silence since the 1960s is an example of this failure.

When *The Living Is Easy* was published in 1948, brisk early sales and reviews that praised the "expert handling of fresh material" (Boyle, "Review" 73) and the "professional ready grace" (Codman, "Review" 48) of the novel's style were indicative of the literary success West had experienced thus far in her career. Even though she was a new novelist, she was already an accomplished writer. While still in her teens she had won a number of prizes for her short stories. She recalls that when she did not win the $10 first prize in the *Boston Post*'s weekly short-story contest, her family "was indignant because they were so used to [her] winning" (McDowell, "Conversations" 269). West left Boston in 1925 to make an entrance in the literary life of Harlem, where she soon moved with her cousin, the poet Helene Johnson, into the apartment that Zora Neale Hurston had vacated to begin her studies with Franz Boas.

Older Harlemites such as Hurston, Countee Cullen, Wallace Thurman, and Claude McKay were much enchanted with the lively, vivacious "Dot." They saw in her an extremely likable, energetic, and talented young writer whose youthful ambitions envisioned few limits. She continued to publish short stories, both in papers like the *New York Daily News,* a forum whose questionable literary status was justified among her peers by the ever-present need to pay rent, and in more literary organs such as *Opportunity* and *The Messenger.*

Her career also extended well beyond her publications. She played a bit part in DuBose Heyward's original production of *Porgy and Bess,* an event that no doubt later influenced *The Living Is Easy.* In 1932 she left Harlem as the only woman writer to accompany Langston Hughes and twenty other Americans invited to Russia to make a film about the plight of black life in America, noting that, "My little joke is that they tried and failed to make a communist out of me" (McDowell, "Conversations" 271). For a number of reasons—including a wretched script that Hughes was unable to salvage—the film never materialized. An unconverted although enthusiastic West returned to the United States in 1933.[7]

Dissatisfied with the dwindling communal spirit of her fellow black writers, West started the journal *Challenge* in 1934 during the waning days of the Harlem Renaissance, and it appeared sporadically until 1937. It was during her work on the journal that she came into conflict with Richard Wright. The roots of their disagreement are entrenched in much of the same ground as her later critical exclusion. West's attachment to what may broadly be categorized as a middle-class position cast her in a role at odds with Wright's post-renaissance proletarian artistic vision. Under West, the early issues of the journal sought writing that aimed toward high art and to this end featured well-published writers such as Bontemps, Cullen, and James Weldon Johnson, who provided the introduction for the opening issue.

Although the older writers buttressed the venture by adding much needed name recognition, West was convinced that the diminishing renaissance fire could only be stoked by exposing new talent. She was extremely disappointed, however, in what she perceived to be the poor quality of most of the submissions from the younger generation of writers. Against her professed lack of interest in politics but following what she rightly perceived to be the flow of current black writing, West found it necessary to change the editorial goals of the journal. She willingly reformatted it into *New Challenge* in 1934, with Wright as its associate editor, and the result was writing more politically informed by a working-class social consciousness. In addition to printing Ellison's first published piece, the journal marked its more radical tone, in what turned out to be its only issue, by including Wright's well-known "Blueprint for Negro Writing." Walter Daniel has speculated that the journal's failure can in part be traced to a clash between West's reluctance to abandon her desire for nonpolitical, "quality" black writing and Wright's radical agenda that privileged writing inspired "from below rather than above" ("*Challenge* Magazine" 501). Despite her brief flirtation with communism in Russia and despite any editorializing that hinted otherwise, West was never truly comfortable with her fellow writers' overtly naturalistic tone or their explicitly politicized, radical agendas.

Leaving left-wing politics behind completely, West turned to work on *The Living Is Easy*. Early on, sections of the novel were to be printed in

Ladies Home Journal, but, according to West, the board of editors were nervous about the inclusion of a black-authored novel about black characters and refused to serialize it (McDowell, "Conversations" 276). Random House, however, recognized a marketable book and accepted it.

When *The Living Is Easy* was published, West had, for several decades, played an active, if at times oppositional, role in twentieth-century African-American literary life. By the time she entered the era of *Brown v. Board of Education,* she had a novel, dozens of short stories, and the editorship of a significant journal on her literary vita. But her involvement was to end abruptly. Starting her second novel soon after the publication of her first, West had the first hundred pages of it rejected by Houghton Mifflin. She incorporated the fragment into a third novel entitled *The Wedding,* which Harper and Row accepted at an early stage and which progressed with the aid of a Mary Roberts Rinehart fellowship. And that, from one point of view, concludes the most significant chapter of her literary life. Despite the fact that West published stories in the *New York Daily News* throughout the 1960s, *The Wedding* lay long dormant as she retired into writing a local newspaper column for the *Vineyard Gazette* on Martha's Vineyard (Cromwell, "Afterword" 350). Finally, in an unexpected literary revival, *The Wedding* was published in 1995, more than three decades after it was begun, to favorable review in the *New York Times.*

Both West's retreat from the dominant black literary circles of the late 1950s and 1960s and her long silence may in part be traced to her projection of an antagonistic readership composed from within the black population. In a world increasingly caught up in urban riots, church bombings, restaurant sit-ins, and freedom rides, West could not dismiss her fear that the militant black reviewing public would have a heyday with anyone naive enough to publish a novel like *The Wedding,* which is about middle-class manners, or even one condemning or satirizing the black middle class. Her projected reader synecdochically represented the black arts extension of the black power movement. West has observed that "it was fear of such criticism that prevented me from continuing work on my novel. It coincided with the Black Revolution, when many Blacks believed that middle-class blacks were Uncle Toms. I feared, then, what the reviewers would say. . . . I feared that some black reviewer would give 'The Wedding' a bad review, because it was a book about Black professional people" (McDowell, "Conversations" 278).

The severe reviews she projected were like some that greeted *Invisible Man.* West invites comparison to Ellison, for both writers published first novels that were favorably received in the mainstream, white press during the same period after the war, then decades passed and neither published a second novel before Ellison's death in 1994. The leftist-nationalist rhetoric that targeted *Invisible Man* during the 1950s and 1960s (and no doubt helped to forestall his long-awaited second novel) suggest that West had reason to worry about the reception of her manuscript. Without dwelling on the well-documented criticisms of Ellison's decidedly un-Wright-like novel, one may recall, for example, the *Daily Worker*'s characterization of *Invisible Man* shortly after its 1952 publication: "439 pages of contempt for humanity, written in an affected, pretentious, and other worldly style to suit the king pins of world white supremacy" (Neal, "Ellison's Zoot Suit" 108). The novel was still under attack at the New School Conference in 1965 attended by such black intellectuals as John Henrick Clarke and the novelist John O. Killens (Cruse, *Crisis* 507–9). Earlier, Killens wrote in Paul Robeson's journal *Freedom* that "the Negro people need Ralph Ellison's *Invisible Man* like we need a hole in the head or a stab in the back. It is a vicious distortion of Negro life" (Neal, "Ellison's Zoot Suit" 108).

Ellison always addressed such attacks head-on, but West, who is particularly sensitive to her reviews, withdrew in silence from a reviewing climate that drew such assessments. In the broadest sense, the era demanded explicitly programmatic and essentialist novels that offered theme-centered celebrations of black, typically male, identity. This black aesthetic position not only denied a place to the middle-class, female subject of *The Wedding,* but it also set an exclusive and excluding critical agenda from which a novel like *The Living Is Easy* has yet been unable to recover. Deborah McDowell has noted how black aestheticians such as Addison Gayle have perceived one of their critical roles to be that of granting "racial image awards" to "positive" characterizations of black manhood and womanhood ("Boundaries" 56–57). Although the limitations of such binary, racially essential categories have been ably critiqued by McDowell and a host of others—especially black feminist critics—an abiding tendency to "continue to use the yardstick that measures the 'positive' racial self" (57) helps explain why *The Living Is Easy* remains a problematic text in black literature.[8] Measured by this ruler, the novel's protagonist, Cleo, would appear to have come up short. By imagining Cleo as a complex, archetypal trickster whose resistance to the binary is out of the folk tradition, however, West ably transgresses "the rhetoric of opposition that excludes women from creative agency" (59).

The Living Is Easy charted original ground in African-American and women's narrative expressions, both in its use of satire and its revision of the fugitive, male migration novel. Yet the novel's structure is fairly conventional, not only as it follows the general structure of the migration novel form but also in the way it revoices the familiar country-to-city romance. An outsider from humble beginnings (South Carolina-born Cleo Jericho) comes to the big city, marries fortuitously (to Boston's "black banana king," Bart Judson), uses her freshly acquired social status to grasp at middle-class respectability (a ten-room house at a recognizably "proper" address), orchestrates a magisterial display of her social position once it is seemingly secured (a lavish holiday party), and then falters when her economic fulcrum is undercut by outside forces (blocked fruit shipments brought on by the beginning of World War I). Cleo's rise to fortune once she comes to Boston recalls those of any number of like-minded urban newcomers, and her fall at the end likewise recalls so many other stories that warn against a multitude of perilous evils associated with city life.[9] If the structural similarities to the popular form suggest a certain conventionality to *The Living Is Easy*, however, it is only in the most superficial way. West's highly original treatment of Cleo's ambiguous relationship between south and north, country and city, transcends the form's limitations.

By satirizing the black middle class, West provided a groundbreaking view of black life. In the hands of African-American writers, satire aimed toward its own population was a delicate matter, especially given the defensive pose writers frequently had to strike. The climate in which they wrote was clouded by the demands and prejudices of a white publishing and reading public, an oppositional structure of feeling that did not encourage reform-minded critiques of the black population as a group. Despite these limitations, however, fully developed, novelized satire was not new to black fiction. George Schuyler's *Black No More* (1931) and Wallace Thurman's *Infants of Spring* (1932) both explored the ironic implications of intra-racial conflict. Schuyler's target was black and white America's fixation on color. Thurman was well-disposed to satire—Langston Hughes called him a "strangely brilliant black boy, who had read everything, and whose critical mind could find something wrong with everything he read" (*The Big Sea* 234)—and he renounced the pretensions of the New Negro generation through thinly veiled caricatures of its better-known members. The middle class had also been the subject of fiction before West by Jessie Fauset and Nella Larsen. Fauset's *There Is Confusion* (1924) was "the novel that the Negro intelligentsia have been clamoring for" (Locke, "Younger" 162). But West's ironic depiction of Boston's black bourgeoisie made her the first African-American woman to place extended satire in a middle-class setting. Her most complex satiric position concerns her protagonist, Cleo.

Cleo's behavior is characterized by intrigue, deception, and a dazzling forthrightness. She operates as a master signifier whose skill at indirect manipulation and verbal maneuvering is the highly effective adaptive response she imports from the oral tradition of her southern folk roots. Readers of the novel, for example Adelaide Cromwell, have credited West with her strikingly original creation of Cleo. She is like no "familiar black woman in American literature" ("Afterword" 360). But while Cleo's uniqueness elevates her above the demeaning stereotypes that the black arts movement proponents eschewed, she remains a forceful character yet decidedly unsuited for mythic elevation—a point repeatedly borne out in appraisals that paint her high-spirited, manipulative actions as negative embodiments of womanhood. She has been called "a woman smitten by the virus of Agrippinas of all races, the predatory female on the loose, a wholly plausible tantalizing creature" (Codman, "Review" 48), a "vixenish heroine" created with a "steady hand" and "sardonic wisdom" (Bontemps, "Review" 16), and a "castrating female" with a capacity for "bitchery" (Bone, *Negro Novel* 188).

These descriptions—especially the last, which has elicited outrage from several recent critics—are linked by their implication that Cleo requires a critical warning for the reader. This woman, "on the loose" (from what?), like the Roman mother with whom she is paired, seeks to be the agent of her own fortune. Although this prospect may condemn her in reviewers' minds rather than separate her from "mythic" literary foremothers, her self-determination, more pointedly, aligns her with the likes of Sojourner Truth, Harriet Jacobs, and Janie Crawford. Cleo lacks the warmth of the mammy figure or the tragic element of the mulatto (Christian, *Black Feminist Criticism* 1–7). Instead, she comes to wield power in a superficial, class-conscious northern environment that would never give a less forceful woman of her background a second look.[10] Henry Louis Gates, Jr., has observed that motivated signifying "functions to redress an imbalance of power, to clear a space, rhetorically" (*Signifying Monkey* 124). Cleo seizes power whether loud-talking a maid into submission to keep her class distinction intact, invoking the force of her own silence as a means to extract more money from her husband's tightly guarded pockets, or craftily playing the role of signifying monkey among her sisters and their husbands—turning each against the other to lure her sisters north into her own home. Her modus operandi is simple: "If you could tell a bold enough lie, you could get anyone to believe you" (*Living Is Easy* 153).

John Roberts has noted that tricksters have traditionally been prompted by "feelings of rebelliousness against the values of the system which denied opportunities for self-definition" (*From Trickster* 121). The same impulse, called on as a means of resisting dominant power structures and seizing agency in a racist discursive and social environment, is repeatedly thematized throughout African-American literature, especially as it has been enacted in the drive toward freedom and literacy. But Cleo pursues her ends by an anticommunal, antisocial, and race-hating means from within her own black population. Roberts further observes that "the rebellious animal trickster, in adopting behaviors that were not only socially unacceptable by the values of the slave system but also 'morally tainted,' jeopardized the well-being of enslaved Africans within the slave system that was their only source of values and identity" (21). Cleo analogously falls outside the values of her adopted Boston culture as well and never makes a successful transition out of her liminal posture, neither free of her attachment to her adolescent roots nor fully integrated into the black bourgeoisie.[11]

But it is not just Cleo who is "tainted." West's strongest satiric indictment is reserved for the social world where acceptance predicates such behavior. Just as the animal trickster as a normative model cannot "be understood within a conceptual framework which envisions slavery as the primary source of [its] values" (Roberts, *From Trickster* 21), West's "counterfeit bourgeoisie" is satirized as an entirely inadequate norm as well. The values that are missing from Boston society are to be found within the folk culture of Cleo's premigration southern childhood. Thus, the ongoing, implicit juxtaposition of these social, geographic, and psychic poles makes Cleo's participation in the Great Migration the linchpin of West's satire.

Before the second "renaissance" of black women's fiction that has occurred since the 1970s, *The Living Is Easy* joined Larsen's *Quicksand* as the only novels by women to address the Great Migration. Explanations for the relative lack of attention given to the subject are no doubt tied into the overall structures of American women's writings. It is a critical commonplace to contrast the kinetic impulse, which drives the migration novel form, with the more static, communal, relationship-based imperative of black women's writing. Women's communal structures have been characterized by what woman-centered psychologists isolate as a collective vision of social life that challenges male-centered interpretive categories of the self-in-relationships defined by alienation, abstraction, and independence.[12] Men have long written about abandoning confining spaces for the open road, the city, the sea, the river, and other locations that threaten their sovereignty, whereas women writers, black and white, have more often either chosen or been forced to write inside a domestic space looking out on the rest of the world.[13] The narrow compartment above her grandmother's shed where Harriet Jacobs spent seven long years watching the world from her peephole remains the most dramatic African-American counter-expression of the male migratory impulse. The antipodes of a static female heroine and her peripatetic male counterpart begin, if in a limited way, to account for the comparative absence of women writers within the form. This opposition also speaks to the limitations of masculinized ascent as an all-encompassing means of delineating black success.

To this end, when, more recently, African-American women writers such as Rosa Guy, Toni Morrison, and Marita Golden began to look beyond a stationary setting to write about migration, they have more often concentrated on themes associated with the tradition of their domestic genres than with male-authored migration and journey stories. Showing minimal interest in exploring the liberating powers of the journey itself, these writers, following the lead of West and her predecessor, Nella Larsen, have focussed instead upon both the difficulties and the benefits associated with replacing one home with another.

As the earliest women to novelize a conventional version of the south-to-north migration experience, West was selective in drawing on and departing from the form's conventions. As the previous chapters suggested, the male version of migration fiction frequently conceives of migration along the same trajectory as the slave narrative, wherein movement emanates from the desire for freedom and comes as a heroic response to violent white oppression. West refigures this convention entirely, subsuming the need to migrate not in the oppression of race but in that of gender. Cleo is portrayed as too free, too wild in the South, and when she comes of age her mother sends her north with a white woman who is unmarried, a "conscientious custodian" guarding Cleo against the inevitable advances of "coachmen and butlers and porters" (*Living Is Easy* 25). But having been displaced from the South, from the communal bonds of her doting sisters, Cleo assumes a posture similar to that of other migrants. An adolescent questing figure, she enters a liminal phase, seeking admittance into a new order. Her quest is to realize a feminized version of ascent, but the quest is elusive as she remains perched between a moral center associated with the South and the misdirected normative values of the middle-class black north. Robert Bone contends that, "south and north cannot unite, even by Cleo's force of will" (*Negro Novel* 190). The reason for this schism lies not in the fact that black north and black south are irreconcilably divided. It is because Cleo's black north falsely emulates acquisitive, individualistic, hierarchical white ideals and in so doing distances itself from the folk roots of the black south. In making this point, West consciously sought to avoid alienating her readership, which was drawn from a combination of the black population she satirized and the middle-class whites on whom her fictional Boston black society falsely models itself—and who thereby became secondhand targets of her satire.

The powerful presence of the South manifests itself most fully in the feminine ties that bond mother to daughter and sister to sister. They establish a relationally oriented communal paradise, a southern pastoral norm against which West will later balance her satire of the urban north. Although Cleo's daily misdeeds and domineering theatrics are rooted in her attempt to steal some of her mother's love from her three sisters, her mother enacts a female model of emotional connection by spreading her love unselfishly and equally among her daughters. Cleo's premigration, youthful outrageousness puts her at the center of her sisters' hearts, making for the happiest time of her life: "So long as her sisters were within sight and sound, they were the mirrors in which she would see Mama. They would be her remembering of her happy, happy childhood" (*Living Is Easy* 22).

The novel's title affirms the ideal of a southern family connection. It would seem logical to assume that "the living is easy" refers to middle-class Boston black society having achieved a certain social and economic level of comfort, but such a reading is misdirected. Recalling that West had a role in *Porgy and Bess,* the phrase comes from librettist DuBose Heyward's first line of the opening number of George Gershwin's folk opera. "The living is easy" does not signify a world of middle-class ease; rather, it connotes an affinity with the idyllic southern paradise depicted in the plaintive lines of "Summertime," where one is sheltered by protective parents and cooperative nature:

> Summertime an' the livin' is easy,
> > Fish are jumpin', an' the cotton is high.
> Oh, yo' daddy's rich, and yo' ma is good lookin',
> > So hush, little baby, don' you cry.
> One of these mornin's, you goin' to rise up singin',
> > Then you'll spread yo' wings an' you'll take to the sky.
> But till that morning there's nothing can harm you
> > With Daddy an' Mammy standin' by.

The contrast between this version of the South and postmigration north is stark enough to put Cleo in "a state of suspension" (*Living Is Easy* 28). Her liminality both divides her and complicates her. On the one hand, she clings to the family bonds forged in her southern childhood, always "storing impressions" from behind the mask of a southern outsider sneering at those she outwardly professes to emulate. But another part of her despises her birthright and openly mocks the "poor darkies" from the South (260). She wholeheartedly buys into the material preoccupations of black Boston society and will purchase a place in the society's inner sanctum at any price. Her fond memories of the central place she held in her sisters' affections cause her to manipulate Bart craftily into paying for the sisters to come visit her. The fact that the sisters must sacrifice family duties to come is of little consequence to Cleo, an attitude indicative of her important distinction between the family bond and the marriage bond (which reflects the contrast that West draws between relationships among women by themselves and between women and men). Cleo finds excuses to extend her sisters' stay well beyond a normal visit. They desert their husbands, and Cleo comes close to realizing her goal of forging communal, family connections from down home with the social stature that she finds in the North. The northern and southern halves are to be symbolically fused in front of the outside world at a New Year's Eve party that Cleo throws in her new South End mansion.

The party functions—like that most famous of twentieth-century literary parties held in Mrs. Dalloway's Bloomsbury home—as a creative act of domesticity designed to exhibit the social artistry of the hostess, the "hour which gave her whole life meaning" (245). It signals that her migration, and thus her home, is complete. But the intrusive Septimus Smith of Cleo's world enters in the form of her southern guest of honor, who has been invited to speak on behalf of a falsely imprisoned southern laborer. Rather than honor his request for financial support, Cleo deftly reduces his speech to a social gaffe, a horrifying and inappropriate intrusion into her otherwise flawless party. Having already extracted what she most wanted from the South by reclaiming her sisters, she rejects his plea for racial solidarity outright and thus negates the possibility of communal ascent.

In Cleo's act of denial, West locates the primary flaw of both her protagonist and black Boston. To be an accepted part of this society she must outwardly cut all social and psychological ties to her southern roots and disclaim her past, even though she inwardly needs to be fortified by her recollections of its effect on her: "You had to be born there. . . . And when you were, her thinking ran dreamily, all you remembered were the happy days of your childhood, when being alive was a wild and glorious thing" (143).

West's task is to illustrate the false center of a black northern culture so obsequiously formal that one "hankered to pick a bone and talk with [one's] mouth full." Northern characters are dramatically laden with ironic satire: "Mr. Hartnett failed in business, and blew his brains out just like a white man. Everybody was a little proud of his suicide" (112). The North is a place where children "learned to dissolve when grown-ups were talking," where upper-class blacks move away when "old second-class niggers from way down South" (45) move in next door, and where the "chaff" of the South will "forever" be perceived as a "cross to bear" by the "wheat" of the North (46). Black middle-class northerners are better off embracing the culture of the South as an inevitable and positive extension of their culture. Their salvation from extinction lies not "in a daily desperate effort to ignore their racial heritage" (105), but in embracing the South's capacity for unchecked joy and preference for the "salt flavor of lusty laughter" (44), "boisterous mirth," and an unrestrained affection for its folk roots.

Having watched her husband leave her in the final scene of the novel, Cleo asks herself, "But who will love me best? Who?" (347). The plea captures the essence of her singular quest. She has mistakenly looked to high living, a lavish income, and social prestige as a false means of achieving the same kind of fulfillment provided by her "happy, happy childhood" and founded in the unconditional love and adulation of her sisters down home. I describe these almost universal aspirations as false because in West's satiric characterization of middle-class black Boston such trappings of success must be secured at the price of one's racial birthright. The models of racial pride—the newspaper editor Simeon Binney, Dean Galloway, and Cleo's brother-in-law, Robert Jones—serve Cleo only as annoying reminders of a heritage best soon forgotten. In the traditional context of African culture, the initiand makes the transition from the liminal phase to incorporation (*rite d'agregation*) into the new society only after having been instructed in the importance of communal living.

In privileging the selfish, acquisitive values of Boston's black elite, Cleo fails to make the transition that honors foremost "the revered ethical values of the group." (V. Turner, "Myth and Symbol" 177). Her final, forced posture of "solitude" inside her "oppressive environment" demonstrates the concluding stage of her ascent (Stepto, *From Behind the Veil* 167). The novel concludes in West's grand signification on the insufficiency of Euro-American avenues to success and assimilation, having been placed squarely within an African-American, community-based, folk cosmology.

The Migrant as Communal Individualist: *Invisible Man*

> But I know what the relief really is. It is the relief from
> responsibility. Yes, you know what the relief is. It is the flight
> from the reality you were born to.
>
> Robert Penn Warren

With the narrator's migration from the heart of Dixie to the streets of
Harlem framing its narrative, *Invisible Man* is the climactic fictional expression of the African-American Great Migration novel form. The novel
was published in 1952 on the heels of half a century of migration fiction
favoring narrative modes of expression emphasizing the environmental
sources of the migrant character's thought and action. In his *Paris Review*
interview of 1955, reprinted in his landmark book of essays *Shadow and
Act* (1964), Ellison explains the novel's style as a shift from naturalistic to
expressionistic to surreal, each stage of which reflects the invisible man's
state of consciousness as he moves from south to north, from "the relatively stable to the swiftly changing" (178). This multivalent prose style
breaks free of the migration novel form's surface of social realism.

Ellison recasts his narrator's northward journey in the mythic, psychological, and experimental terms necessary to sound out its manifold complexities. His narrative, in brilliantly foregrounding the interplay between
geography and the self, confronts the material realities of the urban north
as more than just so many crumbling buildings and racial barriers. For
Ellison, the settings of pre- and postmigration life cannot be comprehended
apart from the mental frame through which they are experienced. In link-
ing the physical with the psychological, Ellison produces the most formally
innovative and ambitious examination of what it means for a migrant to
be displaced from the roots of southern culture.

Although Ellison's mode of expression represents an original development in migration fiction, his thematic emphasis is of a piece with earlier
migration novelists. *Invisible Man* continues the lengthy African-American narrative project of searching for an inhabitable community. As the
itinerant narrator conceives the process, he struggles to be liberated from
society's perverse efforts to "Keep this Nigger-Boy Running" (33). The
dream-induced phrase emphasizes the kinetic nature of the narrator's quest
and ties it into the geography of his surroundings. Ellison records his hero's story within a framed retelling of the journey that takes him from the
battle royal of his hometown to the liminal "border area" of Harlem, where
he composes his tale while a larger, communitywide battle royal rages

above. His progress is made difficult not only by his own well-document-ed personal flaws but also by the formidable social and physical barriers he is forced to confront as both migrant outsider and black American. Ellison's surreal vision of Harlem—with its myth-charged subterranean locations, psychological forms of reality, and all too real class and racial warfare, evictions, murders, and riots—is every bit as severe and menac-ing as the jarring urban naturalism of Richard Wright and Carl Offord.

The narrator's task is to reconstitute his northern environment, amid all its deficiencies, within the context of a usable southern cultural and communal tradition. He encounters numerous authentic models for do-ing so along the way, from his interaction with various characters (his grandfather, Mary Rambo, Petey Wheatstraw, Brother Tarp, and DuPre), to folk art forms (the blues, jazz, folk tales, and folk rhymes), linguistic styles (boasts, jokes, masking, the dozens, and signifying), and folk figures based in oral traditions (B'rer Rabbit, Stakolee, and one of the novel's central metaphors, the running man).[14]

By creating a Harlem setting whose essential character is dependent on its migrant roots, Ellison indicates the cultural importance of the Great Migration. By the novel's conclusion, his prized briefcase is filled with remnants of these interactions, including an odd assortment of migrant artifacts. Rather than liberating him, however, they are tokens of racial inferiority and oppression, and despite his best efforts he cannot seem to get rid of them. Bledsoe's letters of introduction, Mary's bank, Brother Tarp's leg chain, Tod Clifton's Sambo puppet, and even the briefcase itself project unusable, demeaning images of down home. When he burns the briefcase's contents, he renounces these false vehicles of community and the authority they represent. He sits underground, putatively ready to emerge but alone, disillusioned, and having "overstayed" his hibernation. He has ended where he began, at a remove from kinship and seemingly trapped, to use Michael Cooke's phrase, in a "narrative of solitude" (*Afro-American Literature* 109).

Considering his apparent talent as a public speaker and the range of expressive possibilities that his heritage offered, how does the narrator end up there? Measured against the experience of earlier migrant characters, does his posture of stasis point to the impossibility of ascent? Or does Ellison, in reproducing the migration novel's quest for communal ascent, imagine the conditions necessary for the narrator to transcend his solitude? Positing an emphatic yes to this final query relies on discerning the all-important implications of moving, as the narrator does, from the search for an intensely personal version of his identity (the *I* that constitutes the novel's first word) to one that resides within the long cultural struggle for equality in African-American life (the *you* that constitutes the final word).

My interest in *Invisible Man* is focused not so much on definitively answering such questions as on recognizing the full range of their implications in the context of Ellison's relation to migration. An examination of the migratory trajectory of his personal history, together with those of his novel and essays, points to the centrality of migration for Ellison's career as well as for the essential, even culminating, position of *Invisible Man* among the many novels that have been so far considered. Unlike lesser-known migration novelists, Ellison's critical reputation needs no remedying. The multitude of evaluations of *Invisible Man* are among the most penetrating of those addressing any American novel. Just as Ellison's work remains central to any systematic appraisal of African-American and American literature and culture, his emphasis on the migrant's quest for identity, which Ellison has labeled *"the* American theme" (*Shadow and Act* 177), likewise positions *Invisible Man* as an indispensable literary expression of the issues and consequences surrounding the Great Migration.

Harlem: Ellison's Migration

By exploring geography's effect on identity, Ellison wrote within a literary lineage that was more pervasive than even he himself seemed ready to acknowledge. In an earlier chapter, I noted how he balked at acknowledging the influence of slave narratives as structuring devices in his writing. He also pointedly asserted that *Invisible Man* is not an autobiographical work (*Shadow and Act* 167). Yet Ellison had firsthand experience with northward migration and inscribed for his narrator roughly the same geographic route that he followed in his youth. The invisible man's effort to interpret his physical surroundings through a psychological filter follows out of Ellison's mythic projections of his own Oklahoma background. He was particularly well equipped to write about the relationship between self and place, having not only migrated from Alabama to Harlem after his junior year of college but also having grown up in the "border area" of American racial politics. Born in 1914, just seven years after statehood, he was one of Oklahoma's early native sons. That his origins were neither of the South nor North but of the Southwest defined Ellison's conception of himself as a writer. Speaking of black Oklahoma pioneers in an interview, he notes that "they had a sense of what it meant to come to the frontier because they had come looking for better conditions for themselves and for their children. . . . The people who went out there were trying to determine their fate. . . . And they did this quite actively" (H. West, "Growing Up" 11). When he writes in *Going to the Territory* that "it is no accident that much of the symbolism of our folklore is rooted in the imagery of geography," and follows by pointing out that Oklahoma "had been a sanctuary for runaway slaves," a "territory of hope," and "a land of opportunity" (131–32), he pointedly establishes his birthplace as something far different from what he calls the South's "indigenous tradition of chattel slavery" (*Shadow and Act* 198).

In 1979 Ellison spoke before an East Coast audience at Brown University in honor of Dr. Inman Page, a Brown alumnus and Ellison's Oklahoma City Frederick Douglass High School principal. Ellison refers to the "then wild territory of Oklahoma—and I assure you that it was wild! Yes, but wild mainly in the sense of its being a relatively unformed frontier state" (*Territory* 134). To misread Ellison's version of his background tempts one to mythologize the Oklahoma of his youth into a sort of free-standing border outpost at the edge of the American wilderness. In the same speech he recalls the scene in Francis Parkman's *The Oregon Trail* where the explorer comes upon the "a snug little cottage, far on the other side of the great prairie, wherein he discovered vintage French wines and the latest French novels" (134). Ellison wants to point out that such "incongruous juxtapositions" occupy the heart of frontier life and were very much a part of his childhood world. At the same time, his reference to Parkman points to his willingness to lay claim to a particularly untamed, romanticized version of his birthplace.

Ellison's retrospective appraisal has led critics to construct his past within a frontier framework of the kind delineated in Frederick Jackson Turner's famous essay "The Significance of the Frontier in American History," which viewed American civilization in the context of the settling and closing of the American West. Such appraisals no doubt contain kernels of truth.[15] As a destination for homesteaders, Oklahoma was what Turner called a "safety valve," an open territory available to people who coveted a fresh start, needed a chance to erase their past, and, in the case of African Americans, wanted a home with economic opportunity where they had control over their own lives. The most famous singular example of frontier settlement was the one-day Oklahoma land run in April of 1889. Among approximately fifty thousand homesteaders, more than seven thousand blacks gathered at the Oklahoma border for a signal to begin the race for free quarter-sections of land. At the sound of a starter's pistol at noon on April 22, they rushed south into the presumptively "unassigned" and open territory (which had been variously purchased and confiscated from Native

American residents), where they staked their claims as legal participants of the land rush.

Over the next two decades, as many as one hundred thousand more blacks followed, including Ellison's parents.[16] The legacy of these independent settlers was strong. They established longstanding, stable urban black enclaves in Tulsa and Oklahoma City and created some twenty-five all-black communities around the state, a few of which, like Boley and Langston, still flourish. Originally conceived as utopian settlements, these communities were mostly designed to appeal to likeminded religious and sociopolitical sects, although a few sprang up spontaneously in places where settlers sought to profit from the untapped natural wealth of the territory.[17]

For the generation of African-American southerners represented by Ellison's parents, Oklahoma territory was perhaps the most appealing destination in the country. With an abundance of available land and no history of black-white confrontation, it was a far more realistic promised land than the urban North, yielding in reality what places such as Chicago and New York seemed destined only to deliver in folk mythology and song. Ellison indeed had the good fortune to come of age in a location whose unique situation, in John Reilly's words, "exempted its society, for a time, from the equilibrium of rigid caste relationships prevalent in the Old South and the fixed systems of power characteristic of capitalist industrial sectors of the United States" ("Testament" 49).

Describing Ellison's past through the nostalgic reconstruction of a frontier paradigm offers much in the way of populist allure. With surprising backwater savvy, America's premier black novelist emerged untainted from beyond the margin of America's racial original sin. Through academic and musical virtuosity, he earned a scholarship to attend Booker T. Washington's black Harvard of the South; he also migrated to the black mecca, wrote the best novel of the postwar generation, and became the literary world's most eloquent spokesperson on race.

For all its appeal, however, this version of Ellison's biography tells only a partial story. He did not emerge from a frontier of dime novel iconography. He was a child of the city. In 1914, the year Ellison was born, Oklahoma City already had much in common with other American urban centers. By the late teens and early 1920s it was a thriving metropolitan area approaching one hundred thousand that shared a similar physical and social infrastructure, including segregation, with its older counterparts. With a central business district, railroads, a flourishing livestock industry and farm trade, and a money-rich, petroleum-based economy, the city had grown by fits and starts since it was settled following the land run. Soon after statehood, Oklahoma was already producing one-quarter of all the oil produced in the nation, and as the hub of this economic boom Oklahoma City was a well-established commercial crossroads with limitless resources and unexpected cultural sophistication. "Oklahoma was a great oil state in those days," Ellison recalled in the *Daily Oklahoman* on January 11, 1993, "and there was a lot of money in circulation. Much of that great pool of oil was on the northeast side and much of that property was owned by Negroes." He has added that "people are surprised when I tell them I knew a few millionaires who were black" (H. West, "Growing Up" 13). Although his recollection was meant to correct misperceptions about Oklahoma City's economic opportunities for blacks, it also broaches the more complex subject of black agency by appearing to give credence to the myth that racial inequalities are reducible to, and correctable by, financial terms and arrangements.

As a boy, Ellison was "all over Oklahoma City," where racial and ethnic intermingling was far more common than in the South. Jewish neighbors lived around the corner from the Ellison family, he recalled in the *Daily Oklahoman,* and an English couple, whom Ellison knew, owned the Blue Front Grocery across the street from the Baptist church. Oklahoma City's main area of white residential wealth was clustered in Heritage Hills, whose southern border was Tenth Street, less than a mile north of the Ellison family's rooming house on First Street in the downtown black section called Deep Second. Heritage Hills contained a large assortment of stately mansions whose enormous size, impressive architectural adornments, art collections, continental furnishings, and general air of privilege easily rivaled such better known wealthy enclaves as Shaker Heights, Ohio, or Whitefish Bay, Wisconsin. Among the many lavish homes near Ellison's neighborhood, for example, the Hefner estate, a Greco-Georgian mansion, was built in 1917 and located on Fourteenth Street. It rested on grounds displaying imported fountains and English gardens. Its furnishings included Persian, Chinese, and Turkish rugs, Czechoslovakian, French, and Italian chandeliers, Belgian lace curtains, and other adornments from its owners' world travels (Goins and Morris, *Oklahoma Homes* 174).

With Oklahoma City informally following the strict segregation laws outlined in the Texas constitution, however, the only access available to a black child was through the many servants' quarters lining the rears of Heritage Hills' spacious lots. In contrast, the "festive center" of Ellison's world was Slaughter's Hall, home to Jimmy Rushing, the blues singer who later gained fame as a recording artist and singer with Count Basie's band

and Bennie Goodman's orchestra. Above the "steady clanging of bells and a great groaning of wheels along the rails" from the Rock Island roundhouse near Ellison's home, he recalls hearing Rushing's voice cry out four blocks away. The contrast between the soon-to-be-famous singer's local nightspot and Heritage Hills' continentally furnished mansions indicates the young city's cultural diversity. The very existence of Heritage Hills only a few blocks from the "sweet, high-floating sound" (*Shadow and Act* 242) of Jimmie Rushing demands a careful appraisal of what can be said to constitute a "frontier" existence.

When he writes that "ours was a chaotic community, still characterized by frontier attitudes" (*Shadow and Act* xiii), Ellison refers to a *sensibility,* a feeling for what it meant to reside in the young state. He sensed growing up that the defining quality of the frontier seemed to be its absence of tradition. It was Oklahoma City's "ignorance of the accepted limitations of the possible" (*Shadow and Act* xv) that allowed a poor, fatherless black boy to assume his natural right to strive toward becoming, by his own estimation, a "renaissance man." But he would come to discover that he was decidedly not an early-day Jay Gatsby, formulating a romantic identity out of Platonic self-invention. Although for a time Ellison allowed himself the adolescent illusion, the "boyish ideal," of perceiving his artistic palette as a democratic tabula rasa, his true education began when he recognized the extent to which his musical notes and written words were enveloped by tradition and entrenched within the kind of diverse historical community encompassing his Oklahoma boyhood. Exploring the many nuances of this discovery would become the overarching subject of his fiction and essays. "Behind each artist there stands a traditional sense of style, a sense of the felt tension indicative of expressive completeness; a mode of humanizing reality and of evoking a feeling of being at home in the world. It is something which the artist shares with the group, and part of our boyish activity expressed a yearning to make any- and everything of quality *Negro American;* to appropriate it, possess it, re-create it in our own group and individual images" (*Shadow and Act* xvii).

In 1933 Ellison hopped a freight train for Alabama's Tuskegee Institute, where he had been given a music scholarship. Beginning as a "lark," the trip was, for the young and adventurous boy, "the next best thing to floating down the Mississippi on a raft." Whatever literary fantasies his journey provoked about freedom and independence, however, were undercut in Decatur, Alabama, when two railroad detectives, brandishing revolvers, pulled him and forty or fifty others off the train and lined them up. Although he was able to escape and hide under a loading dock before catching "the first thing that was smoking" the next morning, his realization that he had almost been detained in the town where the *Scottsboro* case was currently being tried made his brush with the law a particularly chilling first lesson in southern hospitality (*Territory* 324–25).

In Ellison's three years at Tuskegee, he made great strides in coming to understand the relation between his nascent aesthetic vision and the geographic legacy of his surroundings. Reading T. S. Eliot's *Wasteland* in his second year at college unlocked Ellison's recognition of the power of tradition, confirming for the young writer that "he 'had been involved in folklore back in Oklahoma' and that many of his ideas about life were shaped by folk rhymes, stories, dances, ritual, and music" (O'Meally, *Craft* 20–21). Living in the South gave him an important understanding of the complicated cultural purchase of southern blacks; it also made him realize that to put to work the roots of his past as an African American he must embrace the language and folklore of the region's folk past. This crucial recognition would develop into the major thematic (and comedic) drive behind *Invisible Man*.

Following his junior year, Ellison left Tuskegee and traveled to Harlem, intending, like his fictional counterpart, to spend a summer earning money and making contacts and then return south to school. The depression economy and the enticements of Harlem soon ended Ellison's college plans, however. Excepting a winter spent in Dayton, Ohio, following his mother's death, a wartime stint in the merchant marines, and several brief residences associated with academic positions, he lived in New York City from 1936 until his death in 1994. It is thus no surprise that Ellison is preeminently an urban writer.

Shortly after he arrived in Harlem, his writing career commenced with the encouragement of Richard Wright, who assigned Ellison to review Turpin's *These Low Grounds* for the fall 1937 issue of *New Challenge*. He became a steady reviewer and essayist for *New Masses* and, for a time, seemed a willing disciple of Wright's communist agenda and radical literary preferences. But by 1945, when Wright himself had abandoned the party and when Ellison first wrote the novel's opening sentences at a friend's home in Wakesfield, Vermont, he had become very much his own artist. He had developed the themes, style, suspicion of partisan politics, and high regard for technique and aesthetic integrity that would set him apart from his mentor and would ultimately lead to his famous rejection of Wright as a dominant literary ancestor (*Shadow and Act* 114–43).

Invisible Man is not the earliest text in which Ellison explored the urban self in relation to the folk south. His fullest discussion of migrant psychology is found in the "Harlem Is Nowhere" chapter from *Shadow and Act*. Originally written in 1948 and previously unpublished, the short chapter is, among Ellison's essays, a curious piece whose strident voice of protest is oddly out of sync with the rest of the collection. It is one of the few points in his career where he addresses the subject of oppression in extended prose. It is also one of the most profound analyses of the psychological trauma that the Great Migration produced. In his diagnosis of this trauma, he summed up the tensions operating in Harlem and other black ghettoes of the postwar 1940s. His representation of the move northward as a dynamic, dialectical process offering the possibilities of both transcendence and madness, liberation and enslavement, helps bring into full relief *Invisible Man*'s complex view of the relation between the physical environment and personality.

Commencing with a description of Lafargue Psychiatric Clinic, Ellison characterizes the men and women inhabiting this institution for the underprivileged as inevitable by-products of Harlem's deplorable physical, social, and economic conditions. Absent is the optimism found in the Harlem of the educated New Negro, which lay before James Weldon Johnson, Langston Hughes, and even Ellison like "a glamourous place, a place where wonderful music existed and where there was a great tradition of Negro American style and elegance"—a "Mecca of equality." Instead, Harlem is a "ruin" offering a "labyrinthine existence among streets that explode monotonously skyward with the spires and crosses of churches and clutter under foot with garbage and decay" (295). "Overcrowded and exploited politically and economically, Harlem is the scene and symbol of the Negro's perpetual alienation in the land of his birth" (296).

Many of the chapter's passages on the setting's "sordid reality" register the same tone of frustration and fury driving Wright's *Twelve Million Black Voices,* a book that had a profound influence on Ellison. In a long personal letter, Ellison praised the work for "[squeezing] out of us what we leave unspoken." The work, Ellison wrote, engaged his "deepest memories and thoughts; those which are sacred and those which bring the bitterest agonies and the most poignant remembrances and regrets" (Bentson, *Speaking for You* 210–12). Like Wright's African-American folk history and sermon on migration, Ellison's essay is profoundly deterministic. But he is less interested in the "forces which generate this confusion" than in the mental "character that arises from the impact between urban slum conditions and folk sensibilities." As existential metonyms for African-American culture as a whole, Lafargue's patients exhibit the psychopathology of a people who have been swept "from slavery to the condition of industrial man in a space of time so telescoped (a bare eighty-five years) that it is possible literally for them to step from feudalism into the vortex of industrialism simply by moving across the Mason-Dixon line" (*Shadow and Act* 295–96). On levels at once mythic, technological, sociological, and psychological, Ellison undercuts the mythology of northern freedom to summarize the deleterious consequence of leaving behind the bonds of southern community.

As a commentary on the northward exodus, the essay's most striking feature is Ellison's linkage between Harlem's "unreality" and the northern migrant's folk past. In *Invisible Man*, the narrator states in the Epilogue: "In going underground, I whipped it all except the mind, the *mind.*" Worse than the slums in which migrants are forced to live is the inevitable mental toll of "trying to give pattern to the chaos" (580). Even when the agony of urban poverty is visibly manifested in its grim physical surroundings, Ellison realizes that the less perceptible but far more damaging toll on northern slumdwellers is their complete loss of faith in the existence of potential. Ellison, in another essay, notes how Richard Wright's migration produced "changes within the 'inner world.' In the North energies are released and given *intellectual* channelization—energies which in most Negroes in the South have been forced to take either a *physical* form . . . or to be expressed as nervous tension, anxiety and hysteria" (*Shadow and Act* 88).

In a summation of the migrant condition that prefigures Robert Stepto's definition of ascent, Ellison lyrically summarizes his version of the equivocal results of ascending north and failing to remain attached to the psychological foundation of what he calls "Southern Negro rationality":

> In the North [the African American] surrenders and does not replace certain important supports to his personality. He leaves a relatively static social order in which, having experienced its brutality for hundreds of years—indeed, having been formed within it and by it—he has developed those techniques of survival to which Faulkner refers as "endurance," and an ease of movement within explosive situations which makes Hemingway's definition of courage, "grace under pressure," appear mere swagger. He surrenders the protection of his peasant cynicism—his refusal to hope for the fulfillment of hopeless hopes—and his sense of being "at home in the world" gained from confronting and accepting (for day-to-day living, at least) the obscene absurdity of his predicament. Further, he leaves a still authoritative religion which gives his life a semblance of metaphysical wholeness; a family structure which is relatively stable; and a body of folklore—tested in life-and-death terms against his daily experience with nature and the Southern white man—that serves him as a guide to action. (*Shadow and Act* 298–99)

Ellison counters the mythology of the North as a New Canaan by cataloging the bulwarks of folk life lost in the transition to this wasteland. Taken together, the "peasant cynicism," the "sense of being 'at home in the world,'" and religion, family, and folklore allow southern blacks to retain their belief in a future of "full democracy." Lacking such expressions of communal consciousness, Harlemites coin a meaning-packed rhetoric summarizing their situation. Songs such as "Blow Top Blues" and vernacular declarations like "frantic," "buggy," and "mad" represent feeble rhetorical attempts to neutralize the conditions they name. They respond to the greeting "How are you?" with a formulaic "I'm nowhere, man," a phrase whose casual ubiquity ritually summarizes the homelessness, the facelessness, and the estrangement of these "displaced persons." With his usual foresight, Ellison anticipates, and frames within African-American cultural discourse, one of the white literary academy's central insights—the disappearance of the subject (and the author)—a full generation before poststructuralism initiated its own vocabulary of displacement. But in contrast to poststructuralism, Ellison was aware that the social construction of agency is something that individual Harlemites take personally. When hearing the plaintive phrase "I'm *nowhere*," he refuses to replace persons with subject positions. Evoking Ellison's title "Harlem Is Nowhere," the phrase expands in significance from a "gesture, a seemingly trivial word" to become, as he uses it here, a passive response to fate, a phatic and tragi-comic answer to the broad query of where the modern urban African American resides in American society.[18]

This same query is central to *Invisible Man*. But by a cunning shift in terms from the essay to the novel, Ellison transforms the pathological burden of being "nowhere," which haunts Harlem and accounts for the "personality damage" of the patients in the Lafargue Institute, into that far bolder but more ambiguous condition of being "invisible," the doubly conscious state wherein the narrator is capable of seeing but not being seen, acting but not being acted upon. As Ellison's narrator opens with the famous declarative "I am an invisible man," his words denote a lamentation and a call to action. He announces in the opening paragraph of chapter 1, "I am nobody but myself" (15). Simultaneously negating and confirming a self, this seemingly tautological assertion of individualism masks his long-term, often floundering search for communal affiliations and belies the complicated migratory path that has led him to this conclusion. Several times during his career, Ellison invokes Heraclitus' famous pronouncement: "A man's character is his fate." But in a (perhaps conscious) act of misquoting, he transforms the axiom into "geography is fate"

(*Territory* 198; H. West, "Growing Up" 11). The phrase, substitution intact, underscores Ellison's stake in exploring the relationship among identity, place, and community. *Invisible Man* contains Ellison's vision of how the intersection of these subjects shapes African-American (and American) consciousness. The novel's narrative charts the narrator's effort to reconstitute himself from an individualistic American hero—an Adam repeatedly cast from the garden and forced in motion from one set of social arrangements to another—into a communal man who can settle into a fixed place of habitation within a tradition of shared narratives and practices.

From the moment the narrator enters the "main ballroom of a leading hotel" to deliver his Washingtonian graduation speech on "humility as the essence of progress" (17) and finds, to his dismay, that he is a bit player and his speech merely a prop in a grotesque stage play of racial authority, he suffers disillusioned blow after blow to his youthful idealism. In no way individual, his drive toward selfhood is a series of attempts to align himself with role models who represent liberatory modes of community. He seeks "communal ascent," that seemingly contradictory expression of freedom that conceives of mobility, self-expression, and self-reliance in relation to a rooted community. Ellison is his own best critic when he identifies this process as the narrator's struggle "to create an individuality based upon an awareness of how it relates to his past and the values of the past" (O'Brien, *Interviews* 75).

But Ellison portrays his hero's relationships in such a way that none is wholly satisfying. With gullible optimism the narrator puts his faith in a range of authority figures—from the southern college president, Bledsoe, "the example of everything I hoped to be," and the northern industrialist, Norton, who tells him, "Whatever you become, and even if you fail, you are my fate" (44), to Brother Jack and the brotherhood. Each conception of community these men of power represent is flawed and fails him, as Ellison observes, "despite [the narrator's] unquestioned willingness to do what is required of him by others as a way to success" (*Shadow and Act* 177). Viewed within the migration novel form—and within the African-American literary tradition at large—such failures are predictable and even to be expected. Always looking to advance beyond the bounds of an individual self, the narrator repeatedly identifies himself with communities that overemphasize his localized alliance to specific persons or groups who themselves reflect the values of power-based hierarchies. Expressed within the language of Toni Morrison's observations about the distinctive nature of black literature, the narrator's failure results from not heeding the guidance of an "ancestor," one of those "timeless people whose relationships to the characters are benevolent, instructive, and protective and [who] provide a certain kind of wisdom" ("Rootedness" 342). In the heat of whatever moments his tenuous loyalties arise, he fails to embrace the kind of broadminded definition of community that would properly situate him within a historically informed, culturally invested, sense of his relation to others.

If Ellison provides a model for who such an ancestor might be, it is personified in Mary Rambo, the southern migrant whom the narrator meets soon after arriving in New York. To heed George Kent's correct contention that *Invisible Man* is constructed on folk foundations is to register, in a symbolic sense, how the entire novel represents the narrator's attempt, as he says during the riot, "to get to Mary's" (Kent, *Blackness* 98, 484). It is significant that he first comes to live with her immediately following his encounter with the lobotomy machine, Ellison's particularly chilling omen of the effect of northern technology on the migrant's imagination. But even as she nurses him back to health, he is not ready to understand what she has to offer. To his frustration, she "usually think[s] in terms of 'we' while I have always tended to think in terms of 'me'" (316). Although it takes him more than two hundred pages to work through the ramifications of this difference, the transition from "me" to "we" is tantamount to accepting the "socially responsible role" he must be ready to play before he can end his hibernation. In the meantime, he has to endure a more complicated, more painful experience within another kind of community—the "bigger 'we'" (316) represented by Jack and the Brotherhood. The problem with the Brotherhood's community is its false basis of affection. With no real sense of shared culture and language that are not artificial, it demands affection based on loyalty to theory rather than to the more realistic bond of experience. In a statement that links the narrator's search for community within the organization to the more wide-ranging search for meaning laid out in "Harlem Is Nowhere," the narrator explains: "Outside the Brotherhood we were outside history; but inside of it they didn't see us. It was a hell of a state of affairs, we were *nowhere*" (499–500).

In contrast, Mary is both the living embodiment of communal ascent and a notable success story among literary migrants. Instead of trying to adapt herself to an unyielding urban environment, she resides there physically but remains immersed in the food, the language, the dress, the sensibilities, and the kinship patterns of down home. Her rooming house is a middle ground. From within the confines of this lively, disheveled setting, although not always prospering, she at least thrives. As she says, "I'm in New York, but New York ain't in me" (255). She superficially resembles the traditional mammy figure, a blues-singing widow carrying the world's burden, but she subverts the stereotype through her self-sufficiency. She resides in a black-only world and nurtures not the master's white child, as Claudia Tate notes, but the young black protagonist (Benston, *Speaking for You* 168). As the narrator's surrogate parent, she names him, offers him a comfortable, familiar home, and recognizes in him the potential for leadership and responsibility. As a blues figure, Mary sees no value in simple endurance, which is a static notion in contrast to the kinetic impulse that brought her to Harlem. Following Ellison's well-known characterization of the power of the blues, she offers the narrator a model for transcending the limitations of her experience through creative resourcefulness.[19]

The value of Mary's micro-community can be measured by contrasting it with the two other dominant modes of community posited by Ellison. His representation of the college and the Brotherhood foregrounds the pitfalls associated with inadequate communal topos. With the "honeysuckle and purple wisteria heavy from the trees and white magnolia mixed with their scents in the bee-humming air" (34), the college is initially revived in the narrator's imagination in a fanciful burst of bucolic imagery. The Oakley plantation in *The Sport of the Gods* offers the appropriate cautionary tale about such apparent southern arcadias. As long as nothing challenges the facade of benevolent community, the illusionary surface remains intact. The invisible man's real education comes outside the classroom as he confronts the entanglement of selfish motivations and prejudices that turn the college into an instrument of private ambitions. This particular Eden is fueled by decidedly unsouthern, unpastoral sources of power. Down the road rests a black dynamo, "engines droning earth-shaking rhythms in the dark, its windows red from the glow of the furnace" (34). The powerful dynamo reflects the school's technological alliance with the postmigration industrial city and, as Bernard Bell notes, serves as a fitting emblem of the college's president, Bledsoe, the figure at the school's controls (*The Afro-American Novel* 197–99). Bledsoe's power is all the more potent because he has ruthlessly mastered the art of the trickster. In betraying his racial birthright to maintain his position he masks his personal influence behind the mythic past of the founder and the economic machinery of the northern millionaires, who "descended" yearly on Founders' Day to deposit sizable checks in the school coffers.

Although Ellison differentiates between the college's founder and Booker T. Washington, the distinction should not be read as the author's denial that his Tuskegee experience provided the material for his fiction. Ellison is not the first migration writer to call on Tuskegee to insinuate the corrosive effect of northern industry and money on the South. Helga Crane, in Nella Larsen's *Quicksand* (1928), vents her frustrations with the school's elitist pretensions via the same mechanical metaphor: "The great community, she thought, was no longer a school. It had grown into a machine. It was now a show place in the black belt, exemplification of the white man's magnanimity, refutation of the black man's inefficiency. Life had died out of it" (4).

Ellison also took pains, whenever asked, to separate the Brotherhood from the Communist Party, even though his fictional representation accurately summarizes his frustrations with party politics while writing for Marxist journals in the 1930s. His denial of these connections is more about his view of art than about his refusal to be aligned autobiographically with his protagonist. That any appraisal of the college and the Brotherhood can be better understood within the historical framework of Ellison's experience need hardly be argued. Nonetheless, he has always demanded that readers consider the modernist implications of his work apart from his own life. The particular and the concrete are important insofar as they comment on the general, the mythic, and the symbolic. A leg iron and a bank are not mere objects; a journey north is not simply an excursion to a different place. They are respective avenues into slavery, reconstruction, and a broad consideration of where African Americans can and cannot reside in American culture. Likewise, however historically mimetic the college and the Brotherhood can be shown to be, they reflect Ellison's commitment to recording how certain kinds of black and white institutions in general mask an insidious self-interested politics of conflicted alliance.

Insofar as he transmutes the personal into a grander social dimension, Ellison's terms of analysis frame his particular version of modernism in historical and communal terms. One scene in particular illustrates the characteristic basis of his analysis. Not long after arriving in Harlem, the narrator happens onto an old couple's eviction, which allows him to leave Mary's rooming house and enter into the Brotherhood. By commencing his career as a public speaker, he tries unsuccessfully to cut himself off from the culture of his grandfather, Mary, Harlem, and that "self-mocking image" of southern discrimination, the shattered "grinning darky" bank (319).

Although it would be hard to account in every case for the large social forces that may have affected how Ellison staged the scene, no issue was more central to the overall interests of African Americans than where they were going to live. The scene is important because Ellison directly confronts the implications of "dispossession." Freely evoking the term in his remarks to the angry crowd, the narrator broaches the critical larger dilemma of how the evicted couple's situation reflects the alienated condition of all transplanted southerners living in Harlem. The snow-filled streets are littered with the couple's belongings, each one a powerful relic of a real and very much alive African-American cultural past no less symbolically charged than the personal items the narrator totes in his briefcase.

The details of the eviction come closer than anywhere else in the novel to reenacting the urban wasteland Ellison describes in "Harlem Is Nowhere." As in the essay, the narrator links the material effects of dispossession with their psychological results. Responding to something "working fiercely inside me," the narrator identifies the "warm, dark, rising whirlpool of emotion" (270), which drives and unites the crowd, as an emotion of shame for its impotence and for the plight of the old couple. Contrary to what the narrator believes, it is hardly his speech—a sometimes articulate, mostly ironic mishmash of false starts, contradictions, and half-formed responses to the angry calls of his listeners—that moves the mob to action. Their energy is driven by the same fury that makes all Harlem blacks feel as if "I'm nowhere," as if "one wanders dazed in a ghetto maze, a 'displaced person' of American democracy" (*Shadow and Act* 300). The scene's force generates from the collision between conscience and public law, between the crowd's indignant recognition that what is legal is not necessarily just and the white marshal's lament that he merely enforces the orders of other, more powerful men. This tension, as Ellison recognized it in his Harlem neighbors, leads to "free-floating hostility . . . a hostility that bombards the individual from so many directions that he is often unable to identify it with any specific object. . . . Sometimes it provokes dramatic mass responses, and the results are the spontaneous outbreaks called the Harlem riots of 1935 and 1943" (*Shadow and Act* 301).

"Harlem Is Nowhere" and the eviction, together with the novel's climactic riot scene, collectively offer powerful accounts of the psychological basis of group aggression. There are also larger, less personal issues at play. Ellison composed *Invisible Man* at a time when American cities were undergoing their most profound change since industrialization began. Much of this change resulted from a nationwide urban housing crisis caused by the sheer number of migrants who needed homes. Contrary to general perception, more blacks migrated north during the 1940s than in the preceding three decades. The disastrous results of federal housing policy designed to respond to the inner-city shortage make the narrator's speech on "dispossession" of national as well as local urgency.

With migrants and returning service personnel in competition for housing, by 1945, the year Ellison began to write, it is estimated that 20 to 30 percent of the American population was housed in physically substandard residences, with the figure for African Americans considerably higher (Chudacoff, *Evolution* 285). Washington lawmakers responded with a massive plan to improve conditions and relieve the shortage. For the first time, in a plan that came to be known as the Wagner-Taft-Ellender Housing Act, the federal government expressed interest in improving the inner-city residential areas whose rapid deterioration had been so graphically conveyed by Richard Wright in Bigger Thomas's spare one-room Chicago tenement, by Ann Petry in Lutie Johnson's decrepit apartment in *The Street* (1946), and by Ellison in the "dark little apartment that smelled of stale cabbage" (281) from which the eighty-seven-year-old Provos are evicted. After much fine-tuning, Harry S. Truman signed the plan into law in 1949.

Nowhere in the evolution of federal-city relationships did the distance between theory and reality turn out to be so great, however. Far from achieving its purpose, the act turned thousands of inner-city black migrants into a culture of the dispossessed. Its purpose was to provide funding for building large-scale public housing projects, redeveloping inner-city slum areas, and expanding mortgage insurance, which made it the first piece of federal legislation directly concerned with central cities. Its passage signaled that Congress was at last coming to terms with the fact that urban areas such as Harlem and South Chicago were central to the national welfare. Because both liberal and conservative interests were piqued by the potential for urban redevelopment, it was, it seemed, a bill designed to please everyone. The real estate industry saw it as a way to reclaim and develop valuable but decayed central city land sites. Mayors and city commissioners recognized its potential for luring the money of wealthy suburbanites back into the urban core. City planners viewed it as a means of rationalizing and controlling the burgeoning physical structure of the metropolis. Social reformers applauded its emphasis on improving slum conditions. Middle-class city-dwellers relied on the mortgage insurance it provided to buy FHA-funded single-family suburban homes. And the poor, inner-city residents whose homes were targeted for demolition and replacement saw it as a sign that the federal government, for the first time in history, cared about the kind of home in which each of them lived.

Such optimism, however, was short-lived for all. Administering the act quickly became a nightmare of complications, fraught with labyrinthine red tape, multiyear lag times, and overly complex legal requirements. The private enterprise required by law to help finance projects showed far less interest than anticipated. Of the redevelopment projects undertaken under the act's famous Title I, the majority leveled blighted residential slums and replaced them not with better housing for the poor but with structures designed to boost property values: parking lots, factories, shopping centers, and up-scale housing well out of the reach of the area's displaced residents. New York City even received federal money to clear land and build a coliseum. Contrary to all intentions, between the passage of the act and 1960 more inner-city homes were destroyed than were built. Estimates indicate that slum-clearance and urban-renewal programs caused a net loss of 200,000 housing units a year between 1950 and 1956 and 475,000 a year between 1957 and 1959, which led critics to charge that urban renewal was merely a euphemism for "Negro removal" (Chudacoff, *Evolution* 288). The leveled areas held primarily low-rent dwellings; the new buildings were a combination of high-rent homes and the massive, hideous institutional public structures that were mistakenly envisioned at the time as innovative solutions to the country's public housing dilemma.

White upper- and middle-class residents responded to this deficiency with a quick exodus to the suburbs. From 1945 to 1950 FHA-financed housing starts jumped tenfold, from 41,000 to nearly 500,000 new single-family homes. White resettlement was eased by low-interest FHA loans and small down payments, both of which, because of blatantly racist federal regulations, were almost entirely unavailable to blacks.[20] As white flight surged forward with Washington's blessing, black residents who wanted to own homes had to find their own means to finance their purchase. In Lorraine Hansberry's *A Raisin in the Sun,* only the ironic financial benefit that Walter Younger's death provides allows his family to exit the inner city. But in spite of the play's concluding image of family unity and hope, such windfalls were the exception. As cities were stripped of their most politically powerful and economically stable constituency, those left behind, the majority of them black migrants, were left with little political clout and even less hope for escaping deteriorating inner cities.

When viewed within the housing act's original goal of providing "a decent home and a suitable living environment for every American family," the situation of these inner-city African Americans elevates the narrator's extemporaneous speech on the responsibilities of "law-abiding" citizens in Harlem to a cruel parody of national racial justice. The act, with its implications of governmental neglect, racial hostility, and self-interested class politics, provides a fitting gloss on the postwar urban environment in which Ellison composed *Invisible Man.*

Although Ellison did not, it seems, comment publicly on the act itself, his deeply felt concern for the general urban issues surrounding its passage, the results of which are still in evidence, found expression almost two decades later when in August 1966 he was called to testify as an expert witness before a Senate subcommittee on urban disarray. The legislation played a major role in creating the deplorable urban conditions leading up to the unrest of the 1960s and, as much as any single event, was instrumental in making a fortune-teller out of Ellison. The evidence of his prescience is no where better registered than in *Invisible Man*'s final riot scene, which documents the effects of a population on the verge of a war with itself. The tragi-comic image of Ras the Destroyer appearing on horseback at the height of the riot clearly evokes the tragic political downfall of Marcus Garvey several decades earlier, all the while anticipating the appearance of a new kind of urban nationalist warrior, fearless and defiant, who would make a mark on the urban scene during the 1960s.

Having been driven underground in the riot, the narrator finds himself trapped in the coal cellar, burning the contents of his briefcase to illuminate the darkness. His position represents not only the concluding, if temporary, site of his long search for a community and a home but also serves as an appropriately double-edged culminating emblem for the history of literary migration. Ellison repeats an image of unsteady stasis first set down in the conclusion of Dunbar's *The Sport of the Gods*. His narrator sits waiting, unable to leave the safety of his hole until the conditions above him improve. He has not, it seems, completed the migrant's quest of concluding his narrative inside the embrace of a livable community. His posture, in one sense, affirms the typicality of his ascent as Stepto has described it. He has lost contact with his past, emblematized in the governing image of the childhood mealtime gathering that opened this book, but has survived to become articulate and literate. Nonetheless, even within the material limitations of pre–civil rights America, he, as a lone individual, has taken the next important step in planning his immersion back into the community. Substantial changes have occurred in the half-century since Berry and Fanny Hamilton came home to the South, unable to negotiate the perils of the modern city and permanently trapped by the limitations of their plantation imaginations. The invisible man has replaced the "'heart of darkness' across the Mason-Dixon line" for all-black Harlem (579). He has transformed the tokens of his oppression into usable energy. He has gradually remade his cellar into a meaningful site of potential transcendence. He has thus found a means to redeem a hitherto unredeemable space.

He has also temporarily abandoned a city verging on social and physical chaos and retreated into the safer recesses of his mind, using imagination to exercise control over the script of existence. By instilling order, sense, and purpose into a setting where external control has proven impossible to maintain, he has entered into what Raymond Williams identified as "a community of the medium" (*Politics* 45). Stepto earlier established this concluding posture as one of "hibernation" beyond the reaches of either ascent or immersion. The hibernation narrative is one "in which the narrator eventually gains complete authorial control of the text of the narrative, and of the *imagination* as a trope subsumed within that text (*From Behind the Veil* 193, my emphasis). Through his hibernation, which he announces is "over," the narrator is joined to the large community of literate African Americans who excavate their history to reclaim and reconstruct an oppositional environment. Fugitive slaves, on the pages of their personal stories, repeatedly performed such heroic acts of creative agency. It is no coincidence that Frederick Douglass's portrait, which hangs in his Brotherhood office, looms over the invisible man as a dominant ancestral presence. Like each of the former slave's three narratives, where he looked back on his Maryland childhood and struggled to root out its meaning, to order, even to control his history and thereby his historical reputation, Ellison's narrator transcends the limitations of his setting by the act of composition. With this gesture, he begins to envision a world of "infinite possibility," where "imagination" gives order to "chaos" (576) and where he will "shake off the old skin and come up for breath" (580). The narrator makes the novel's most pointed statement of how his identity rises from his community of affiliation when he emerges from the modernist retreat into hibernation by coming to realize that "even an invisible man has a socially responsible role to play" (581). By affirming that the communal sphere offers a potent avenue to liberation, Ellison verifies, finally, the overarching value that he places on the folklore, stories, figures, people, and events—the collective history—to which the narrator must align himself to discover who he is.

By the conclusion of his tale, the narrator no longer appears held back by the self-imposed limitations that plagued him throughout his journey. His midnight "mugging" of the anonymous tall blond man and his subway meeting with Norton suggest that he has learned to put the lesson of his grandfather into action and is ready to leave the liminal site of his hole. But these encounters also indicate that even though the smoke of the riot has cleared, the world above remains hostile. With this insight, Ellison closes the novel, having created a hero who has made the necessary strides to emerge from his isolation but also having concluded that in 1952—two years before *Brown v. Board of Education* and a decade before the civil rights movement began to register tangible results—the migration novel pattern still falls short of fulfilling the urban dream of an inhabitable geography. *Invisible Man* marks a watershed moment in migration history and literature by bringing up to date the material impact of the city on African-American culture while simultaneously anticipating the widespread changes about to occur in the national racial landscape. The novel's ultimate significance rests on Ellison's capacity to capitalize on the materials of the past as he simultaneously apprehends their imprint on the future.

.

Epilogue:
Post–Ellison Migration Novels

> Where does one run when he's already in the promised land?
>
> Claude Brown

The Great Migration ended the same decade that its negative effects were registered in nearly every major city in America. From the summer of 1964, beginning with a violent outburst in Harlem, through the aftermath of Martin Luther King's assassination in April of 1968, seventy-five major riots erupted in sixty-seven cities across the country. They were, in the words of the controversial Kerner Commission charged with investigating them, "unusual, irregular, complex, and in the present state of knowledge, unpredictable social processes" (*Report of the National Advisory Committee* 109–15). Although there were no "typical" riots, they shared some fundamental similarities. Most began as seemingly inconsequential scuffles between residents and police before escalating into communitywide violence, looting, and arson. Unlike the racial disorders of earlier decades, which usually involved fighting between blacks and whites over disputed neighborhoods, the rioters' attacks were focused on property and businesses owned by nonblacks, a pattern that would repeat itself in the 1992 Los Angeles riot. They involved so many residents—upward of ten thousand in Newark, Detroit, and other large cities where the most violent riots occurred—that civil control was impossible to maintain. Whatever their initiating causes, the explanation for the riots, as the Kerner Commission noted, was tied into "the growing concentration of impoverished Negroes in our major cities resulting from Negro migration from the rural South" (204).

In his groundbreaking sociological work *The Truly Disadvantaged,* William Julius Wilson confirmed this conclusion by persuasively arguing that after more than a century of migration, the movement's most profound effects were registered not during the years surrounding World War I, but from the period following *Invisible Man* through the 1960s and into the Reagan era. The riots reflected the residents' ongoing sense of fury and futility as they sought to create a home in the segregated inner city. With limited resources for improving their squalid physical surroundings and psychologically debilitated by the hopelessness of daily life, the rioters protested their condition in the most immediate manner imaginable: by declaring war on their environment. The news coverage, film footage, and photographs of these skirmishes brought the frustrations of living in slums into middle-class homes and provided the country with an enduring set of images of how a culture of migrants responded to the accumulated burdens of ghetto life.

Whatever their media appeal, the riots told only the sensational part of a larger, more complex story. At the same time that the dream of black progress in northern cities continued to decline, the civil rights movement was reshaping the domestic homeland of African Americans into what had optimistically come to be called the New South. The results of the movement were often slow to arrive and hard to detect, yet they were tangible enough that thousands of once-hopeful migrants abandoned the city and moved back to their places of origin. Migrants had, since the end of slavery, made a habit of traveling down home on social and work-related visits, so the trip north had always been, in a certain sense, circular. But as the 1960s ended, census data recorded a more permanent change in the pattern. For the first time since the Civil War, the northward movement reversed itself. Between 1970 and 1975, 238,000 African Americans left the South, but more than 300,000 returned, the majority of whom had either been born or had previously lived in the South. Statistically, the change was not terribly significant. By this time, African Americans were a fully entrenched urban culture: 74 percent resided in metropolitan areas, and 58 percent lived in inner cities (Johnson and Campbell, *Black Migration* 154–55). Symbolically, however, the change meant the end of the Great Migration.

This watershed moment did not spell the end of novels that recorded the experience of moving north, but it altered the terms by which migration was examined. The demographic shift southward, together with the collapse of the inner city, affirmed the historical difficulty of finding a livable home at the same time these developments opened other avenues for envisioning this quest.

Three general categories reflect the range of novels related to migrant culture since *Invisible Man*. The first are not true migration novels but are made up of urban narratives that occur after the exodus, where migration lies in the distant background. The geographic mobility that helped bring about the creation of the inner city is, in these works, no longer viewed as the inhabitants' mode of deliverance. Expressing their goals less in the language of freedom than of survival, characters have become prisoners of the city. The fictional landscapes are on the verge of chaos, engulfed in paranoia and straining to keep the streets from exploding. The range of these narratives is reflected in Frank Lloyd Brown's novel about life in the inner-city projects, *Trumball Park* (1959); Chester Himes's camp detective series, including *The Real Cool Killers* (1959) and *Cotton Comes to Harlem* (1965); Kristen Hunter's tragic story about the effects of poverty, racism, and sexism on a young woman, *God Bless the Child* (1964); Claude Brown's autobiographical *Manchild in the Promised Land* (1965); John A. Williams's apocalyptic *The Man Who Cried I Am* (1967); Gloria Naylor's *The Women of Brewster Place* (1982); and John Edgar Wideman's *Philadelphia Fire* (1990).

Employing various modes of psychological and social realism, these novels descend from *Native Son*—an alliance that Williams freely acknowledged in his Wright-inspired characterization of Harry Ames, the "father" of recent black fiction. It is not Wright, however, but W. E. B. Du Bois in his autobiography *Dusk of Dawn* (1940) who best encapsulates the feelings of alienation and defeat shared by the novels' protagonists. In defining the imprisoning quality of caste segregation, he concludes:

> It gradually penetrates the minds of the prisoners that the people passing do not hear; that some thick sheet of invisible but horribly tangible plate glass is between them and the world. They get excited; they talk louder; they gesticulate. Some of the passing world stop in curiosity; these gesticulations seem so pointless; they laugh and pass on. They still either do not hear at all, or hear but dimly, and even what they hear, they do not understand. Then the people within may become hysterical. They may scream and hurl themselves against the barriers, hardly realizing in their bewilderment that they are screaming in a vacuum unheard and that their antics may actually seem funny to those outside looking in. They may even, here and there, break through in blood and disfigurement, and find themselves faced by a horrified, implacable, and quite overwhelming mob of people frightened for their own very existence. (*Writings* 650)

The second category, closely related but not a part of the Great Migration novel form, employs a more optimistic means of dismantling the North as the mythic land of promise. It is composed of narratives of southern re-colonization that look closely to the legacy of Zora Neale Hurston. Mildred D. Taylor's Newberry Award–winning *Roll of Thunder, Hear My Cry* (1976), Alice Walker's *Meridian* (1976) and *The Third Life of Grange Copeland* (1970), Raymond Andrews's *Appalachee Red* (1978), Toni Cade Bambara's *The Salt Eaters* (1980), Gloria Naylor's *Mama Day* (1988), Thulani Davis's *1959* (1992), and Bebe More Campbell's *Your Blues Ain't Like Mine* (1992) are among the growing number of novels that challenge the conception that black and northern urban culture are becoming ever more synonymous. Even in the midst of the political turmoil associated with civil rights, these recol-onization novels recuperate a sweep of southern geographies where loyalty to the ideal of community is the critical underpinning of black life.

Spinning off these stories are the many novels that return to the ritual ground of slave life and figure it as the site of heroic individual responses to southern white oppression. These neo-slave narratives include Marga-ret Walker's *Jubilee* (1966), Ernest Gaines's *The Autobiography of Miss Jane Pittman* (1971), Ishmael Reed's *Flight to Canada* (1976), Charles Johnson's *Oxherding Tale* (1982), Sherley Anne Williams's *Dessa Rose* (1986), and Toni Morrison's *Beloved* (1987).

Hazel Carby has questioned the extent to which the blossoming inter-est in the "ideology of the folk"—embodied in these novels and, as she describes it, in the academic enshrinement of Hurston—is less an act of cultural authentication than an attempt to override the all-over painful signs of black urban America in crisis. In the face of the alarming decay of cities, even since the riots of the 1960s, Carby asks whether the con-temporary privileging of Hurston's work as an appropriate classroom vehicle for the expression of black culture constitutes an irresponsible denial of contemporary reality ("Politics" 40–42). She is rightly concerned about how and why criticism produces specific cultural meanings. Her critique of the academy's resurrection of Hurston, however, seems to dis-count the demographic reality of remigration and the fact that African-American culture, because it has been predominantly rural for all but the past few generations, makes folk attachments, in the minds of many north-ern residents, more real than imaginary.[1] The larger issue within the de-bate concerns whether the Hurston revival offers a needed corrective that infuses concepts of community and heritage into the urban canon of Rich-ard Wright's descendants or whether it establishes a willful literary era-sure of the Great Migration because the experience has not turned out as well its participants may have wished.

A small but growing number of novels written since *Invisible Man* fall conventionally within the migration novel form. Comprising the third and final category, they verify that writers have remained committed to positioning the South as African-American culture's locus of identity even as they have sought to come to terms with its overall urbanization. William Melvin Kelly's *A Different Drummer* (1962) and Charles Johnson's *Faith and the Good Thing* (1974) kept the form alive during the decades in which each appeared. More recently, Rosa Guy's *A Measure of Time* (1983), Marita Golden's *Long Distance Life* (1989), Connie Porter's *All Bright Court* (1991), and Toni Morrison's *Jazz* (1992) join Rita Dove's Pulitzer Prize-winning collection of poetry *Thomas and Beulah* (1987) and August Wilson's Pulitzer Prize–winning drama *The Piano Lesson* (1990) as expressions of a revival of interest in the south-to-north journey, especially among women writers.

The first two categories, by exploring the Great Migration's considerable aftereffects, do not address individual acts of migration directly but envision the movement as an ongoing cultural phenomenon still in evidence long after the journey is completed. The third category, in contrast, moves outside of the post-civil rights realities of African-American life to consider migration in either mythic or nostalgic terms. (The exception is Porter's *All Bright Court,* which begins in a housing project in Lackawanna, New York, in the 1960s and moves into the present.) When mythic, like *A Different Drummer* and *Faith and the Good Thing,* the narratives are only peripherally connected to the historical figures, events, and locations that play so prevalent a role in characterizing earlier examples of the form. When nostalgic, like *A Measure of Time, Long Distance Life,* and *Jazz,* the novels rely on well-known south-to-north structuring devices and set their stories in an earlier part of the century when the utopian mythology surrounding relocation still seemed real. Within these mythic and nostalgic impulses the quest for communal ascent has remained alive, but by inscribing their stories outside contemporary events recent novelists have confirmed the difficulty of creating new racial geographies that are either markedly different or more optimistic than those of their predecessors.

Faith and the Good Thing, A Measure of Time, Long Distance Life, and *Jazz* all record how their protagonists are drawn to the city in search of different versions of the promised land. Faith Cross seeks "the Good Thing" in Chicago (Johnson, *Faith* 47); Dorine Davis wants to be "her own black self" in the midst of the Harlem Renaissance (Guy, *Measure* 123); Naomi Johnson simply craves a world in Washington "away from seeing my daddy sharecropping" (Golden, *Long Distance Life* 32); and Violet and Joe Trace realize "the minute they arrive at the train station or get off the ferry and glimpse the wide streets and the wasteful lamps lighting them, they know they are born for it" (Morrison, *Jazz* 33). Numerous scenes depict the urban setting as a zone of liberation where oppressive racial structures are abolished, class hierarchies are dissolved (within fixed racial categories), and the material and cultural benefits of mass culture are everywhere in evidence. Predictably, each of these migrants comes to be disillusioned by the same moral, social, and economic barriers that have become the touchstone of the mass experience. Each is forced to make the usual sacrifices and accommodations to keep from succumbing to the combined pressures of their environments, but, importantly, all of them eventually turn to the strength of their shared cultural origins to lighten their urban burdens.

Johnson offers the most inventive demonstration of how African-American culture trades on the strength of the folk. When Faith dies of burns suffered in a hotel fire in Chicago, her ghost returns to Georgia. Her quest turns to recapturing the beauty of the past, which eludes her except as she can recover it in her imagination. She becomes an important imaginative artifact of her Georgia community when her ill-fated attempt to find the "good thing" up north becomes an often-repeated folk tale. In more traditional narratives, both Dorine Davis and Naomi Johnson live to see their children go back to the "region of quiet and inertia" (Guy, *Measure* 318) to participate in the civil rights movement. Returning to Washington after the death of Martin Luther King, Naomi's daughter voices the contradictions of geography that have pulled at her family for three generations: "Esther relived every moment of her time in the South, the land that had nurtured her kin, and then spat them out like a mutinous taste in the mouth into the arms of the North. And yet the South its cadence its promise and betrayal, flourished inside all of them, as strong as a heartbeat. Esther had ventured into that seething terrifying land to change it and, in the end, submitted to its more willful touch, felt the South mold and shape her, momentarily break her" (Golden, *Long Distance Life* 177–78). Morrison's *Jazz* reflects a similar ambivalence about Harlem in an earlier era. Animating the whirlwind culture around Lenox Avenue in 1926, the novel is a pastiche of fragments loosely organized around a quirky, adulterous love triangle that pits Joe Trace's wife Violet against her young rival, Dorcas Manfred. When Joe shoots Dorcas and Violet cannot resist taking a knife to Dorcas's corpse at her funeral, the tone for Morrison's view of Jazz Age Harlem appears to favor the bizarre in the midst of familiar resonances about filling the void of community created by two decades in "the City."

As an expression of forms and characterization associated with earlier migration novels, *Jazz*'s conventional themes are framed within an unconventional postmodern style and articulated by a one-of-a-kind narrator, who at every turn challenges the notion that any act of storytelling reflects a "true" version of events. The narrator's voice is filled with silences, revisions, self-corrections, improvisations, and alterations, all demanding that readers not only listen carefully but also supply missing notes to her jazz-inspired tapestry of words. That the novel so easily moves into the reader's space reflects Morrison's genius for breaking down customary artistic divisions between text and audience. As in her other novels, she seeks to inscribe a collective history through the singular lives of characters while remaining well aware of the limitations of language for fully encapsulating that history. Even within the failures and blank spaces of Joe and Violet's pasts, they manage to end their odyssey "inward toward each other" (Morrison, *Jazz* 228). From "under the covers" where their ecstatic sharing of cherished common memories is so meaning-filled and personal that the envious narrator is finally rendered unable to speak, Morrison concludes her tale, affirming that the truest expression of community lies in the "remembering" that joins its individual members.

Kelly's *A Different Drummer* fits less neatly into a communal category. Yet as one of the most provocative and underappreciated novels to appear since *Invisible Man* it offers an ideal point of exit for analysis of the migration novel form. Kelly moves his narrative outside the boundaries of conventional geography and history to consider the epic implications of the Great Migration. It is a racial romance constructed on the premise that a lone act of defiance by a single man sets in motion a "spontaneous" (191) out-migration of every African American living in a mythical southern state. Characterized in apocalyptic terms, the exodus begins after Tucker Caliban liberates himself from the land once occupied by his slave ancestors by salting his field, shooting his livestock, and burning his farmhouse. Small in stature, brooding and uncommunicative, Caliban is an unlikely hero but one who affirms the northern-born, Harvard-educated author's appreciation for the relative power of the black masses.

The magnitude of the movement can be measured in the wary responses of the white southerners left behind. Drawing on one of Faulkner's central insights, Kelly points to the way in which the fate of the white south is immutably dependent on the region's African-American presence. Despite whatever illusions the town's sharecroppers and Mister Harper, their self-appointed philosopher and mouthpiece, possess about shouldering the historical burden of their oppressed neighbors, the black withdrawal leaves them angry, paralyzed, and doubting their cultural autonomy.

One of Kelly's major achievements is to weigh the repercussions of migration within the South, especially—and here he is delving into unexplored material—considering it from the white population's point of view. The radical tenor of his vision is muted, however, by the fact that his exodus has a point of departure but no identifiable destination. As if stymied by the same inability to imagine a livable home that plagued earlier novelists, Kelly's vision of postmigration life remains completely uncharted. In Bennett T. Bradshaw, the novel offers a northerner who understands the importance of what Caliban has begun when he inquires, "Don't you feel you're on the site of some significant event, reminiscent of the Bible or the Iliad?" (125). But the "Ivy-educated" Bradshaw fails miserably in helping to open the doors of the promised land. Instead, this comically bourgeois agent of change foolishly travels south, where, besieged by whites bent on revenge, he becomes the sacrificial scapegoat of their collective cultural loss.

A Different Drummer offers a befitting point for concluding an examination of migration fiction because its conception of the Great Migration assumes symbolic significance that is, perhaps for the first time in African-American literature, fully commensurate with its monumental historical importance. Although other historical and literary events and movements would seem qualified for equally grandiose claims, they have, when measured by their comparative impact, fallen short—with the exception of emancipation. Despite whatever momentary racial compensation was exacted in, for example, Nat Turner's and Denmark Vesey's violent rebellions, they brought about little real change in the structure of slave culture. Likewise, the various attempts at establishing all-black colonies—ranging from the plan to take possession of Texas outlined by the hero of Sutton Griggs's curious novel *Imperium in Imperio* (1899) to Marcus Garvey's unsuccessful back to Africa movement—all failed to offer viable separatist options for relocation. *A Different Drummer* similarly registers the folk south's designs for self-liberation. But in contrast to these other efforts, the act of collective migration leads to a full-scale successful revolution. Regardless of the barriers faced in creating a livable urban home, regardless of whether, in the words of Morrison's narrator in *Jazz*, "the streets will confuse you, teach you or break your head" (72), Kelly underscores how, in the simple process of quietly walking away one by one, millions of African-American southerners have altered the course of their own, and all of America's, history.

Notes

Introduction

1. Ellison, *Invisible Man;* citations to specific pages are given in the text for this book and for the others I will discuss.

2. As the criticism of African-American literature has burgeoned, a number of studies have played important roles in charting the contours of that literary tradition and advancing critical understanding of it. Among the major studies that have been useful to me are: Andrews, *To Tell a Free Story;* Baker, *Blues, Ideology;* Bell, *The Afro-American Novel;* Carby, *Reconstructing Womanhood;* Christian, *Black Women Novelists;* Gates, Jr., *The Signifying Monkey;* Scruggs, *Sweet Home;* Smith, *Self-Discovery and Authority;* Stepto, *From Behind the Veil;* and Sundquist, *To Wake the Nations.* I also want to acknowledge the strong reception of Griffin's *"Who Set You Flowin'?"* which is a study that sets up its own compelling typology of migration narratives. It came to me too late in this project to address fully.

3. Although most blacks living in the United States are descended from slaves and are thus tied to a lineage of involuntary migration, there has been an ever-growing voluntary migration of black people into the country.

4. For brief discussions of the migration and the ramifications of available statistical information, see Jones, *Labor of Love,* 153–56; Myrdal, *An American Dilemma,* 185; Renshaw, "The Black Ghetto," 41; Sherman, ed., *The Negro and the City,* 5; Still, *Urban America,* 277; and Spear, *Black Chicago.* These and other studies that include demographic information on the migration draw on statistics from the decennial reports of the U.S. Census Bureau; see, for example, their special volume, *Negro Population in the United States, 1790–1915.* It has been common among historians to use the term *Great Migration* to refer to the wave of southern blacks who moved to northern cities during the peak, from 1916 to 1918. As the meaning of the term has broadened, however, it has become common practice, which is followed here, to refer to the entire twentieth-century period of northern relocation as the Great Migration.

5. From Washington, "The Rural Negro." For a discussion of the debate over migration see Grossman, *Land of Hope*, 38–65; also see Painter, *Exodusters*, 234–55. Painter gives an especially good account of the national responses, black and white, to the Kansas Exoduster movement, around which occurred one of the clearest and most compressed debates over southern migration. She contrasts the strong support of the radical abolitionists—Sojourner Truth, William Lloyd Garrison, Wendell Phillips, Henry Highland Garnet, and George T. Downing—with the "maverick stance" of Frederick Douglass, who was a surprisingly active opponent of the exodus. Claiming that the present situation of southern blacks was "exceptional and transient," Douglass felt it the duty of southern residents to stay where they were and not surrender by going to "a strange land" and "regard the present agitation of an African Exodus from the South as ill-timed, and in some respects hurtful" (Painter, *Exodusters* 248).

6. Miller is quoted in Marks, "Black Workers," 173; also see Griggs, *The Negro's Next Step*, 29–31.

7. Donald, "The Negro Migration of 1916–1918"; Scott, *The Negro Migration during the War*; Woodson, *A Century of Negro Migration*. For an excellent historiographic narrative that positions these early migration scholars see Cohen, "Lever for Social Change."

8. Important historical studies of migration include Farley and Allen, "The Redistribution of the Black Population"; Gottlieb, *Making Their Own Way*; Grossman, *Land of Hope*; Harrison, ed., *Black Exodus*; Johnson and Campbell, *Black Migration in America*; Katzman, "Black Migration"; Lemann, *The Promised Land*; Painter, *Exodusters*; and Trotter, *The Great Migration*.

9. For a review of migration historiography traced through its various phases, see Trotter, "Introduction: Black Migration in Historical Perspective: A Review of the Literature," in *The Great Migration*, 1–22.

10. In this vein, Carby has written that "black women blues singers, musicians, and performers dominated the black recording industry and vaudeville circuit throughout the twenties, and they are the central figures in the emergence and establishment of an urban blues culture. However, in order to acknowledge their roles as the primary cultural mediators of the conditions of transition and the producers of a culture of migration we have to challenge the contemporary histories of the formation of a black urban culture as a history of the black middle class" ("Policing" 754).

11. With the exception of those noted internally, the titles and blues lines are quoted as follows from Oliver, *Blues Fell This Morning*: Trixie Smith (63), Bill Casey (38), Bene Campbell (24), Wheatstraw (53), and Sykes (40). Oliver provides in his discussion of migration and the blues a good sampling of migration-related lyrics; see especially 12–68 (an appendix provides a discography for all of the references). Also see Oliver, *Blues Off the Record*, 156–74; Rowe, *Chicago Breakdown*, 26–62; and Barlow, *Looking Up at Down*, 288–318.

12. The significance of these letters can be illustrated by their inclusion in nearly

every study of any importance on the subject of the Great Migration. Marks, Grossman, and Henri are among those who rely on the letters for primary information.

13. Fisher, "City of Refuge"; citations to specific pages are given in the text.

14. In *Drama, Fields*, Victor Turner explores (166–230) the pilgrimage as a social process, equating the "believing actor" on a pilgrimage to the threshold status of the limen. He concludes that "as in the liminality of initiation rites, such an actor-pilgrim is confronted by sequences of sacred objects and participates in symbolic activities which he believes are efficacious in changing his inner and, sometimes, hopefully, out condition from sin to grace, or sickness to health. He hopes for miracles and transformations, either of soul or body."

15. See Park, "Human Migration," and Park's student, Stonequist, *The Marginal Man*.

16. I have found Carby's construction of the "ideology of the folk" a useful and provocative characterization. Although her primary task, as I read it, is to understand why slavery as a principal subject occupies so little space in the twentieth-century black novelist's imagination and her conclusion is founded on recognizing the romanticized distortions that result from conflating slavery and sharecropping, many of the novels under consideration—especially those falling in to the fugitive mode—link themselves to slavery and the South in such a way as to undermine, if not negate, some of these distortions.

17. Thurman, Johnson, and the blues lines are quoted from Levine, *Black Culture and Black Consciousness*, 262, whose discussion of folk sources of black consciousness, including those pertaining to the impulse of migration, remains the standard treatment of the subject.

18. The significance of Stepto's work should not be undervalued, but, as with any seminal study, his book has been widely debated and has generated much healthy criticism. If there is a weakness to his theory it is in his methodological articulation of that theory rather than in its inherent validity. His is perhaps too ambitious a claim of universality, given the choice of texts he uses to make his argument. Deborah McDowell and other black feminist critics have taken Stepto to task for the male-centeredness of his book, and some reviewers have noted his propensity for difficult theoretical argot, which in their view dulls the force of the book's major points.

19. Because of the terms' obvious significance to this study, I quote Stepto's definition of ascent and immersion at length: "The classic ascent narrative launches an 'enslaved' and semi-literate figure on a ritualized journey to a symbolic North; that journey is charted through spatial expressions of social structure, invariably systems of signs that the questing figure must read in order to be both increasingly literate and increasingly free. The ascent narrative conventionally ends with the questing figure situated in the least oppressive social structure afforded by the world of the narrative, and free in the sense that he or she has gained sufficient literacy to assume the mantle of an articulate survivor. As the phrase 'articulate survivor' suggests, the hero or heroine of an ascent narrative must be willing to forsake fa-

milial or communal postures in the narrative's most oppressive social structure for a new posture in the least oppressive environment—at best, one of solitude; at worst, one of alienation. This last feature of the ascent narrative unquestionably helps bring about the rise and development of an immersion narrative in the tradition, for the immersion narrative is fundamentally an expression of a ritualized journey into a symbolic South, in which the protagonist seeks those aspects of tribal literacy that ameliorate, if not obliterate, the conditions imposed by solitude. The conventional immersion narrative ends almost paradoxically, with the questing figure located in or near the narrative's most oppressive social structure but free in the sense that he has gained or regained sufficient tribal literacy to assume the mantle of an articulate kinsman" (*From Behind the Veil* 167).

For migration fiction, *symbolic south* and *symbolic north* are key terms because they open ascent to more than just one kind of geographic movement. By inseparably yoking freedom with literacy, the latter term becomes not only the ability to read but also to comprehend all manner of northern, urban codes, from recognizing a con artist like Fisher's Mouse Uggams to distinguishing among dangerous and inhabitable urban spaces. The ascent of an escaped slave from southern bondage to northern freedom, and who pays the price of leaving his family behind, parallels the ascent of the migrant who flees the South to avoid economic slavery but pays the price of social ostracism in urban housing segregation and intra-racial antagonism from the entrenched northern black culture.

20. For example, among recent broad theories of African-American narrative practice, are Carby, *Reconstructing Womanhood;* Willis, *Specifying;* Gates, Jr., *The Signifying Monkey;* and Kubitschek, *Claiming the Heritage.*

21. I use the term *usable past* here and throughout the study as a blend of its original formulation by Van Wyck Brooks and Lewis Mumford and as it has been examined more recently within the context of immigration in a study such as Bodnar, *The Transplanted.* In both cases, the term suggests an excavating of the past—whether historical or creative—not so much as a means of justifying present concerns but as a way of locating within the structures and languages of the present moment aesthetic, social, and cultural artifacts of experience that ignite within individuals a sense of their shared communal bonds. For further discussion, see C. Blake, *Beloved Community,* 224, 296–303.

Chapter 1: The Early Migration Novel

1. My notion of the term *symbolic geography* draws from Stepto's characterization and the influence of Victor Turner's similar concept of "ritual topography": "I should mention that my working definition of symbolic geography, in all its obvious indebtedness to the ideas of Professor Turner, focuses on the idea that a landscape becomes symbolic in literature when it is a region in time and space offering spatial expressions of social structures and ritual grounds on the one hand, and of *communitas* and *genius loci* on the other. The distinction between the two

pairings has to do quite simply with time: social structures and ritual grounds exist in time, while spatial expression of *communitas* and *genius loci* are, as Turner says, of *communitas* alone, 'moments in and out of time'" (*From Behind the Veil* 67).

2. The general tenor of the early criticism of *The Sport of the Gods* was negative. In 1930 Chamberlain found the novel inferior to the works of Charles Chesnutt; see "The Negro as Writer." In a pathbreaking 1948 study, *Negro Voices in American Fiction,* Gloster called it "amateurish in execution" (50). Turner set the critical tide of the black arts era for Dunbar. In "Paul Laurence Dunbar" he argued that the writer was (unfavorably) a bitter and scathing member of the protest tradition. Likewise, in a thesis opposite mine, Bone complained in *The Negro Novel in America* that "the novel reiterates the plantation-school thesis that the rural Negro becomes demoralized in the urban North," and thus he concluded, "that at the height of the post–Reconstruction repression, with the Great Migration already under way, Dunbar was urging Negroes to remain in the South, where they could provide a disciplined labor force for the new plantation economy. His only fear was that the stream of young Negro life would continue to flow northward, a sacrifice to 'false ideals and ambitions'" (42).

In *Native Sons,* Margolies followed Bone's lead in suggesting that the novel, in the mode of Booker T. Washington, "implicit[l]y urges negroes to submit to small town or plantation values—despite racial injustices—since cities, by their nature, are degenerate and corrupt" (30). More recent critical appraisals not only treat the novel more kindly but also make strong cases for the fact that earlier critics completely misread the novel. In "We Wear the Mask," an important reassessment of *The Sport of the Gods,* Candela refutes Turner, Bone, and Margolies by demonstrating convincingly the critical fallacy of viewing the novel as merely another advocate of the plantation tradition.

Candela, as well as subsequent critical revisions by Bell in *The Afro-American Novel,* Baker in *Blues, Ideology,* and Revell in *Paul Laurence Dunbar,* pays attention to close readings of plot, characterization, and theme. Assuming different critical agendas, the critics nonetheless converge in a similar point of agreement. Refuting what Candela calls "the body of misdirected or damaging criticism" ("We Wear the Mask" 60) that reduces Dunbar to a plantation writer voicing his anti-urban biases, the critics have forcefully demonstrated the satiric, masking power of *The Sport of the Gods.*

3. Fredrickson, *Black Image,* 97–130. Brooks remarked that "Howells was perhaps the only critic in the history of American literature who has been able to create reputations by a single review." *The Confident Years,* 142, quoted in Wagner, *Black Poets* 77.

4. K. Williams, "Masking of the Novelist," 165.

5. That the conditions of racial conflict often associated with Reconstruction were more a part of the latter decades of the nineteenth century is the general assumption of Woodward's classic study of the period, *The Strange Career of Jim*

Crow. The several-decade scholarly response to the work constitutes one of the major debates in the historical profession, a debate made no less complex by the fact that *Strange Career* has gone through four revised editions during its first twenty years of publication. As Rabinowitz notes, "During the process of revision, *Strange Career* evolved from a lecture series meant for a local, predominantly southern audience, which aimed to provide a historical foundation for hopes that desegregation would be peaceful and successful, into the most widely used survey text on the nature of American race relations since the Civil War" ("More Than the Woodward Thesis" 844).

At the heart of the work is what has come to be called the Woodward thesis, which generally stated that intensifying racial separation was institutionalized into law during the 1890s and that legal segregation was largely a creation of that decade rather than of slavery or Reconstruction. The thesis has been challenged on numerous fronts, most notably by Rabinowitz and Williamson (*Crucible of Race*), who have both demonstrated that the racial particulars of the 1890s, especially in regard to segregation, had ample precedent in the North and the South in Reconstruction laws and in de facto practice during the antebellum period. There are also defenses of Woodward's argument, however. See, for example, Cell, who in *The Highest Stage* challenges details of Woodward's thesis while generally endorsing his argument.

6. Despite the general prevalence of Jim Crow mandates, there were many examples throughout the South where local units resisted state-mandated segregation. See, for example, Meier and Rudwick, "The Boycott Movement."

7. For a thorough discussion of the black-degeneracy, white-supremacist hypothesis and the beast image of blacks, see Fredrickson, *Black Image*, 228–82; for an extended discussion of pre–Civil War white fiction as it treated black characters, see Yellin, *The Intricate Knot*.

8. See *Plessy v. Ferguson* 163 U.S. 537 (1896), in Olsen, *Thin Disguise*.

9. The critical literature on the plantation tradition continues to burgeon. See, among many, Gloster, *Negro Voices in American Fiction*, 23–30; Yellin, *The Intricate Knot*, 19–81; Andrews, *The Literary Career of Charles W. Chesnutt*, 49–55; and MacKethan, "Plantation Fiction." MacKethan usefully divides the plantation tradition into three representative strains: the benevolent paternalism of Joel Chandler Harris's folktales; the traditional tales of Thomas Nelson Page, grounded in their assumptions of black bestiality and inferiority; and the subversive tales of Charles Chesnutt, whose parodies of the form were for the most part lost on his white readers.

10. In Baker's theoretical consideration of *The Sport of the Gods*, he takes strong exception to the protest reading of the novel, which he suggests comes from over-historicizing Dunbar's fictional concerns. Diverting his reading from the plane of history to that of myth, he seeks to deemphasize a textual world of "the simpleminded, passive, migratory, black victim hopelessly cut off from nurturing (though paradoxically subjugating) southern roots and inarticulately stranded in the urban

North" (*Blues, Ideology* 121). Although it is problematic to dismiss the suggestive possibilities of readings that are historically informed, particularly in so complex a racial era, the manner in which Baker traces the "blues energy" of the text is among the most captivating and persuasive arguments for the novel's importance.

11. Bruce traces a number of contemporary reactions to Dunbar. He notes that Dunbar's wife, Alice, whose stormy relationship with her husband eventually led to divorce, was particularly angry over the minstrel tones of his second theatrical venture, *Uncle Eph's Christmas.* Dunbar's collection of stories that followed *The Sport of the Gods, In Old Plantation Days* (1903), is marked by its return to plantation stereotypes, with Dunbar unapologetically setting himself apart in "detached amusement" from his folk characters in, for example, the Brother Parker stories; see *Black American Writing,* 56–98.

12. For a photograph of the cover, see the entry on Chesnutt in the *Dictionary of Literary Biography.*

13. See, for example, "The Framing of Charles W. Chesnutt," Werner's ingenious theorizing of him as a protomodernist whose use of masks and other means of verbal indirection prefigures contemporary theoretical enterprises.

14. For the classic account of black stereotypes, see S. Brown, "Negro Character."

15. The passage to which I refer casts New York in the similar role of enticer: "New York is the most fatally fascinating thing in America. She sits like a great witch at the gate of the country, showing her alluring white face and hiding her crooked hands and feet under the folds of her wide garments—constantly enticing thousands from far within and tempting those who come from across the seas to go no farther. And all these become the victims of caprice. Some she at once crushes beneath her cruel feet; others she condemns to a fate like that of galley-slaves; a few she favours and fondles, riding them high on the bubbles of fortune; then with a sudden breath she blows the bubbles out and laughs mockingly as she watches them fall" (Johnson, *Autobiography* 65–66).

16. The two very different novels were published seven years apart, but Johnson had already written a draft of the first two chapters during the spring of 1905, just three years after the appearance of *The Sport of the Gods* and two years before Dunbar's untimely death. In his true autobiography *Along This Way,* Johnson mentions showing a draft of "my more serious work" to Brander Matthews, the renowned professor of English at Columbia University, in the spring of 1905. "He read the manuscript and told me he liked the idea and the proposed title, and that I was wise in writing about the thing I knew best" (193). Johnson makes no explicit mention of having read *The Sport of the Gods,* but the high esteem in which he held Dunbar's work—he called his inscribed copy of *Lyrics of Lowly Life* "one of my most treasured books" (*Along This Way* 152)—and the fondness with which he describes his relationship to Dunbar, as well as his interest in black urban life (*Black Manhattan*) would strongly suggest that the well-read Johnson knew his friend's novel.

17. Other critics, notably Stepto (*From Behind the Veil*), Bruce (*Black American Writing*), MacKethan ("Black Boy and Ex-Coloured Man"), and Smith (*Self-Discovery and Authority*), have discussed the ways in which Johnson looks to earlier black sources as well as to such contemporaries as Du Bois. My reading is indebted to their respective analyses.

18. The novel was originally published in 1912 by Sherman and French, a small publishing house. Among the popular subjects that a number of Johnson's critics have addressed are the similarities between the author and his protagonist and the sources of his story. Such questions are more critical than they might otherwise be because they provide insight into Johnson's perceptions of what has proven to be an enigmatic character. In "Irony and Symbolic Action," Skerrett demonstrates in a close reading of Johnson's *Along This Way* that the author lived and traveled in some of the same settings as his narrator, but the true source of his protagonist was a light-skinned boyhood friend. Despite the fact that Johnson was in many ways the antithesis of his cowardly narrator, he clearly was pleased by the novel's reception as an authentic autobiography and did not claim authorship until Alfred A. Knopf reissued the book in 1927. He set the record straight in 1933 in *Along This Way*. For a discussion that speculates on the reasons behind the surprising dearth of first-person narrators in nineteenth-century black fiction, see Yarborough, "The First-Person in Afro-American Fiction."

19. James Weldon Johnson to Sherman, French and Company, February 17, 1912, James Weldon Johnson Collection, Beineke Library, Yale University.

20. For an account of the trip, see Hemenway, *Zora Neale Hurston*, 84–103.

21. For an in-depth discussion of this scene, see Sundquist, *Hammers*, esp. 42–43.

22. Collier is the earliest of several critics who have noted Johnson's astute anticipation of the Harlem Renaissance; see "The Endless Journey," 372–73.

Chapter 2: Migration and the Harlem Renaissance

1. There are numerous historical, cultural, and literary evaluations of the Harlem Renaissance. The standard historical treatment of Harlem is Osofsky, *Harlem*. Other works I have found useful include Anderson, *This Was Harlem*; Bremer, *Urban Intersections*; De Jongh, *Vicious Modernism*; Huggins, *Harlem Renaissance*; Kramer, ed., *The Harlem Renaissance*; Lewis, *Five Families*; Singh et al., eds., *The Harlem Renaissance*; and Wintz, *Black Culture*. The liveliest and most interesting portraits of the period are still found within the biographies and autobiographies of its individual members. Hemenway's *Zora Neale Hurston* and Rampersad's first volume of *The Life of Langston Hughes* are both exemplary, and Hughes's autobiography *The Big Sea* remains the classic account, one that Rampersad notes "would never be surpassed as an original source of insight and information on the age" (379).

2. Finding that Locke's *The New Negro* "constitutes a high point for energies

set in motion at the turn of the century," Baker calls attention to the anthology's urban sensibility. It is "a kind of manual of maroonage, a voice of a northern, urban black population that has radically absented itself from the erstwhile plantations and devastated country districts of the South" (*Modernism* 122).

3. McKay's willingness to look at all facets of Harlem culture led one black reviewer to write that in *Home to Harlem* McKay had "out-niggered Mr. Van Vechten." *The Tattler,* March 16, 1928, as quoted in Singh, *Novels of the Harlem Renaissance,* 44.

4. Citations to *Cane* are from the reprinted edition edited by Darwin Turner.

5. Not everyone felt that exploring southern vernacular themes was the task of the renaissance writer. White patron Carl Van Vechten recognized this in paying Hughes a curious and backhanded compliment when he wrote, "You and I are the only colored people [in Harlem] who really love *niggers"* (in Davis, *Nella Larsen* 230). Hughes himself recorded a headline from the Pittsburgh *Courier,* "LANGSTON HUGHES' BOOK OF POEMS TRASH," and recalls being labeled by the Chicago *Whip* as "the poet lowrate of Harlem" because of the "vulgarity" of his poems (*The Big Sea* 266). But by measuring blackness only by the yardstick of the talented tenth, which neglected the folk roots of the ever-growing majority of northern African Americans, these assessments manifested ineffectual symptoms of off-target elitism and were not reflective of the feelings of most Harlemites.

6. When White wrote *Flight* he had published one previous novel, *Fire in the Flint* (1924), but was known mostly for his work with the NAACP as its assistant executive secretary. Owing to White's reputation and his novel's timely and "undeniable significance," as one commentator wrote, *Flight* was widely reviewed in standard major publications. Carl Van Vechten, who had become quite close to White after endorsing his first novel enthusiastically, also reviewed *Flight* favorably, noting that "with this second book Mr. White takes on quite a new stature" (*New York Herald Tribune,* April 11, 1926, 3). But on the whole, although there were various positive qualifications, the novel was greeted with disappointment. The quotations from reviews are drawn from the *New York Times,* April 11, 1926, 9; *New Republic,* September 1, 1926, 48; and *Survey,* September 1, 1926, 56.

7. Quoted in Davis, *Nella Larsen,* 281. In addition to Locke's review, Davis (277–81) quotes from and summarizes Du Bois's review and a range of other contemporary notices to indicate the generally positive reception of *Quicksand.*

8. Willis, to whom my reading of Hurston is indebted, provocatively labels her willingness to ignore some obvious material and historical realities of black life in favor of descending into the Florida Everglades a "utopian betrayal of history's dialectic" (*Specifying* 48).

9. Charles S. Johnson, a University of Chicago-trained black sociologist, has discussed how the depression economy inflicted disproportionate damage on black workers in both agricultural and industrial settings. See "Incidence upon the Negroes" and "The Conflict of Caste and Class." For a discussion of depression-era migration demographics, see Johnson and Campbell, *Black Migration in Ameri-*

ca, 90–100; for descriptive historical theorizing, see Yans-McLaughlin, *Immigration Reconsidered,* 141–44; and Lieberson, *A Piece of the Pie,* 239–52.

10. Perhaps the most famous example of a family on relief was Richard Wright's. Wright was living in Chicago in October 1929 when the stock market crashed. As Fabre writes of the period, "In a few months the exuberance of the South Side was entirely extinguished. Evicted tenants' furniture on the sidewalk, bread lines, workers hunting for odd jobs, the unemployed sleeping in the parks, famished children scrounging in garbage cans—all this was the new face of ruined America" (*Unfinished Quest* 81). Wright was a substitute employee with the postal service but was let go when the service was forced to reduce its hours. Despite high scores on his competitive examinations, no better position became available, and his salary plummeted from $30 to $5 a week. For the next few years, what might be said of Wright was true for almost all black writers who came of age during the era of the New Negro: Whatever energy had been available during the 1920s to work on and develop the craft of writing was sapped by the agonizing day-to-day need to find work and food. Wright's situation at the beginning of the depression makes a strong case for the unavoidably large impact that material concerns have on artistic production.

Chapter 3: The Fugitive Migrant Novel's Critique of Ascent

1. See Bone, "Richard Wright," and Fabre, *Unfinished Quest.*

2. The philosophic and literary nature of Wright's relationship to existentialism is thoroughly covered in Wright criticism, particularly in discussions of his patently existential novel *The Outsider* (1953). The place to begin locating the roots of Wright's fascination with existentialism is in Fabre's masterful biography *Unfinished Quest,* the best and most thorough of the many accounts of Wright's life (esp. 322–23, 326–27, 374–76, and 528–29). Also see Widmer, "Black Existentialism."

3. Wright's substantial contribution to the literature of the Great Migration is also much in evidence in his posthumously published first novel, *Lawd Today* (1963); his collection of short stories, *Uncle Tom's Children;* his introduction to Horace Cayton and St. Claire Drake's *Black Metropolis;* and his prose essay, *Twelve Million Black Voices* (1941). The collective effect of this variety of texts is to suggest the overarching presence of migration in Richard Wright's consciousness throughout the time he lived and wrote in the United States.

4. For a thorough reading of Wright's debt to mainstream modernism in *Native Son,* see Werner, "Bigger's Blues."

5. In spite of his somewhat clumsy handling of controversial themes, Offord remains one of the few migration authors to conceive of his novel in the context of larger global events. As Trilling summed up many reviewers' opinions, "Mr. Offord's book may not be a good novel but it is a chilling account of something that is much more than a footnote to the problems confronting us on the home

front" ("Fiction" 816). Bell also noted that "even if one concedes that Mr. Offord's bitterness had led to touches of exaggeration, this story of life in Harlem, showing how injustice and ignorance have been exploited by the forces of Fascism, is close enough to the grim truth to leave one depressed and shaken" ("Review" 16). As his reviewers note, Offord's examination of the unsteady relationship between German fascism and black nationalism was a timely subject that played an ideologically important role in offering an African-American version of the anti-fascist sentiment that white American liberal and radical writers held during the years of World War II (cf. Aaron, *Writers on the Left* 155–57).

6. Of the two "polar types," Matthews notes, "All human relationships could be classified either as communal, based on unreflecting tradition, like-mindedness, personal knowledge of the 'others,' or as societal, based upon conscious utilitarian calculation of the means required to realize conscious goals. Most relationships have an element of both, all societies do, but in historical terms one can characterize societies by whichever type of association is dominant. Thus primitive and peasant societies are characterized by a preponderance of *Gemeinschaft* or communal relations, whereas relations in modern societies are mainly *Gesellschaft* or associational" (*Quest* 40).

7. For my understanding of the Chicago School's relation to literature, I am especially indebted to Bone, "Richard Wright," a seminal article that firmly establishes the important presence of the Chicago Renaissance and the backdrop of sociological theory and practice that helped to define it, and to Maxwell, whose unpublished "Down-Home to Chicago" intelligently configures the Chicago School in relation to Wright's communist sympathies and Hurston's anthropological model of human behavior. For more historically and social science-based approaches to Robert Park and Chicago sociology, see Bulmer, *The Chicago School;* Lal, *The Romance of Culture;* Lyman, *The Black American;* Matthews, *Quest;* and Persons, *Ethnic Studies;* as well as Park, "Human Migration."

8. The influences that Park and Washington had on each other were substantial. In *Shadow and Act* Ellison writes that Park was "the power behind Washington's throne" (307). O'Meally derisively labels a summary of black "disposition" in Park and Burgess's *Introduction to the Science of Sociology,* which was used as a Tuskegee University textbook, as "a ridiculous reduction of the Washingtonian 'ideal Tuskegee student': merrily expressive, mindless, and cloaked in frills" (*The Craft of Ralph Ellison* 22–23).

9. See Park, "Racial Assimilation," in *Collected Writings of Robert E. Park,* ed. Hughes et al., 1:204–20.

10. For an extended discussion of Park's theories on black migration and acculturation, see Lal, *The Romance of Culture,* 124–59, esp. 151–59. Park's quote is taken from Lal, "Black and Blue," 555.

11. See, for example Hunton, "The Adventures of the Brown Girl"; Hurston, "Stories of Conflict"; and Wright, "Between Laughter and Tears."

12. For accounts of the debate prefigured by Frazier, *The Negro Family,* see,

among many, Clark, *The Dark Ghetto;* Lewis, *Five Families;* Valentine, *Culture and Poverty;* and, more recently, Lemann, who notes that "today the Moynihan Report stands as probably the most refuted document in American history" (*The Promised Land,* esp. 170–77).

13. For a refutation of Baldwin's characterization of Wright, see Gibson, "Wright's Invisible Native Son."

14. My biographical information for Attaway was culled from Garren, *Dictionary of Literary Biography,* 76:3–7; Sims Jr., *Lives of Mississippi Authors,* 14–16; and the *Daily Worker,* February 26, 1939, 8.

15. See also O'Meally, ed., *New Essays on* Invisible Man, 43–44.

16. In corroboration of this point, it was Ellison in his early review of *Blood on the Forge* in *New Masses* who first alluded to the family's organic structure by noting how each brother represents a traditional, complementary aspect of folk culture: Chinatown embodies the pagan/hedonistic impulse; Melody, the artistic; and Big Mat, foreshortened from the biblical Matthew, the religious ("The Great Migration" 23–24).

17. Arna Bontemps anticipated the more positive critical appraisal of slave narratives by more than a decade. By the late 1960s he and a small group of scholars were already touting the slave narratives' importance. He wrote: "From the [slave] narratives came the spirit and the vitality and the angle of vision responsible for the most effective prose writing by black American writers from William Wells Brown to Charles W. Chesnutt, from W. E. B. Du Bois to Richard Wright, Ralph Ellison, and James Baldwin. Consciously or unconsciously, all of these reveal in their writing a debt to the narratives, a debt that stands in marked contrast to the relatively smaller obligations they owe the more recognized arbiters of fiction or autobiography in their time" (*Great Slave Narratives* 10). Bontemps preceded Blassingame's *The Slave Community* and Genovese's *Roll Jordon, Roll* by three years, both of which were instrumental in taking the focus of studies of slavery out of the hands of slaveowners and putting it into the mouths and hearts of the slaves themselves. For details on this extremely important historiographic progression, which is in a large degree tied into the scholarly exchange surrounding Blassingame's book and Elkins, *Slavery,* see Lane, *The Debate over Slavery,* and Van Deburg, *Slavery and Race.* The best general discussion on the use of slave narratives by historians and on the gamut of issues surrounding slavery in historical literature is found in Meier and Rudwick, "The Historiography of Slavery," 239–76. I thank an anonymous reader for calling attention to this important book.

18. The standard study for countering these earlier assessments of slave narratives and laying a claim to the slave narrative's centrality in African-American literature is Andrews, *To Tell a Free Story,* esp. 265–91.

19. The preciseness of Olney's article outside his central thesis lends itself well to being quoted in length. For overviews of the conventions that govern slave narratives, see also Stepto, *From Behind the Veil,* esp. 3–31; Hedin, "Strategies of Form"; Osofsky, "Introduction," in *Puttin' on Ole Massa;* Klotman, *Another Man*

Gone, 10–23; Nichols, *Many Thousand Gone;* and Gates, Jr., "Binary Oppositions."

Although I adopt Olney's categories, I am less persuaded by his thesis. His paradigms are useful to the extent that they allow generalization about certain commonalities inherent in so large a body of literature. A summary assessment of the narratives states: "An autobiography or a piece of imaginative literature may of course observe certain conventions, but it cannot be only, merely conventional without ceasing to be satisfactory as either autobiography or literature, and that is the case, I should say, with all the slave narratives except the great one by Frederick Douglass" ("'I Was Born'" 168). The implications of such a claim raise a number of questions. What are the criteria for determining, for example, where a member of any genre—for example, *Paradise Lost*—ceases being a "merely conventional" epic and thereby becomes "satisfactory"? What separates a genre such as Japanese haiku or a Pindaric ode—whose success is in part defined by its adherence to rigid conventions—from "looser" genres such as slave narratives? What features of Douglass's narratives are specifically not conventions that somehow elevate them above other narratives? Would a wholly unconventional narrative—or any other generic member—necessarily be more satisfactory?

20. My use of the concept of intertextuality favors Roland Barthe's gloss of the term, to which he assigns a wide enough range of possibility to allow a multitude of ways to investigate the relationship among texts. Asserting that intertextuality "clearly cannot be reduced to a problem of sources and influences," and generalizing about what he calls "a prerequisite for any text," he writes that "every text is an intertext; other texts are present in it, at variable levels, in more or less recognizable forms: the texts of the previous culture and those of the surrounding culture; every text is a new fabric woven out of bygone quotations. Scraps of code, formulas, rhythmic patterns, fragments of social idioms, etc. are absorbed into the text and redistributed in it, for there is always language prior to the text and language around it. A prerequisite for any text, intertextuality cannot be reduced to a problem of sources and influences; it is a general field of anonymous formulas whose origin is seldom identifiable, of unconscious or automatic quotations given without quotations marks" ("Théorie du texte"). Julia Kristeva is stricter in her definition, referring to intertextuality as "a mosaic of quotations" and implying from this that intertextuality occurs when, and only when, one text can be shown to have directly borrowed from another text (*Semeiotike* 146).

21. The numerous precedents for the father as enslaver are well established within slave literature; even the wives of slave owners viewed the large number of master-sired slave children as a built-in part of the system. Consider, for example, where Harriet Jacobs writes that "Southern women often marry a man knowing that he is the father of many little slaves. They do not trouble themselves about it. They regard such children as property, as marketable as the pigs on the plantation" (*Incidents* 57). Frederick Douglass recalled that "slaveholders have ordained, and by law established, that the children of slave women shall in all cases follow

the condition of their mothers; and this is done obviously to administer to their own lusts, and make a gratification of their wicked desires profitable as well as pleasurable; for by this cunning arrangement, the slaveholder, in cases not a few, sustains to his slaves the double relation of master and father" (*Narrative* 2).

22. In a 1968 study Margolies was one of the earliest critics to recognize the importance of *Blood on the Forge*. In writing about the boxcar migration scene, he astutely noted that it conjures up both ends of the life-cycle: It is a womb out of which the brothers will be propelled into the industrial north and a coffin that signals the death of their essential attachments to southern folk culture (*Native Sons* 55).

Chapter 4: The Communal Migrant's Recuperation of Immersion

1. For a discussion of the politics of community in both critical theory and in American women's and African-American literature (particularly in *Song of Solomon*), see Clayton, *Pleasures of Babel*, 99–106, 130–45.

2. In *Modernism*, Baker links modernism and African-American writing by defining the term in the context of black writers normally excluded from the modernist equation. His argument is that the enforced separateness of black writing within white culture makes all African-American writing, to a degree, modernist. Marginality can be viewed thus not as a sign of aesthetic or cultural inferiority, but as a literary virtue.

3. Both Williamson (*Crucible of Race* 409–13) and Sundquist (*To Wake the Nations* 459–67) find a distinctly Hegelian position underlying Du Bois's later writings, and Sundquist traces the "messianic dimensions of Du Bois's intellectual efforts and public leadership" (463) back to *The Souls of Black Folk*.

4. Greene, "Black Novelists," 394. Greene's assessment was not harsh enough to keep him from writing an introduction and editing a new edition of the novel for the University of Alabama Press's Library of Alabama Classics series, published in 1989. Conditionally more praiseworthy in his useful introduction, he positions the novel as a stylistic precursor to Toni Morrison's *Bluest Eye* (1970) and as an early affirmation of southern experience that would find later expression in the works of Ernest Gaines.

5. Christian offers personal reflections on the ever-changing, mostly improving contours of black feminist criticism in "But What Do We Think We're Doing Anyway" (esp. 64–65). McKay recounts a personal, institutional development of black women's criticism, especially as it takes place in predominately white academic institutions ("Literature and Politics"). Also see Werner (*Black American Women Novelists*) for a highly useful description of the institutional, historical progression of black feminist criticism as it has occurred through its various historical waves of critical "mothers" and "grandmothers."

6. One of the few extended discussions, Bone's early treatment of *The Living Is Easy* in *The Negro Novel in America*, found it to be a novel of some merit, al-

though his conclusions about the novel's protagonist were later severely criticized by Smith and others (*Towards a Black Feminist Criticism*). Huggins in *Harlem Renaissance,* Lewis in *When Harlem Was in Vogue,* and Wintz in *Black Culture and the Harlem Renaissance* do not mention West in any significant way. Recent critical focus on her has been limited to interviews and Clark's descriptive article that contextualizes her place among African-American Boston writers ("Boston Black and White"). Rampersad has conjectured a possible romantic link between West and Langston Hughes (*Life* 268). The most informative and sympathetic treatment of *The Living Is Easy,* drawn with an eye toward West's biography and offering a sociological perspective on the novel, is Adelaide Cromwell's afterword in the Feminist Press edition of the novel (1977).

7. The biographical material for West has been collated from the Dorothy West Papers, Mugar Library, Boston University; Cromwell, "Afterword"; Daniel, "*Challenge* Magazine"; Ferguson, "Dorothy West"; Guinier, "Interview"; Newson, "An Interview"; and McDowell, "Conversations."

8. Nellie McKay has observed that the ascendancy of black women writers (and the tension between them and their male counterparts) is in part due to the manner in which they have avoided racially essential categories: "While black men projected visions of a world in which race provided almost the only area of conflict between black and white men in the struggle for manhood and power, black women writers have always rejected such binary oppositions and created fictional worlds in which the self is in constant interaction with a variety of issues, including race" ("Literature and Politics" 94).

9. The various conventions that identify the genre and so emphasize its consistency are considered in Wohl ("The 'Country Boy' Myth") and Siegal (*Image of the American City*), both extended examinations of these popular traditions.

10. There is a marked contrast between West's protagonist and the stereotyped black women honoring plantation ideals of loyalty and devotion that Christian describes. West ingeniously locates just such a normative perception of black women in Cleo's first northern white benefactress and then undermines the stereotype entirely. Nowhere is her satire more obvious than when she writes, "From what Miss Boorum had read of southern colored people they were devoted to what they quaintly called 'my white folks,' and quite disdainful of their own kind, often referring to them as 'niggers.' They like to think of themselves as an integral part of the family, and preferred to die in its bosom rather than any place else. It was to be hoped that Cleo would show the same sterling loyalty" (*Living Is Easy* 27).

11. My reference to liminality invokes the term as it was discussed earlier in the introduction. Characterized by Victor Turner, the "liminal phase" of rites of passage is characterized as the tenuous period after which "an individual or group either from an earlier fixed point in the social structure, from a set of cultural conditions (a 'state'), or from both" has reached a "cultural realm that has few or none of the attributes of the past or coming state" (*Drama, Fields* 94).

12. I refer here especially to the work of Nancy Chodorow and Carol Gilli-

gan. The role of community in black women's writing is especially prevalent in the criticism of and on Toni Morrison. See, for example, Gillespie and Kubitschek, "Who Cares?"

13. Writers are not the only artists to try and come to terms with such an opposition. Consider the following well-known blues lines: "When a woman gets the blues, she hangs her li'l head an' cries, / When a woman gets blue she hangs her head an' cries, / But when a man gets the blues, he flags a mail train and rides" (Oliver, *Blues Off the Record* 159).

14. Given the charge, particularly during the black arts era, that Ellison's novel is by its assertion of universality necessarily antiblack, the numerous commentaries on the indelible imprint of African-American folklore on the entire structure of the work have done much to foreground Ellison's profound understanding of the relation between folk forms, black experience, and American culture at large. A list illustrating but not exhausting critical interest in Ellison's use of the folk includes Blake, "Ritual and Rationalization," 121–36; Dance, *Shuckin' and Jivin'*; Kent, *Blackness,* 152–63, 184–201, and "Ralph Ellison," 95–104; Forrest, "Luminosity," 308–21; Neal, "Ellison's Zoot Suit," 105–25; and O'Meally, *The Craft of Ralph Ellison.* For a discussion of the running man motif, see Klotman, "The Running Man," 277–88.

15. See, for example, references to Ellison's "frontier belief in a free and open territory" (Busby, *Ralph Ellison* 2) and his "frontier paradigm of liminality" (Ostendorf, "Ralph Waldo Ellison" 99).

16. My estimates for the number of participants in the land run, including the number of blacks who participated and followed soon after, are from Grossman, *Land of Hope,* 24; and McReynolds, *Oklahoma,* 289–92.

17. Johnson and Campbell, *Black Migration in America,* 64–65. For further discussion of all-black Oklahoma communities, see Hill, "The All-Negro Communities of Oklahoma."

18. Among the few critical articles touching on the chapter, Wright's "Shadowing Ellison" is particularly illuminating in viewing Ellison's portrait of the Lafargue Clinic as a "backdrop of . . . tragic adaptation of symbolic action to social pathology" (70). Reilly briefly touches on the essay in "The Testament of Ralph Ellison," 58–60, and proclaims "Harlem Is Nowhere" as the place in which Ellison "comes nearer than anywhere else to attempting a total analysis of the Afro-American condition" (59).

19. Ellison's definition of the often improvised twelve-bar stanzas divided into three sections with an *a-a-b* rhyme scheme known as the blues is quoted in *Shadow and Act:* "The blues is an impulse to keep the painful details and episodes of a brutal experience alive in one's aching consciousness, to finger its jagged grain, and to transcend it, not by the consolation of philosophy but by squeezing from it a near-tragic, near-comic lyricism. As a form, the blues is an autobiographical chronicle of personal catastrophe expressed lyrically" (78–79).

20. For damning accounts of the racist basis of FHA policy, see Abrams, *Forbidden Neighbors*, 229–37; Friedman, *Government and Slum Housing*; Jackson, "The Spatial Dimensions"; and McEntire, *Residence and Race*. Abrams observes, "The Federal housing Administration, created under the National Housing Act of 1934, was launched in an effort to encourage home-building and mortgage-lending during the depression. FHA adopted a racial policy that could well have been culled from the Nuremberg laws. From its inception FHA set itself up as the protector of the all-white neighborhood. It sent its agents into the field to keep Negroes and other minorities from buying homes in white neighborhoods. It exerted pressure against builders who dared to build for minorities, and against lenders willing to lend on mortgages. This official agency not only kept Negroes in their place but pointed at Chinese, Mexicans, American Indians, and other minorities as well" (229–30).

Epilogue

1. Few writers have expressed the complex feelings that northerners hold toward the South any better than James Baldwin, who was born in Harlem. In the opening of "Nobody Knows My Name," he observes, "Negroes in the North are right when they refer to the South as the Old Country. A Negro born in the North who finds himself in the South is in a position similar to that of the son of the Italian emigrant who finds himself in Italy, near the village where his father first saw the light of day. Both are in countries they have never seen, but which they cannot fail to recognize. The landscape has always been familiar; the speech is archaic, but it rings a bell; and so do the ways of the people, though their ways are not his ways" (*Price* 183).

Selected Bibliography

Aaron, Daniel. *Writers on the Left Episodes in American Literary Communism.* New York: Harcourt, Brace and World, 1961.

Abrams, Charles. *Forbidden Neighbors.* New York: Harper and Brothers, 1955.

Anderson, Jervis. *This Was Harlem.* New York: Farrar, Straus & Giroux, 1982.

Andrews, William L. "Charles Waddell Chesnutt." In *Dictionary of Literary Biography,* vol. 50: *Afro-American Writers before the Harlem Renaissance,* 36–51. Edited by Trudier Harris and Thadious M. Davis. Detroit: Gale Research, 1986.

———. *The Literary Career of Charles W. Chesnutt.* Baton Rouge: Louisiana State University Press, 1980.

———. *To Tell a Free Story: The First Century of Afro-American Autobiography.* Urbana: University of Illinois Press, 1986.

Attaway, William. *Blood on the Forge.* New York: Doubleday, 1941. Reprint. New York: Macmillan, 1970.

———. *Let Me Breathe Thunder.* New York: Doubleday, 1939.

Baker, Houston. *Blues, Ideology, and Afro-American Literature.* Chicago: University of Chicago Press, 1984.

———. "Modernism and the Harlem Renaissance." In *Modernist Culture in America,* 107–25. Edited by Daniel Joseph Singal. Belmont: Wadsworth, 1991.

———. *Modernism and the Harlem Renaissance.* Chicago: University of Chicago Press, 1987.

———. *Singers of Daybreak Studies in Black American Literature.* Washington, D.C.: Howard University Press, 1974.

———, ed. *Twentieth-Century Interpretations of* Native Son. Englewood Cliffs: Prentice-Hall, 1972.

Baker, Houston, and Patricia Redmond, eds. *Afro-American Literary Study in the 1990s.* Chicago: University of Chicago Press, 1989.

Bakhtin, M. M. *The Dialogic Imagination.* Translated by Carol Emerson and Michael Holquist. Edited by Michael Holquist. Austin: University of Texas Press, 1981.

Baldwin, James. *Go Tell It on the Mountain.* New York: Dell Publishing, 1953.

———. *Notes of a Native Son.* New York: Dell, 1963.

———. *The Price of the Ticket.* New York: St. Martin's/Marek, 1985.

Barlow, William. *"Looking up at Down": The Emergence of Blues Culture.* Philadelphia: Temple University Press, 1989.

Barthe, Roland. "Theorie du texte." In *Encyclopaedia universalis.* Volume 15. Paris: Seuil, 1973.

Bearden, Romare, and Harry Henderson. *A History of African-American Artists from 1792 to the Present.* New York: Pantheon, 1993.

Bell, Bernard. *The Afro-American Novel and Its Tradition.* Amherst: University of Massachusetts Press, 1987.

Bell, Lisle. "Review." *Weekly Book Review,* 16 May 1943, 16.

Benston, Kimberly W., ed. *Speaking for You: The Vision of Ralph Ellison.* Washington, D.C.: Howard University Press, 1987.

Berry, Mary Frances, and John W. Blassingame. *Long Memory: The Black Experience in America.* New York: Oxford University Press, 1982.

Blackwell, James. *The Black Community: Diversity and Unity.* New York: Harper and Row, 1985.

Blake, Casey Nelson. *Beloved Community.* Chapel Hill: University of North Carolina Press, 1990.

Blake, Susan L. "Ritual and Rationalization: Black Folklore in the Works of Ralph Ellison." *PMLA* 93 (Jan. 1979): 121–36.

Bland, Aldon. *Behold a Cry.* New York: Charles Scribner's Sons, 1947.

Blassingame, John W. *The Slave Community.* New York: Oxford University Press, 1972.

Bloom, Harold, ed. *Modern Critical Views: James Baldwin.* New York: Chelsea House Publishers, 1986.

Bodnar, John. *The Transplanted: A History of Immigrants in Urban America.* Bloomington: Indiana University Press, 1985.

Bone, Robert. *The Negro Novel in America.* New Haven: Yale University Press, 1965.

———. "Richard Wright and the Chicago Renaissance." *Callaloo* 28 (Summer 1986): 446–68.

Bontemps, Arna, and Jack Conroy. *Anyplace but Here.* Garden City: Double, Doran, 1945. Reprint. New York: Hill and Wang, 1966.

Bontemps, Arna, ed. *Great Slave Narratives.* Boston: Beacon Press, 1969.

———. "The Negro Renaissance: Jean Toomer and the Harlem Writers of the 1920s." In *Anger, and Beyond: The Negro Writer in the United States,* 22–32. Edited by Herbert Hill. New York: Harper and Row, 1966.

———. Review of *The Living Is Easy. New York Herald Tribune Weekly Book Review,* 13 June 1948, 16.

Botkin, B. A. *Lay My Burden Down: A Folk History of Slavery.* Chicago: University of Chicago Press, 1945.

Bowles, Gladys K., A. L. Bacon, and P. N. Ritchey. *Poverty Dimensions of Rural-to-Urban Migration: A Statistical Report.* Washington, D.C.: Economic Research Service, United States Department of Agriculture, 1973.

Boyle, F. A. Review of *The Living Is Easy. Library Journal,* 1 May 1948, 73.

Bradbury, Malcolm, and James McFarlane. "The Name and Nature of Modernism." In *Modernism, 19–55.* Edited by Malcolm Bradbury and James McFarlane. New York: Viking Penguin, 1978.

Bremer, Sydney. *Urban Intersections: Meetings of Life and Literature in United States Cities.* Urbana: University of Illinois Press, 1992.

Brooks, Van Wyck. *The Confident Years, 1885–1915.* New York: Dutton, 1952.

Brown, Claude. *Manchild in the Promised Land.* New York: New American Library, 1965.

Brown, Henry Box. *Narrative of the Life of Henry Box Brown. Written by Himself.* Manchester: Lee and Glynn, 1849.

Brown, Milton. *Jacob Lawrence.* New York: Dodd, Mead, 1974.

Brown, Sterling A. "Negro Character as Seen by White Authors." *Journal of Negro Education* 2 (1933): 179–203.

———. "The New Negro in Literature, 1925–1955." In *The New Negro Thirty Years Afterward, 57–72.* Edited Rayford W. Logan. Washington, D.C.: Howard University Press, 1955.

———. *Southern Road.* New York: Harcourt, Brace, 1932.

Brown, William Wells. *Narrative of William Wells Brown, a Fugitive Slave. Written by Himself.* Boston: American Anti-Slavery Society, 1847.

Bruce, Dickson. *Black Writing from the Nadir: The Evolution of a Literary Tradition, 1877–1915.* Baton Rouge: Louisiana State University Press, 1989.

Bulmer, Martin. *The Chicago School of Sociology: Institutionalization, Diversity, and the Rise of Sociological Research.* Chicago: University of Chicago Press, 1984.

Busby, Mark. *Ralph Ellison.* Boston: Twayne Publishers, 1991.

Candela, Gregory. "We Wear the Mask: Irony in Dunbar's *The Sport of the Gods.*" *American Literature* 48 (1976): 60–72.

Carby, Hazel. "Ideologies of Black Folk: The Historical Novel of Slavery." In *Slavery and the Literary Imagination, 125–43.* Edited by Deborah E. McDowell and Arnold Rampersad. Baltimore: Johns Hopkins University Press, 1989.

———. "Policing the Black Woman's Body in an Urban Context." *Critical Inquiry* 18, no. 4 (1992): 738–55.

———. "The Politics of Fiction, Anthropology, and the Folk: Zora Neale Hurston." In *History and Memory in African-American Culture, 28–44.* Edited by Geneviève Fabre and Robert O'Meally. New York: Oxford University Press.

———. *Reconstructing Womanhood: The Emergence of the Afro-American Woman Novelist.* New York: Oxford University Press, 1987.

Carroll, Charles. *The Negro as Beast.* St. Louis: American Book and Bible House, 1900. Reprint. Salem, N.H.: Ayer, 1991.

Cell, John W. *The Highest Stage of White Supremacy: The Origins of Separation in South Africa and the American South.* New York: Oxford University Press, 1980.

Chamberlain, John. "The Negro as Writer." *Bookman* 70 (1930): 603–11.

Chesnutt, Charles W. *The Colonel's Dream.* New York: Doubleday, 1905. Reprint. Upper Saddle River: Gregg Press, 1968.

———. *The Conjure Woman.* Boston: Houghton Mifflin, 1899. Reprint. New York: Cambridge University Press, 1983.

———. "The Goophered Grapevine." In *The Collected Stories of Charles W. Chesnett,* 1–13. Edited by William L. Andrews. New York: Penguin, 1992.

———. *The House Behind the Cedars.* Boston: Houghton Mifflin, 1900. Reprint. New York: Penguin, 1993.

———. *The Marrow of Tradition.* Boston: Houghton Mifflin, 1901. Reprint. New York: Penguin, 1993.

Christian, Barbara. *Black Feminist Criticism.* New York: Pergamon, 1985.

———. *Black Women Novelists: The Development of a Tradition, 1892–1976.* Westport: Greenwood Press, 1980.

———. "But What Do We Think We're Doing Anyway: The State of Black Feminist Criticism(s); or, My Version of a Little Bit of History." In *Changing Our Own Words: Essays on Criticism, Theory, and Writing by Black Women,* 58–74. Edited by Cheryl A. Wall. New Brunswick: Rutgers University Press, 1989.

Chudacoff, Howard P. *The Evolution of American Urban Society.* Englewood Cliffs: Prentice-Hall, 1981.

Clark, Edward. "Boston Black and White: The Voice of Fiction." *Black American Literature Forum* 19 (1985): 83–89.

Clark, Kenneth. *The Dark Ghetto* New York: Harper and Row, 1965.

Clayton, Jay. *The Pleasures of Babel.* New York: Oxford University Press, 1993.

Codman, Florence. Review of *The Living Is Easy. Commonweal,* 25 June 1948, 48.

Cohen, William. "Lever for Social Change." In Alfredteen Harrison, *Black Exodus: The Great Migration from the American South,* 72–82. Jackson: University Press of Mississippi, 1991.

Collier, Eugenia. "The Endless Journey of an Ex-Colored Man." *Phylon* 32 (1971): 372–85.

Cooke, Michael G. *Afro-American Literature in the Twentieth Century: The Achievement of Intimacy.* New Haven: Yale University Press, 1984.

Cromwell, Adelaide M. "Afterword." In Dorothy L. West, *The Living Is Easy.* Old Westbury: Feminist Press, 1982.

Cruse, Harold. *The Crisis of the Negro Intellectual.* New York: Morrow, 1967.

Cullen, Countee. *One Way to Heaven.* New York: Harper, 1932.

Dance, Daryl. *Shuckin' and Jivin'.* Bloomington: Indiana University Press, 1978.

Daniel, Walter C. "*Challenge* Magazine: An Experiment That Failed." *CLA Journal* 19 (1976): 493–503.

Davis, Arthur P. *From the Dark Tower: Afro-American Writers, 1900–1960.* Washington, D.C.: Howard University Press, 1981.

Davis, Charles T., and Henry Louis Gates, Jr., eds. *The Slave's Narrative.* New York: Oxford University Press, 1985.

Davis, Thadious M. *Nella Larsen: Novelist of the Harlem Renaissance.* Baton Rouge: Louisiana State University Press, 1994.

De Jongh, James. *Vicious Modernism: Black Harlem and the Literary Imagination.* New York: Cambridge University Press, 1990.

Dixon, Melvin. *Ride Out the Wilderness: Geography and Identity in Afro-American Literature.* Urbana: University of Illinois Press, 1987.

Dixon, Thomas. *The Clansman: An Historical Romance of the Ku Klux Klan.* New York: Grosset and Dunlap, 1905. Reprint. Cutchogue, N.Y.: Buccaneer, 1990.

————. *The Leopard's Spots.* New York: Doubleday, Page, 1902. Reprint. New York: Irvington, 1979.

Donald, Henderson H. "The Negro Migration of 1916–1918." *Journal of Negro History* 4 (1921): 383–498.

Douglass, Frederick. *My Bondage and My Freedom.* New York: Miller, Orton, and Mulligan, 1855. Reprint. Edited by William L. Andrews. Urbana: University of Illinois Press, 1987.

————. *Narrative of the Life of Frederick Douglass, an American Slave. Written by Himself.* Edited by Benjamin Quarles. Boston: American Anti-Slavery Society, 1845. Reprint. Cambridge: Harvard University Press, 1960.

Dove, Rita. *Thomas and Beulah.* Pittsburgh: Carnegie-Mellon Press, 1986.

Drake, St. Clair, and Horace R. Cayton. *Black Metropolis: A Study of Negro Life in a Northern City.* 2 vols. New York: Harcourt, Brace, 1945. Reprint, with introduction by Richard Wright. New York: Harper and Row, 1962.

Draper, Theodore. *American Communism and Soviet Russia: The Formative Period.* New York: Octagon, 1960. Reprint. New York: Vintage, 1986.

Dreiser, Theodore. *Sister Carrie.* New York: Doubleday, 1900. Reprint. New York: W. W. Norton, 1970.

Drimmer, Melvin. *Issues in Black History: Reflection and Commentaries on the Black Historical Experience.* Dubuque: Kendall-Hunt Publishing, 1987.

Du Bois, W. E. B. "The Browsing Reader." *The Crisis* 35 (June 1928): 202.

————. *The Philadelphia Negro: A Social Study.* Philadelphia: University of Pennsylvania, 1899. New York: Schocken Books, 1967.

————. *The Souls of Black Folk.* Chicago: A. C. McClurg, 1903. Reprint. New York: Signet, 1982.

————. "Strivings of the Negro People." *Atlantic Monthly* 80 (Aug. 1897): 194–98. Reprinted in *The Souls of Black Folk.* New York: Signet, 1982.

————. "The Talented Tenth." In Booker T. Washington et al. *The Negro Problem: A Series of Articles by Representative American Negroes of To-Day,* 31–75. New York: James Pott, 1903.

————. *Writings.* Edited by Nathan I. Huggins. New York: Library of America, 1986.

Dunbar, Paul Laurence. *The Complete Poems.* New York, Dodd, Mead, 1955.

———. *The Fanatics*. New York: Dodd, Mead, 1901. Reprint. Upper Saddle River, N.J.: Gregg, 1970.

———. *Love of Landry*. New York: Dodd, Mead, 1900. Reprint. Westport: Greenwood Press, 1969.

———. *Majors and Minors*. Toledo: Hadley and Hadley, 1896. Reprint. Manchester, N.H.: Ayer, 1992.

———. *In Old Plantation Days*. New York: Dodd, Mead, 1903. Reprint. Westport: Negro University Press, 1969.

———. *The Sport of the Gods*. New York: Dodd, Mead, 1902. Reprint. Miami: Mnemosyne, 1969.

———. *The Uncalled: A Novel*. 1898. Reprint. New York: International Association of Newspapers and Authors, 1901, and Salem, N.H.: Ayer, 1971.

———. *Uncle Eph's Christmas: A One Act Negro Musical Sketch*. New York: Will M. Cook and Paul Laurence Dunbar, 1900.

Elkins, Stanley. *Slavery: A Problem in American Institutional and Intellectual Life*. Chicago: University of Chicago Press, 1959. Reprint. Chicago: University of Chicago Press, 1968

Ellison, Ralph. *Going to the Territory*. New York: Random House, 1986.

———. "The Great Migration." *New Masses*, 2 Dec. 1941, 23–24.

———. "Growing Up." In *Speaking for You*, 11–14. Edited by Kimberly Bentson. Washington, D.C.: Howard University Press, 1987.

———. *Invisible Man*. New York: Random House, 1952. Reprint, with author's introduction. New York: Random House, 1982.

———. *Shadow and Act*. New York: Random House, 1964.

———. "Transition." *Negro Quarterly* 1 (Spring 1942): 90–91.

Equiano, Olaudah. *The Interesting Narrative of the Life of Olaudah Equiano, or Gustavus Vassa, the African. Written by Himself*. 2 volumes. London: The author, 1789.

Fabre, Michel. *The Unfinished Quest of Richard Wright*. Translated by Isabel Barzun. New York: William Morrow, 1973.

Farley, Reynolds, and Walter R. Allen, "The Redistribution of the Black Population and Residential Segregation." In *The Color Line and the Quality of Life in America*, 103–57. Edited by Reynolds Farley and Walter R. Allen. New York: Russell Sage Foundation, 1987.

Faulkner, Howard. "James Weldon Johnson's Portrait of the Artist as Invisible Man." *Black American Literature Forum* 19 (1985): 147–51.

Fauset, Jessie. *Comedy American Style*. New York: Stokes, 1933. Reprint. New York: AMS Press, 1990.

———. *Plum Bun: A Novel without a Moral*. New York: Stokes, 1929. Reprint. Boston: Beacon Press, 1990.

———. *There Is Confusion*. New York: Boni and Liveright, 1924. Reprint. Boston: Northeastern University Press, 1989.

Ferguson, SallyAnn H. "Dorothy West." In *Dictionary of Literary Biography,* vol. 76: *Afro-American Writers, 1940–55,* 187–95. Edited by Trudier Harris and Thadious M. Davis. Detroit: Gale Research, 1988.

Fine, Elsa Honig. *The Afro-American Artist: A Search for Identity.* New York: Holt, Rinehart and Winston, 1971.

Firmat, Gustavo Pérez. *Literature and Liminality.* Durham: Duke University Press, 1986.

Fisher, Dexter, and Robert B. Stepto. *Afro-American Literature: The Reconstruction of Instruction.* New York: Modern Language Association of America, 1979.

Fisher, Rudolph. "The City of Refuge." In *The New Negro,* 57–74. Edited by Alain Locke. New York: Albert and Charles Boni, 1925. Reprint. New York: Atheneum, 1968.

———. *Walls of Jerico.* New York: Alfred A. Knopf, 1928. Reprint. Salem, N.H.: Ayer, 1969.

Fleming, Robert E. "Irony as a Key to Johnson's *The Autobiography of an Ex-Coloured Man.*" *American Literature* 43 (1971): 83–96.

———. *James Weldon Johnson.* Boston: Twayne Publishers, 1987.

Forrest, Leon. "Luminosity from the Lower Frequencies." In *Speaking for You: The Vision of Ralph Ellison,* 308–21. Edited by Kimberly W. Benston. Washington, D.C.: Howard University Press, 1987.

Fowler, Alastair. *Kinds of Literature: An Introduction to the Theory of Genres and Modes.* Cambridge: Harvard University Press, 1982.

Franklin, John Hope, and Alfred A. Moss, Jr. *From Slavery to Freedom.* 6th ed. New York: McGraw, Hill, 1988.

Frazier, Franklin. *The Negro Family in the United States.* Chicago: University of Chicago Press, 1939.

Fredrickson, George M. *The Black Image in the White Mind: The Debate on Afro-American Character and Destiny, 1817–1914.* New York: Harper and Row, 1971.

Friedman, Lawrence M. *Government and Slum Housing.* Chicago: Rand McNally, 1968.

Fussell, Paul. *The Great War and Modern Memory.* New York: Oxford University Press, 1975.

Gaines, Ernest. *A Gathering of Old Men.* New York: Alfred A. Knopf, 1983.

Garren, Samuel. "William Attaway." In *Dictionary of Literary Biography,* vol. 76: *Afro-American Writers, 1940–55,* 3–7. Edited by Trudier Harris and Thadious M. Davis. Detroit: Gale Research, 1988.

Gates, Henry Louis, Jr. "Binary Oppositions in Chapter One of Narrative of *The Life of Frederick Douglass, an American Slave Written by Himself.* In Dexter Fisher and Robert B. Stepto, *Afro-American Literature: The Reconstruction of Instruction.* New York: Modern Language Association of America, 1979.

——. *Figures in Black: Words, Signs, and the "Racial" Self.* New York: Oxford University Press, 1987.

——. *The Signifying Monkey.* New York: Oxford University Press, 1988.

Gelfant, Blanche. *The American City Novel.* Norman: University of Oklahoma Press, 1954.

Genovese, Eugene D. *Roll, Jordon, Roll: The World the Slaves Made.* New York: Random House, 1974.

Gibson, Donald. "Wright's Invisible Native Son." *American Quarterly* 21 (1969): 728–38.

Gillespie, Diane, and Missy Dehn Kubitschek. "Who Cares? Women-Centered Psychology in *Sula.*" *Black American Literature Forum* 24 (1990): 21–48.

Gilpin, Charles. "Charles S. Johnson: Entrepreneur of the Harlem Reniassance." In *The Harlem Renaissance Remembered,* 215–46. Edited by Arna Bontemps. New York: Dodd, Mead, 1972.

Gloster, Hugh. *Negro Voices in American Fiction.* New York: Russell and Russell, 1948.

Goins, Charles R., and John W. Morris. *Oklahoma Homes Past and Present.* Norman: University of Oklahoma Press, 1980.

Golden, Marita. *Long Distance Life.* New York: Doubleday, 1989.

Goldfield, David R., and Blaine A. Brownell. *Urban America: From Downtown to No Town.* Boston: Houghton Mifflin, 1979.

Gottlieb, Peter. *Making Their Own Way: Southern Blacks' Migration to Pittsburgh, 1916–30.* Urbana: University of Illinois Press, 1987.

Grant, Robert B. *The Black Man Comes to the City: A Documentary Account from the Great Migration to the Great Depression, 1915–1930.* Chicago: Nelson-Hall, 1972.

Greene, J. Lee. "Black Novelists and Novels, 1930–50." In *The History of Southern Literature,* 383–98. Edited by Louis Rubin. Baton Rouge: Louisiana State University Press, 1985.

Griffin, Farah Jasmine. *"Who Set You Flowin'?" The African-American Migration Narrative.* New York: Oxford University Press, 1995.

Griggs, Sutton. *Imperium in Imperio.* Cincinnati: Editor, 1899.

——. *The Negro's Next Step.* Memphis: Natural Public Welfare League, 1923.

Grossman, James. *Land of Hope: Chicago, Black Southerners, and the Great Migration.* Chicago: University of Chicago Press, 1989.

Guiner, Genii. "Interview with Dorothy West, May 6, 1978." Black Women's Oral History Project. Cambridge: Schlesinger Library, Radcliffe College, 1981.

Gutman, Herbert G. *The Black Family in Slavery and Freedom, 1750–1925.* New York: Pantheon Books, 1976.

Guy, Rosa. *A Measure of Time.* New York: Henry Holt, 1983.

Hamilton, Cynthia. "Work and Culture: The Evolution of Conspicuousness in Urban Industrial Society in the Fiction of William Attaway and Peter Abrahams." *Black American Literature Forum* 21 (Spring–Summer 1987): 147–63.

Hansberry, Lorraine. *A Raisin in the Sun*. New York: Random House, 1959.

Harper, F. E. W. *Iola Leroy; or, Shadows Uplifted*. Philadelphia: Garrigues Brothers Press, 1892. Reprint. Boston: Beacon Press, 1987.

Harris, Joel Chandler. *Uncle Remus: His Songs and Sayings*. New York: D. Appleton, 1880. Reprint. Marietta: Cherokee, 1981.

Harrison, Alferdteen. *Black Exodus: The Great Migration from the American South*. Jackson: University Press of Mississippi, 1991.

Hedin, Raymond. "Strategies of Form in the American Slave Narrative." In *The Art of Slave Narrative: Original Essays in Criticism and Theory*, edited by John Sekora and Darwin T. Turner. Macomb: Western Illinois University, 1982.

Hemenway, Robert. *Zora Neale Hurston: A Literary Biography*. Urbana: University of Illinois Press, 1977.

Henderson, George Wylie. *Jule*. New York: Creative Age Press, 1946.

Henderson, Harry, and Romare Bearden. *A History of African-American Artists: From 1792 to the Present*. New York: Pantheon, 1993

Henri, Florette. *Black Migration: Movement North, 1900–1920*. Garden City: Doubleday, 1975.

Hill, Mozell. C. "The All-Negro Communities of Oklahoma: The Natural History of a Social Movement." *Journal of Negro History* 31 (July 1946): 254–68.

Hogue, Lawrence. *Discourse and the Other*. Durham: Duke University Press, 1986.

Hollis, Burney. "Waters Turpin." In *Dictionary of Literary Biography*, vol. 51: *Afro-American Writers from the Harlem Renaissance to 1940*, 289–95. Edited by Trudier Harris and Thadious M. Davis. Detroit: Gale Research, 1988.

———, ed. *Swords upon This Hill*. Baltimore: Morgan State University Press, 1984.

Hopkins, Pauline. *Contending Forces*. Boston: The Colored Cooperative Publishing, 1900. Reprint. Carbondale: Southern Illinois University Press, 1978.

Huggins, Nathan. *Harlem Renaissance*. New York: Oxford University Press, 1971.

Hughes, Langston. *The Big Sea: An Autobiography*. New York: Alfred A. Knopf, 1940. Reprint. New York: Hill and Wang, 1993.

———. *Fine Clothes to the Jew*. New York: Alfred A. Knopf, 1927.

———. "The Negro Artist and the Racial Mountain." *Nation*, 23 June 1926, 692–94.

———. *Weary Blues*. New York: Alfred A. Knopf, 1926.

Humphries, Jefferson, ed. *Southern Literature and Literary Theory*. Athens: University of Georgia Press, 1990.

Hunton, W. A. "The Adventures of the Brown Girl in Her Search for Life." *Journal of Negro Education* 7 (Jan. 1938): 71–72.

Hurston, Zora Neale. *Dust Tracks on a Road*. Philadelphia: J. B. Lippincott, 1942. Reprint. Urbana: University of Illinois Press, 1991.

———. "The Gilded Six-Bits." *Story Magazine* 3 (Aug. 1933): 86–93. Reprinted in *The Complete Stories*. New York: HarperCollins, 1995.

———. *Jonah's Gourd Vine*. Philadelphia: J. B. Lippencott, 1934. Reprint. San Bernadino: Borgo Press, 1991.

————. "Stories of Conflict." *Saturday Review of Literature,* 2 April 1938, 32.

————. *Their Eyes Were Watching God.* Philadelphia: J. B. Lippincott, 1937. Reprint. Urbana: University of Illinois Press, 1978.

Jackson, Kenneth T. "The Spatial Dimensions of Social Control: Race, Ethnicity, and Government Housing Policy in the United States, 1918–1968." *Modern Industrial Cities* (1981): 79–128.

Jacobs, Harriet. *Incidents in the Life of a Slave Girl.* New York: Oxford University Press, 1988.

Johnson, Charles. *Faith and the Good Thing.* New York: Atheneum, 1974.

Johnson, Charles S. "The Conflict of Caste and Class in an American Industry." *American Journal of Sociology* 42 (1936): 55–65.

————. "Incidence upon the Negroes." *American Journal of Sociology* 40 (1935): 737–45.

————. "The Negro Migration: An Economic Interpretation." *Modern Quarterly* 2 (1925): 314–26.

Johnson, Daniel, and Rex Campbell. *Black Migration in America.* Durham: Duke University Press, 1981.

Johnson, James Weldon. *Along This Way.* New York: Viking Press, 1933. Reprint. New York: Da Capo Press, 1973.

————. *The Autobiography of an Ex-Coloured Man.* Boston: Samuel French, 1912. Reprint. New York: Penguin Books, 1990.

————. *Black Manhattan.* New York: Alfred A. Knopf, 1930. Reprint. New York: Da Capo Press, 1991.

————. "Making of Harlem." *Survey Graphic* 53 (March 1925): 635–39.

Jones, Gayle. *Corregidora.* New York: Random House, 1975.

Jones, Jacqueline. *Labor of Love, Labor of Sorrow.* New York: Random House, 1986.

Jones, Leroi [Amiri Baraka]. *Blues People: Negro Music in White America.* New York: William Morrow, 1963.

Katzman, David. "Black Migration." In *The Readers' Companion to American History,* 114–16. Edited by Eric Foner and John A. Garraty. Boston: Houghton Mifflin, 1991.

Kelly, William Melvin. *A Different Drummer.* New York: Doubleday, 1962.

Kent, George. *Blackness and the Adventure of American Culture.* Chicago: Third World Press, 1972.

————. "Ralph Ellison and Afro-American Folk and Cultural Tradition. In *Speaking for You: The Vision of Ralph Ellison,* 95–104. Edited by Kimberly W. Benston. Washington: Howard University Press, 1987.

Kinnamon, Keneth. *The Emergence of Richard Wright.* Urbana: University of Illinois Press, 1972.

————, ed. *New Essays on* Native Son. New York: Cambridge University Press, 1990.

Klotman, Phyllis Rauch. *Another Man Gone: The Black Runner in Contemporary Afro-American Literature.* Port Washington: Kennikat Press, 1977.

———. "The Running Man as Metaphor in Ellison's *Invisible Man.*" *CLA Journal* 13 (March 1970): 277–88.

Kramer, Victor, ed. *The Harlem Renaissance Re-examined.* New York: AMS Press, 1987.

Kristeva, Julia. *Semeiotike: Recherches pour une s'analyse.* Paris: Seuil, 1969.

Kubitschek, Missy Dehn. *Claiming the Heritage: African-American Women Novelists and History.* Jackson: University Press of Mississippi, 1991.

Lal, Barbara Ballis. "Black and Blue in Chicago: Robert E. Park's Perspective on Race Relations in Urban America." *British Journal of Sociology* 38, no. 4 (1988): 546–65.

———. *The Romance of Culture in an Urban Civilization: Robert Park on Race and Ethnic Relations in Cities.* New York: Routledge, 1990.

Lane, Ann J. *The Debate over Slavery: Stanley Elkins and His Critics.* Urbana: University of Illinois Press, 1971.

Larsen, Nella. *Quicksand* and *Passing.* Edited by Deborah E. McDowell. New York: Alfred A. Knopf, 1928, 1929. Reprint. New Brunswick: Rutgers University Press, 1986.

Lawrence, Jacob. *The Great Migration.* New York: HarperCollins, 1992.

Lee, George W. *River George.* New York: Macaulay, 1937.

Lemann, Nicholas. *The Promised Land: The Great Migration and How It Changed America.* New York: Alfred A. Knopf, 1991.

Lenz, Günter H. "Symbolic Space, Communal Rituals, and the Surreality of the Urban Ghetto: Harlem in Black Literature from the 1920s to the 1960s." *Callaloo* 11 (Spring 1988): 309–45.

"Letters of Negro Migrants of 1916–1918." *Journal of Negro History* 4 (1919): 290–340, 412–65.

Levine, Lawrence W. *Black Culture and Black Consciousness.* New York: Oxford University Press, 1977.

Levy, Eugene. *James Weldon Johnson: Black Leader, Black Voice.* Chicago: University of Chicago Press, 1973.

Lewis, David L. *When Harlem Was in Vogue.* New York: Random House, 1981.

Lewis, Oscar. *Five Families.* New York: Basic Books, 1959.

Lieberson, Stanley. *A Piece of the Pie: Black and White Immigrants since 1880.* Berkeley: University of California Press, 1980.

Little, Jonathan. "Charles Johnson's Revolutionary Oxherding Tale." *Studies in American Fiction* 19, no. 2 (1991): 141–51.

Locke, Alain. *Negro Art: Past and Present.* New York: Arno Press, 1969.

———, ed. *The New Negro.* New York: Albert and Charles Boni, 1925. Reprint. New York: Atheneum, 1968.

———. "The Younger Literary Movement." *Crisis* 27 (Feb. 1924): 161–62.

Lucas, Curtis. *The Flour Is Dusty.* Philadelphia: Dorrance, 1943.

———. *Third Ward Newark.* New York: Ziff Davis, 1946.

Lyman, Stanford M. *The Black American in Sociological Thought.* New York: Putnam, 1972.

Machor, James L. *Pastoral Cities: Urban Ideals and the Symbolic Landscape of America.* Madison: University of Wisconsin Press, 1987.

MacKethan, Lucinda H. "Black Boy and Ex-Coloured Man: Version and Inversion of the Slave Narrator's Quest for Voice." *CLA Journal* 32 (Dec. 1988): 123–47.

———. "Jean Toomer's *Cane*: A Pastoral Problem." In Jean Toomer, *Cane*, 229–236. Edited by Darwin Turner. New York: W. W. Norton, 1988.

———. "Plantation Fiction, 1865–1900." In *The History of Southern Literature*, 209–18. Edited by Louis Rubin. Baton Rouge: Louisiana State University Press, 1985.

Margolies, Edward. "Introduction." In William Attaway, *Blood on the Forge*, vii–xviii. New York: Collier, 1970.

———. *Native Sons.* Philadelphia: J. B. Lippincott Company, 1968.

Marks, Carole. "Black Workers and the Great Migration Northward." *Phylon* 46 (1985): 148–61.

———. "Lines of Communication: Recruitment Mechanisms and the Great Migration of 1916–1918." *Social Problems* 31 (1983): 73–83.

Martin, Jay, ed. *A Singer in the Dawn: Reinterpretations of Paul Laurence Dunbar.* New York: Dodd, Mead, 1975.

Matthews, Fred H. *Quest for an American Sociology: Robert E. Park and the Chicago School.* Montreal: McGill-Queen's University Press, 1977.

Maxwell, William. "Down-Home to Chicago: The Richard Wright–Zora Neale Hurston Debate and the Literature of the Great Migration." Unpublished essay.

McAdoo, Harriette Pipes, ed. *Black Families.* Beverly Hills: Sage Publications, 1981.

———. *Home to Harlem.* New York: Harper and Brothers, 1928. Reprint. New York: Pocket Cardinal, 1965.

McCluskey, John, Jr., ed. *The City of Refuge: The Collected Stories of Rudolph Fisher.* Columbia: University of Missouri Press, 1987.

McDowell, Deborah E. "Conversations with Dorothy West." In *The Harlem Renaissance Re-Examined*, 265–82. Edited by Victor A. Kramer. New York: AMS Press, 1987.

———. "Introduction." In Nella Larsen, *Quicksand* and *Passing*, ix–xxxvii. New Brunswick: Rutgers University Press, 1986.

McEntire, Davis. *Residence and Race.* Berkeley: University of California Press, 1960.

McFeely, William S. *Frederick Douglass.* New York: W. W. Norton, 1991.

McKay, Claude. *Banana Bottom.* New York: Harper, 1933. Reprint. New York: Harvest, 1970.

———. *Home to Harlem.* New York: Harper and Brothers, 1928.

McKay, Nellie Y. "Literature and Politics: Black Feminist Scholars Reshaping Literary Education in the White University." In *Left Politics and the Literary Profession*, 84–102. Edited by Lennard J. Davis. New York: Columbia University Press, 1990.

McReynolds, Edwin C. *Oklahoma: A History of the Sooner State*. Norman: University of Oklahoma Press, 1960.

Meier, August, and Elliott Rudwick. *Along the Color Line: Explorations in the Black Experience*. Urbana: University of Illinois Press, 1976.

———. "The Boycott Movement against Jim Crow Streetcars in the South, 1900–1906." In *Along the Color Line: Explorations in the Black Experience*, 267–89. Edited by August Meier and Elliot Rudwick. Urbana: University of Illinois Press, 1976.

———. "The Historiography of Slavery: An Inquiry into Paradigm-Making and Scholarly Interaction." In *Black History and the Historical Profession, 1915–1980*, 239–76. Edited by August Meier and Elliot Rudwick. Urbana: University of Illinois Press, 1986.

Millgate, Michael. *American Social Fiction*. New York: Barnes and Noble, 1967.

Moon, Bucklin. *The Darker Brother*. Garden City: Doubleday, Doran, 1943.

Morrison, Toni. *The Bluest Eye*. New York: Holt, Rinehart, and Winston, 1970.

———. "City Limits, Village Values: Concepts of the Neighborhood in Black Fiction." In *Literature and the American Urban Experience*, 35–45. Edited by Michael C. Jaye and Ann Chalmers Watts. New Brunswick: Rutgers University Press, 1981.

———. *Jazz*. New York: Alfred A. Knopf, 1992.

———. "Rootedness: The Ancestor as Foundation." In *Black Women Writers, 1950–1980*, 339–45. Edited by Mari Evans. New York: Anchor Press, 1984.

———. *Song of Solomon*. New York: Alfred A. Knopf, 1977.

Moses, Wilson J. "The Lost World of the Negro, 1895–1919: Black Literary and Intellectual Life before the 'Renaissance.'" *Black American Literature Forum* 21 (Spring–Summer 1987): 61–84.

Moynihan, Daniel P. *The Negro Family: The Case for National Action*. Washington, D.C.: Government Printing Office, 1965.

Myrdal, Gunnar. *An American Dilemma: The Negro Problem and Modern Democracy*. New York: Harper and Row, 1944.

Naylor, Gloria. *Mama Day*. New York: Ticknor and Fields, 1987.

———. *The Women of Brewster Place*. New York: Viking, 1982.

Neal, Larry. "Ellison's Zoot Suit." In *Speaking for You: The Vision of Ralph Ellison*, 105–25. Edited by Kimberly W. Benston. Washington: Howard University Press, 1987.

Nelson, Emmanuel S. "George Wylie Henderson." In *Dictionary of Literary Biography*, vol. 51: *Afro-American Writers from the Harlem Renaissance to 1940*, 96–100. Edited by Trudier Harris and Thadious M. Davis. Detroit: Gale Research Press, 1988.

Newson, Adele S. "An Interview with Dorothy West." *Zora Neale Hurston Forum* 2 (1987): 19–24.

Nichols, Charles H. *Many Thousand Gone: The Ex-Slaves Account of Their Bondage and Freedom.* Bloomington: Indiana University Press, 1963.

O'Brien, John, ed. *Interviews with Black Writers.* New York: Liveright, 1973.

O'Daniel, Therman. *James Baldwin: A Critical Evaluation.* Washington, D.C.: Howard University Press, 1977.

Offord, Carl Ruthven. *The White Face.* New York: Robert M. McBride, 1943.

Oliver, Paul. *Blues Fell This Morning: Meaning in the Blues.* 2d ed. New York: Cambridge University Press, 1990.

———. *Blues Off the Record.* New York: Da Capo Press, 1984.

Olney, James. "'I Was Born': Slave Narratives, Their Status as Autobiography and as Literature." In *The Slave's Narrative,* 148–71. Edited by Charles T. Davis and Henry Louis Gates, Jr. New York: Oxford University Press, 1985.

Olsen, Otto H. *The Thin Disguise:* Plessy v. Ferguson: *A Documentary Presentation.* New York: Humanities Press, 1967.

O'Meally, Robert. *The Craft of Ralph Ellison.* Cambridge: Harvard University Press, 1980.

———, ed. *New Essays on* Invisible Man. New York: Cambridge University Press, 1988.

Osofsky, Gilbert. *Harlem: The Making of a Ghetto.* New York: Harper and Row, 1963.

———, ed. *Puttin' on Ole Massa: The Slave Narratives of Henry Bibb, William Wells Brown, and Solomon Northup.* New York: Harper and Row, 1969.

Ostendorf, Berndt. "Ralph Waldo Ellison: Anthropology, Modernism, and Jazz." In *New Essays on* Invisible Man, 95–121. Edited by Robert O'Meally. New York: Cambridge University Press, 1988.

Ottley, Roy. *The Lonely Warrior: The Life and Times of Robert S. Abbott.* Chicago: Henry Regnery, 1955.

Page, Thomas Nelson. *In Ole Virginia; or, Marse Chan and Other Stories.* New York: Charles Scribner's Sons, 1887. Reprint. Chapel Hill: University of North Carolina Press, 1969.

Painter, Nell Irvin. *Exodusters: Black Migration to Kansas after Reconstruction.* New York: Alfred A. Knopf, 1976. Reprint. Lawrence: University Press of Kansas, 1986.

Park, Robert. "The Bases of Race Prejudice." In *Collected Writings of Robert E. Park,* vol. 1: *Race and Culture,* 300. Edited by E. C. Hughes et al. Chicago: Free Press, 1950.

———. "Human Migration and the Marginal Man." *American Journal of Sociology* 33 (May 1928): 881–93.

———. "Racial Assimilation in Secondary Groups, with Particular Reference to the Negro." In *Collected Writings of Robert E. Park,* vol. 1: *Race and Culture,* 204–20. Edited by E. C. Hughes et al. Chicago: Free Press, 1950.

Park, Robert, and Ernest W. Burgess. *Introduction to the Science of Sociology.* Chicago: University of Chicago Press, 1921.

Persons, Stow. *Ethnic Studies at Chicago, 1905–45.* Urbana: University of Illinois Press, 1987.

Pizer, Donald. *Twentieth-Century American Literary Naturalism: An Interpretation.* Carbondale: Southern Illinois University Press, 1982.

Pratt, Mary Louise. "Interpretive Strategies/Strategic Interpretations: On Anglo-American Reader Response Criticism." *Boundary* 2, no. 11 (1982–83): 201–31.

Pryse, Marjorie, and Hortense Spillers. *Conjuring: Black Women, Fiction, and Literary Tradition.* Bloomington: Indiana University Press, 1985.

Rabinowitz, Howard N. "More Than the Woodward Thesis: Assessing *The Strange Career of Jim Crow.*" *Journal of American History* 75 (Dec. 1988): 842–56.

Rampersad, Arnold. *The Life of Langston Hughes.* Vol 1. New York: Oxford University Press, 1986.

Redding, J. Saunders. "The Negro Writers: Shadow and Substance." *Phylon* (Fourth Quarter 1950): 371–73.

Reilly, John. "The Search for Black Redemption: Jean Toomer's *Cane.*" In *Cane,* 196–206. Edited by Darwin Turner. New York: W. W. Norton.

———. "The Testament of Ralph Ellison." In *Speaking for You: The Vision of Ralph Ellison,* 58–60. Edited by Kimberly W. Bentson. Washington, D.C.: Howard University Press, 1987.

Relph, Edward. *Place and Placelessness.* London: Pion, 1976.

Renshaw, Patrick. "The Black Ghetto, 1890–1940." *Journal of American Studies* 1 (1974): 41–59.

Report of the National Advisory Commission on Civil Disorders [The Kerner Report]. New York: Bantam Books, 1968.

Revell, Peter. *Paul Laurence Dunbar.* Boston: Twayne Publishers, 1979.

Roberts, John W. *From Trickster to Badman: The Black Folk Hero in Slavery and Freedom.* Philadelphia: University of Pennsylvania Press, 1989.

Ross, Stephen M. "Audience and Irony in Johnson's *The Autobiography of an Ex-Coloured Man.*" *CLA Journal* 18 (1974): 198–210.

Rowe, Mike. *Chicago Breakdown.* London: Eddison Press, 1973.

Rubin, Louis D., Jr., ed. *The History of Southern Literature.* Baton Rouge: Louisiana State University Press, 1985.

Rusch, Frederik L. *A Jean Toomer Reader: Selected Unpublished Writings.* New York: Oxford University Press, 1993.

Schuyler, George. *Black No More.* New York: McCauley, 1931.

Scott, Emmett J. "Letters of Negro Migrants of 1916–1918." *Journal of Negro History* 4 (July 1919): 290–340.

———. *The Negro Migration during the War.* New York: Oxford University Press, 1920.

———, comp. "Additional Letters of Negro Migrants of 1916–1918." *Journal of Negro History* 4 (October 1919): 412–75.

Scruggs, Charles. *Sweet Home: Invisible Cities in the Afro-American Novel.* Baltimore: Johns Hopkins University Press, 1993.

Sekora, John, and Darwin T. Turner. *The Art of Slave Narrative: Original Essays in Criticism and Theory.* Macomb: Western Illinois University Press, 1982.

Shackelford, Otis M. *Lillian Simmons; or, The Conflict of Sections.* Kansas City: R. M. Rigby Printing, 1915.

Sherman, Richard B., ed. *The Negro and the City.* Englewood Cliffs: Prentice-Hall, 1970.

Shields, John, ed. *The Collected Works of Phillis Wheatley.* New York: Oxford University Press, 1988.

Siegel, Adrienne. *The Image of the American City in Popular Literature.* Port Washington: Kennikat Press, 1981.

Sims, Moody, Jr. *Lives of Mississippi Authors, 1817–1967.* Edited by James B. Lloyd. Jackson: University Press of Mississippi, 1981.

Singh, Amritjit. *The Novels of the Harlem Renaissance.* University Park: Penn State University Press, 1976.

———, et al., eds. *The Harlem Renaissance: Revaluations.* New York: Garland, 1989.

Skerrett, Joseph T., Jr. "Irony and Symbolic Action in James Weldon Johnson's *The Autobiography of an Ex-Coloured Man.*" *American Quarterly* 32 (1980): 540–58.

Smith, Barbara. *Towards a Black Feminist Criticism.* Trumansburg: Out Out Books, 1977.

Smith, Sidonie. *Where I'm Bound: Patterns of Slavery and Freedom in Black American Autobiography.* Westport: Greenwood Press, 1974.

Smith, Valerie. *Self-Discovery and Authority in Afro-American Narrative.* Cambridge: Harvard University Press, 1987.

Sollors, Werner. *Beyond Ethnicity: Consent and Descent in American Culture.* New York: Oxford University Press, 1986.

———. "A Critique of Pure Pluralism." In *Reconstructing American Literary History,* 250–80. Edited by Sacvan Bercovitch. Cambridge: Harvard University Press, 1986.

Spear, Allan H. *Black Chicago: The Making of a Negro Ghetto, 1890–1920.* Chicago: University of Chicago Press, 1967.

Standley, Fred L., and Nancy V. Burt, eds. *Critical Essays on James Baldwin.* Boston: G. K. Hall, 1988.

Starling, Marion Wilson. *The Slave Narrative: Its Place in American History.* Boston: G. K. Hall, 1981.

Stepto, Robert B. *From Behind the Veil: A Study of Afro-American Narrative.* Urbana: University of Illinois Press, 1979.

———. "Sterling A. Brown: Outsider in the Harlem Renaissance?" In *The Harlem Renaissance: Revaluations,* 73–82. Edited by Amritjit Singh et al. New York: Garland, 1989.

Still, Bayard. *Urban America: A History with Documents*. Boston: Little, Brown, 1974.

Stone, Albert E. "After *Black Boy* and *Dusk of Dawn:* Patterns of Recent Black Biography." *Phylon* 39 (March 1978): 18–34.

Stonequist, Everett V. *The Marginal Man: A Study in Personality and Culture Conflict*. New York: Charles Scribner, 1937.

Sundquist, Eric. *The Hammers of Creation*. Athens: University of Georgia Press, 1992.

———. "Mark Twain and Homer Plessy." *Representations* 24 (Fall 1988): 102–28.

———. *To Wake the Nations*. Cambridge: Harvard University Press, 1993.

Szwed, John F. "The Politics of Afro-American Culture." In *Reinventing Anthropology*, 153–81. Edited by Del Hymes. New York: Random House, 1972.

Takaki, Ronald T. *Violence in the Black Imagination: Essays and Documents*. New York: Putnam, 1972.

Thompson, Thelma Barnaby. "Carl Ruthven Offord." In *Dictionary of Literary Biography*, vol. 76: *Afro-American Writers, 1940–55*, 130–33. Edited by Trudier Harris and Thadious M. Davis. Detroit: Gale Research, 1988.

Thurman, Wallace. *The Blacker the Berry: A Novel of Negro Life*. New York: Macaulay, 1929. Reprint. New York: Arno Press, 1969.

———. *Infants of the Spring*. New York: Macaulay, 1932.

Toomer, Jean. *Cane*. New York: Boni and Liveright, 1923. Reprint. Edited by Darwin Turner. New York: W. W. Norton, 1988.

Trilling, Diana. "Fiction in Review." *Nation,* 5 June 1943, 816.

Trotter, Joe William, Jr. *The Great Migration in Historical Perspective: New Dimensions of Race, Class, and Gender*. Bloomington: Indiana University Press, 1991.

Turner, Darwin. "Paul Laurence Dunbar: The Rejected Symbol." *Journal of Negro History* 52 (Jan. 1967): 1–13.

Turner, Victor. *Drama, Fields, and Metaphors*. Ithaca: Cornell University Press, 1974.

———. "Myth and Symbol." *Encyclopedia of Social Sciences* 10 (1968): 576–81.

Turpin, Waters. *O'Canaan!* New York: Doubleday, Doran, 1939.

———. *The Rootless*. New York: Vintage, 1957.

———. *These Low Grounds*. New York: Harper, 1937.

Tuttle, William. *Race Riot: Chicago in the Red Summer of 1919*. New York: Atheneum, 1970.

Twain, Mark. *Pudd'nhead Wilson*. Hartford: American Publishing, 1894. Reprint. New York: W. W. Norton, 1980.

U.S. Bureau of the Census. *Negro Population in the United States, 1790–1915*. Washington, D.C.: Government Printing Office, 1918.

Valentine, Charles. *Culture and Poverty: Critique and Counter-Proposals*. Chicago: University of Chicago Press, 1968.

Van Deburg, William L. *Slavery and Race in American Popular Culture.* Madison: University of Wisconsin Press, 1984.

Van Gennep, Arnold. *Les rites de passage.* Paris: Emile Nourry, 1909.

Van Vechten, Carl. *Nigger Heaven.* New York: Alfred A. Knopf, 1926.

Wagner, Jean. *Black Poets of the United States: From Paul Laurence Dunbar to Langston Hughes.* Translated by Kenneth Douglas. Urbana: University of Illinois Press, 1973.

Waldron, Edward. *Walter White and the Harlem Renaissance.* Port Washington: Kennikat Press, 1978.

Warren, Robert Penn. "Divided South Searches Its Soul." *Life,* 9 July 1965, 98–114.

Washington, Booker T. "The Rural Negro and the South." *Proceedings of the National Conference of Charities and Corrections* 41 (1914): 121–27.

Webb, Frank. *The Garies and Their Friends.* London: Routledge, 1857. Reprint. Salem, N.H.: Ayer, 1969.

Weimer, David. *The City as Metaphor.* New York: Random House, 1966.

Werner, Craig. "Bigger's Blues: *Native Son* and the Articulation of Afro-American Modernism." In *New Essays on* Native Son, 117–52. Edited by Keneth Kinnamon. New York: Cambridge University Press, 1990.

———. *Black American Women Novelists: An Annotated Bibliography.* Pasadena: Salem, 1989.

———. "The Framing of Charles W. Chesnutt: Practical Deconstruction in the Afro-American Tradition." In *Southern Literature and Literary Theory,* 339–65. Edited by Jefferson Humphries. Athens: University of Georgia Press, 1990.

West, Dorothy, ed. *Challenge,* September 1934.

———. *The Living Is Easy.* Boston: Houghton Mifflin, 1948. Reprint, with Afterword by Adelaide Cromwell. Old Westbury: Feminist Press, 1982.

———. *The Wedding.* New York: Doubleday, 1995.

West, Hollie. "Growing Up Black in Oklahoma . . . from an Ellison Perspective." In *Speaking for You: The Vision of Ralph Ellison,* 11–14. Edited by Kimberly W. Bentson. Washington, D.C.: Howard University Press, 1987.

Wheat, Ellen Harkins. *Jacob Lawrence: American Painter.* Seattle: University of Washington Press, 1986.

White, Morton, and Lucia White. *The Intellectual versus the City.* New York: Oxford University Press, 1962.

White, Walter. *Fire in the Flint.* New York: Alfred A. Knopf, 1924. Reprint. Westport: Greenwood Press, 1969.

———. *Flight.* New York: Alfred A. Knopf, 1926. Reprint. Westport: Greenwood Press, 1969.

Widmer, Kingsley. "Black Existentialism: Richard Wright." In *Richard Wright: A Collection of Critical Essays,* 173–82. Englewood Cliffs: Prentice-Hall, 1984.

Williams, Kenny. "Masking of the Novelist." In *A Singer in the Dawn: Reinterpretations of Paul Laurence Dunbar,* 152–207. Edited by Jay Martin. New York: Dodd, Mead, 1975.

Williams, Raymond. *The Politics of Modernism.* New York: Verso Press, 1984.

Williamson, Joel. *Crucible of Race: Black-White Relations in the American South since Emancipation.* New York: Oxford University Press, 1984.

Willis, Susan. *Specifying.* Madison: University of Wisconsin Press, 1987.

Wilson, Harriet. *Our Nig.* Boston: C. Rand and Avery, 1859. Reprint. New York: Vintage, 1983.

Wilson, William Julius. *The Truly Disadvantaged: The Inner City, the Underclass, and Public Policy.* Chicago: University of Chicago Press, 1987.

Wintz, Cary. *Black Culture and the Harlem Renaissance.* Houston: Rice University Press, 1988.

Woodson, Carter. *A Century of Negro Migration.* Washington, D.C.: Association for the Study of Negro Life and History, 1900. Reprint. New York: Russell and Russell, 1969.

Woodward, C. Vann. "*Strange Career* Critics: Long May They Persevere." *Journal of American History* 75 (Dec. 1988): 857–68.

———. *The Strange Career of Jim Crow.* New York: Oxford University Press, 1974.

Wohl, R. Richard. "The 'Country Boy' Myth and Its Place in American Urban Culture: The Nineteenth-Century Contribution." *Perspectives in American Culture* 3 (1969): 77–156.

Wright, John. "Shadowing Ellison." In *Speaking for You: The Vision of Ralph Ellison,* 63–88. Edited by Kimberly W. Benston. Washington, D.C.: Howard University Press, 1987.

Wright, Richard. "Almos' a Man." *Harper's Bazaar* 74 (Jan. 1940): 40–41, 105–7. Reprinted as "The Man Who Was Almost a Man" in *Eight Men.* Cleveland: World Publishing, 1969.

———. "Between Laughter and Tears." *New Masses,* 5 October 1937, 22, 25.

———. *Later Works: Black Boy, American Hunger, The Outsider.* New York: HarperCollins, 1991.

———. *Lawd Today.* New York: Avon, 1963.

———. *Native Son.* New York: Harper and Row, 1940. Reprint. New York: HarperCollins, 1987.

———. *Twelve Million Black Voices.* New York: Viking, 1941. Reprint. New York: Arno Press and the New York Times, 1969.

———. *Uncle Tom's Children: Four Novellas.* New York: Harper and Row, 1938.

Yans-McLaughlin, Virginia. *Immigration Reconsidered.* New York: Oxford University Press, 1990.

Yarborough, Richard. "The First-Person in Afro-American Fiction." In *Afro-American Literary Study in the 1990s,* 105–21. Edited by Houston Baker and Patricia Redmond. Chicago: University of Chicago Press, 1989.

Yellin, Jean Fagan. *The Intricate Knot: Black Figures in American Literature, 1776–1863.* New York: New York University Press, 1972.

Zangrando, Robert. *The NAACP Crusade against Lynching, 1909–1950.* Philadelphia: Temple University Press, 1985.

Index

LAWRENCE R. RODGERS is head of the Department of English at Kansas State University, where he is associate professor of English and American ethnic studies. He received a Ph.D. from the University of Wisconsin, Madison.

DATE DUE

JAN 0 4 1999			